Hormuzd Rassam

Narrative of the British Mission to Theodore, King of Abyssinia

Vol. II

Hormuzd Rassam

Narrative of the British Mission to Theodore, King of Abyssinia
Vol. II

ISBN/EAN: 9783744754668

Printed in Europe, USA, Canada, Australia, Japan

Cover: Foto ©Suzi / pixelio.de

More available books at **www.hansebooks.com**

NARRATIVE

OF THE

BRITISH MISSION TO THEODORE,

KING OF ABYSSINIA;

WITH NOTICES OF THE COUNTRIES TRAVERSED FROM MASSOWAH, THROUGH THE SOODÂN, THE AMHÂRA, AND BACK TO ANNESLEY BAY, FROM MÁGDALA.

By HORMUZD RASSAM, F.R.G.S.,

FIRST ASSISTANT POLITICAL RESIDENT AT ADEN, IN CHARGE OF THE MISSION.

IN TWO VOLUMES.—Vol. II.

WITH MAP, PLANS, AND ILLUSTRATIONS.

LONDON:
JOHN MURRAY, ALBEMARLE STREET.
1869.

LONDON: PRINTED BY WILLIAM CLOWES AND SONS, DUKE STREET, STAMFORD-STREET,
AND CHARING-CROSS.

CONTENTS OF VOLUME II.

CHAPTER XIII.

THE CAPTIVES REACH KORÂTA.

Theodore at Zagé — Letters from — His inquiries about boat-building — An officer dispatched to Mágdala to release the Captives — Candidates for the Royal Shirt — The Messenger Hailo — Application for Captives' confiscated property — The European artisans reach Koráta from Gáffat — Royal present for the Zoological Society — Royal Revenue — History of Kántiba Hailo, ex-Mayor of Góndar — Correspondence with the King — A difficulty looming in the distance — Theodore proposes to invest the members of the Mission with the Royal Shirt — Intelligence of Dr. Beke's arrival at Massowah — Families of the European artisans reach Koráta — Arrival of the liberated Captives — Their reception by the Author .. .. Page 1

CHAPTER XIV.

TRIAL OF THE CAPTIVES.

Theodore decides on the trial of the Captives — His charges against them — His object — The Captives plead culpable — Mistranslation of Earl Russell's and her Majesty's letters — A dilemma — Arrival of a messenger from Dr. Beke — The Petition from the relatives of the Captives — The Order of "the Cross and Solomon's Seal" — Another present from Theodore — Dr. Beke's mission injudicious — Ôna Mohammed invested with the "Royal Shirt" — Dábterá Dasta in the royal garments — Visit to Theodore at Zagé postponed — Aláká I'ngádá, the royal Scribe — Reception of the Mission at Zagé — Theodore's courtesy — Consults with his Chiefs about the departure of the Mission and Captives — His grievances against M. Lejean, the Coptic Patriarch, a German, and Mr. Speedy — His opinion of his own subjects — Our return to Koráta 31

a 2

CHAPTER XV.

OUR EXODUS SANCTIONED.

Fresh difficulties — M. Bardel and I'ngădă Wark — Intestine troubles — The European artisans — Dr. Beke's mission — Theodore's suspicions aroused — Favourable prognostications — Theodore and his Shirts — Men-milliners — The King's Dispatch-box — Directions given for homeward route — Reasons for preventing a final meeting between the King and the Captives — Theodore dispenses with the interview — Orders our immediate departure — Arrangements made to re-arrest the Captives .. .. Page 66

CHAPTER XVI.

DISGRACE OF THE MISSION.

The released Captives start homewards — The Mission repairs to Zagê and is arrested there — Charges made against the Author — Theodore apologizes — The Mission placed under surveillance — Our baggage ransacked — Present from the King — We destroy all our papers — The Captives arrested and brought to Zagê — A fresh trial — The King's charges against the Captives and against the Author — He determines to retain the Mission — Theodore unchains the Captives — Craves forgiveness of all the Europeans — The Petition from the relatives of the Captives read — Theodore's letter to the Queen — We are to be kept as hostages — Theodore's request for artificers from England — The Author's letter to the British Government — Mr. Flad selected to go to England — A native matricide — Theodore and Abyssinian law — Charges against Samuel and two other Aitos — Sympathy for the Mission 82

CHAPTER XVII.

UNDER ARREST AT ZAGÊ.

Presents from the King — He restores our confiscated property — His studied courtesy — Theodore not a good marksman — "Who is your father?" — Our Queen's birthday commemorated by the King — Another letter from Dr. Beke — Theodore kills a man at a blow — Artillery practice — Theodore's account of his strategy and exploits — His nimbleness — His cruelties at this time — A case of high treason — "Shrimps" and "Bob" — The Itégé's *Márgaf* — The peninsula and town of Zagê — Theodore's "imitation of a steamer" — A native tournament .. 107

CHAPTER XVIII.

FROM ZAGÊ TO DEBRA TÂBOR.

Departure from Zagê in rear of the royal troops — Theodore's courtesy and remorse — We cross the Abai — The King's fickleness — Arrival at Korâta — Cholera in the royal camp — Start for Debra Tâbor — The Mission accompanies the King to Gáffat — Theodore and taxation — Abyssinian etiquette in drinking — The European artisans reach Gáffat from Korâta — Theodore handles a broom — Loses his centre of gravity — The Mission and Captives at Gáffat — The King pays the Author a visit and sips Hennessy's brandy — Claims Alexander the Great as well as Solomon as his progenitor — Abyssinian hagiography — Theodore and the Bible — The Author arraigned again on fresh charges — The old charges against Consul Cameron and Messrs. Rosenthal and Stern repeated — Theodore suspects our Government — Dr. Beke's movements — The King detains the Author at Debra Tâbor — Tame lions — Trial of a Chief for high treason .. .. Page 123

CHAPTER XIX.

FROM DEBRA TÂBOR TO MÁGDALA.

We are to be sent to Mágdala — Theodore changes his plan — Another outburst of royal courtesy — The Author arraigned again — We are confined and guarded in the Treasury — A visit from Theodore — We drink healths all round — The King believes he is mad — The titles "Gêta" and "Aito" — Order to set out with the King to Mágdala — Hailstones on Mount Gûna — We are sent forward to Mágdala under a guard — Arrival at that fortress — We are placed in fetters — The Author's message to Theodore on the occasion — The preliminary location of the Captives — Kindness of the Chiefs — Aito Samuel's services .. 150

CHAPTER XX.

OUR GUARDIANS AT MÁGDALA.

The Mágdala Council — Râs Kidâna Máryam, the Commandant — Râs Bisáwwir — Bitwáddad Damâsh — Bitwáddad Hailo — Bitwáddad Wâsi — Bitwáddad Bâhri — Dajjaj Gojjé — Bitwáddad Bákal — Bitwáddad Hailo, of Chálga — Bitwáddad Dháfar — Our Warders :— Abâ Fâlek — Bâsha Bisáwwir — Yashálaka Âdam — Yashálaka Warké 167

CHAPTER XXI.

LIFE AT MÁGDALA.

Our domestics — A complimentary letter from the King — Relaxation of prison discipline — Samuel and a Tigré Chief at loggerheads — Duties of the petty Chiefs — The Guards at the Gates — Meditated escape — Escape impracticable — The Metropolitan, Abûna Salâma — His character vindicated — His illness and death — His differences with Theodore — Concessions as to quarters — Abyssinian red-tape — The Author's abode — Abortive sanitary efforts — The Captives' quarters — The Captives ménage — Entertainment of public guests — Society and sympathy — Native lady visitors — Water at Mágdala — Soil and climate — Birds — Religious inquiry among the native soldiery — Reform movement — Conversions to Christianity from Islâm — Christian names — Our own worship .. .. Page 187

CHAPTER XXII.

MARRIAGE AND ETIQUETTE.

Abyssinian marriages — Marriage according to the rites of the National Church — How dissolved — Infidelity of the husbands — Continence of wives married sacramentally — Theodore's canonical marriage with the daughter of Râs 'Ali — Obliges Mr. Bell to follow his example — His marriage with the daughter of Dajjáj Oobé — He gets tired of her — Marries Itamanyo, the wife of a Mussulman Galla — Itamanyo's conversion and devotion — Secondary marriages — Third-degree marriages — Native etiquette — "Girding" — The Shámma described — Various styles of wearing the same — Modes of Address — Etiquette in presentation — In drinking — Covering the head, an insult — Privilege of priests, monks, and nuns 215

CHAPTER XXIII.

REBELLION AROUND MÁGDALA.

Theodore's continued courtesy — He sacks Góndar — He receives her Majesty's letter sent by Mr. Flad — Sends it to the Author, requesting him to write for the English artisans to be forwarded on from Massowah — His letter to that effect — The Author's reply — Theodore repeats his request — The peasantry between Debra Tábor and Mágdala become disaffected — The Commandant of Mágdala sent in chains to Debra Tabor — The district of Bagámédēr rebels — Intercourse between Mágdala and the royal camp cut off — Rumours of Theodore's having fled to Kwâra — His bloodthirstiness at this time — Horrible atrocity perpetrated by a band of rebels — The outrage avenged — Theodore learns a new lesson in cruelty — Honesty and fidelity of Abyssinian servants illustrated — Native agents beyond the fortress protect the messengers of the Mission — How regular intercourse was kept up between the Mission and the coast — Scheme organised for rapid intercommunication between Mágdala and Massowah — Kindness makes friends — The devotion of Mr. Stern's native servants — Where is Theodore ? — Rival candidates for the possession of Mágdala — Overtures from Ahmed, the Imâm of the Wello-Gallas — Menilek the king of Shoa's futile display — The Wakshum Gobazé and his army retire on the approach of Theodore — The Wakshum's friendliness towards the British Expeditionary force .. .. Page 227

CHAPTER XXIV.

THEODORE REACHES MÁGDALA.

Theodore hears of the landing of the British troops — Sir Robert Napier's Proclamation — Death of Hailo, a messenger — Submission of the Dalanta people — The road open to Mágdala — Death and burial of Theodore's sister — Transport of artillery — The Author sends dispatches to the British camp — Abyssinian mourning for the dead — Native and five European prisoners forwarded to Mágdala — Theodore's polite messages and speeches — Sir Robert Napier's ultimatum — Theodore in prospect of the impending invasion — He reaches the Dalanta plateau — Breaks faith with the Dalanta people — The Amháras — Messengers arrive from the British camp — The Author released from his chains — Letter and present from Theodore — Communications to and from the British Camp — Theodore reaches the plateau of Saláingé 254

CHAPTER XXV.

THEODORE AT MÁGDALA.

Theodore enters Mágdala — Tries two Priests for defamation and three Chiefs for treason — He returns to Saláingé — His message to the Author about the advance of the British troops — Changes the Mágdala garrison — The European Captives placed under strict watch — Bitwáddad

Hásani as a soldier and a man — Old acquaintances among our new guard — Mágdala garrison re-inforced — We burn our papers — Theodore's second visit to the fortress — Receives the Author in state — His altered appearance — His condescension on the occasion — Is undecided whether he will fight the British or not — Requests the Author to see him buried, in the event of his death — His miscellaneous conversation — Unshackles Dr. Blanc and Lieutenant Prideaux, and receives them graciously — The King " in labour " — Introduces Prince 'Alamáyo to the Author — Abuses his Chiefs at Salámgê — Asks them if they are prepared to fight the British — Damâsh's reply — A sally from Mágdala against the Gallas, an episode — Origin of the expedition — Theodore's charmed rifle — A night attack — The Amhâras are successful — Are pursued by the Gallas on their return march — Rout of the Amhâras — Letters from the British force at Ashángi — The Mission invited to inspect the great mortar " Sevastopol " — Theodore's queries on European warfare — Recounts his troubles — Complains again of Consul Cameron and Mr. Stern — Contrasts his soldiers with the British troops — All the European Captives are unshackled — The Author's proposal to report his Majesty's recent civility to Sir Robert Napier declined — Theodore is anxious for news from the British camp — Espies some of our troops descending into the Bâshilo valley.. .. .. .. Page 279

CHAPTER XXVI.

THE FALL OF THEODORE.

The European Captives summoned to Salámgê by the King — Theodore harangues his troops on the impending invasion by the British — Declines communicating with Sir Robert Napier — Release of some of the native prisoners — Cruel massacre of the remainder — The European Captives sent back to Mágdala — Letter arrives for Theodore from Sir Robert Napier, which he refuses to receive — The native troops are massed at Salámgê — Theodore attacks the British, is defeated, and wishes for peace — Lieutenant Prideaux dispatched to Sir Robert Napier and returns to Salámgê — Is dispatched again with an angry letter from Theodore — The Author and his fellow-captives directed to go to the British camp — The Author's interview with Theodore previous to his departure — The Captives reach the British camp in safety — Theodore's letter of apology and proffered gift of cattle to Sir Robert Napier on the morning of Easter Sunday — The Commander-in-Chief's message in reply — Theodore sets all the European artisans at liberty — Was Theodore deceived ? — The Author's justification 311

CHAPTER XXVII.

ALL'S WELL THAT ENDS WELL.

Narrative of events between the 11th and 13th April, 1868 — Dispatch of the proffered cattle to the British camp — Theodore's impression that hostilities were at an end — Mr. Speedy — The King prepares to escape on hearing that his present had not been accepted — His troops decline to accompany him — Prepares for defence — Is abandoned by most of his followers — Some of the Chiefs surrender themselves to Sir Robert Napier — Theodore attacks a party of British Cavalry — Retreats with a handful of followers and secures the Gates of Mágdala — The fortress stormed by the British — Theodore shoots himself — A summary of his career — His surviving wives and children — Did Theodore, before his death, curse the Author? — Visit to Mágdala after its fall — The Author charged with the burial of Theodore and the care of his family — Disposal of the Chiefs and people of Mágdala — Contrast — Divine intervention — The Army of Rescue — Burial of Theodore — His son, 'Alamáyo, made over by his mother to the care of the British — Dismissal of the Mágdala Chiefs — The Author proceeds to Dalanta with the royal family — Mágdala in flames — Review of the Expeditionary force — Illness and death of the Queen Tĕru-Wark — Dismissal of all Abyssinian followers at Senâfé — Arrival at Zoolla — Journey to Europe — Dispersion of the late European Captives — On British soil once more — Reception by old friends — Recognition by Government of the services and sufferings of the Mission to Abyssinia — Conclusion .. .. Page 329

LIST OF ILLUSTRATIONS

IN THE SECOND VOLUME.

ACTION AT ÁROGÉ	*Frontispiece.*
ORDER OF THE CROSS AND SOLOMON'S SEAL	Page 45
CAPTIVES' QUARTERS AT MÁGDALA	„ 202
MÁGDALA AND SALÁMGÉ FROM THE FOOT OF SALÁSSÉ	*To face page* 279
THE GREAT MORTAR "SEVASTOPOL"	„ 304
PLAN OF THE AMBA MÁGDALA	„ 311
STORMING OF MÁGDALA	„ 329

THE
BRITISH MISSION TO THEODORE,
KING OF ABYSSINIA.

CHAPTER XIII.

THE CAPTIVES REACH KORÁTA.

Theodore at Zagé — Letters from — His inquiries about boat-building — An officer dispatched to Mágdala to release the Captives — Candidates for the Royal Shirt — The Messenger Hailo — Application for Captives' confiscated property — The European artisans reach Koráta from Gáffat — Royal present for the Zoological Society — Royal Revenue — History of Kántiba Hailo, ex-Mayor of Góndar — Correspondence with the King — A difficulty looming in the distance — Theodore proposes to invest the members of the Mission with the Royal Shirt — Intelligence of Dr. Beke's arrival at Massowah — Families of the European artisans reach Koráta — Arrival of the liberated Captives — Their reception by the Author.

WE heard this afternoon that the King had come to Zagé, the capital of Métcha, situated on a high promontory on the southern side of the Lake, about ten miles from Koráta. No one seemed to know anything of his movements, beyond the fact that he had encamped at the bottom of a deep bay formed by the Zagé peninsula—a long neck of land projecting about three miles into the Lake. The Abai enters the Lake ten miles to the north-west of Zagé, runs through it in a strong current round the peninsula, and debouches on the south-eastern side of the bay, about the same distance below Zagé.

16*th*.—To-day I received the following letter from the King, which was sent by water:—

"In the name of the Father, Son, and Holy Ghost—one God.
"From the King of kings, Theodorus. May it reach Aito

Hormuzd Rassam. How have you passed the time? I, God be praised, am well. How have your brothers [Dr. Blanc and Lieutenant Prideaux] passed the time? Ask them from me. After we parted, by the power of God, I found two lion cubs and one young antelope, which I send to you. I have come to Métcha expressly for the purpose of inquiring about your safe arrival at your destination. If God permit, I shall come to see you, by boat."

(Without date.)

This letter was brought by two courtiers, named Lij Kâsa and Lij Abîtu, together with a present from their royal master of two lion cubs and an antelope, which the soldiers had caught on the line of march, in Métcha. The King, having heard that Agafâri Gôlam merely bent to me when we met, sent the poor fellow a severe reprimand, which obliged him, on coming to me for orders this morning, to kneel and kiss the ground. I told him that he might dispense with the ceremony, but he declared that it might cost him his life to disobey the Sovereign's order.

To the foregoing letter from the King I replied as follows:—

"*Korâta, 17th February,* 1866.

"MOST GRACIOUS SOVEREIGN,

"I had the honour of receiving your gracious letter yesterday, by Lijs Abîtu and Kâsa, and was glad to find from its contents that your Majesty was in perfect health. I pray Almighty God to continue His blessings towards you, and to show me the light of your countenance soon.

"The two lion cubs and the antelope, which your Majesty has been good enough to send me, reached me safely, and I return you my best thanks for them, and for the other favours which your Majesty has shown me since I entered your country. By the assistance of our Heavenly Father, I trust never to prove unworthy of your great kindness.

"By your favour, we arrived here safely from Wandigê, by the Lake, on Thursday last, and were received hospitably by

Aito Kâsa and Aito Wandé, in whose houses we are now residing.

"My companions, Dr. Blanc and Mr. Prideaux, desire me to present to your Majesty their respectful compliments; and in recommending you to the protection of our merciful Creator, I remain," &c.

In accordance with the prevailing usage in the country, I had to dispatch one of my own followers, with the returning deputies, to inquire personally for me after the King's health. Being most anxious that Consul Cameron and his fellow-captives should be relieved of their chains as speedily as possible, and knowing, moreover, that Agafâri Gôlam was already charged with the order for their release, I sent his Majesty a verbal message, begging that he would "gladden my heart" by directing Agafâri Gôlam to proceed to Mágdala forthwith and bring the European liberated prisoners to me. I had already learnt enough of the King's character to put me on my guard against irritating him. A letter might reach him when in an angry mood, and any request preferred at such a time was almost certain to be denied or wilfully misapprehended. Hence, I made it a rule, whenever I had any favour to ask which might possibly be refused, always to send the application through a verbal message, charging those who were intrusted with the same, whether my own followers or persons in the King's employ, not to deliver it unless his Majesty was known to be in good humour. Fortunately, all his immediate attendants were on the best terms with me, and readily co-operated in this plan of proceeding.

The same courtiers returned the day after with the following answer to my message on this occasion:—

(After compliments.)

"By the power of God, when I heard of your safe arrival at Korâta I was extremely rejoiced. Be of good cheer; I have ordered Agafári Gólam to proceed at once to release the prisoners and bring them to you, in order that I may send you to your country.

"With respect to the four double-barrelled fowling-pieces and eight double-barrelled pistols, with their moulds and appurtenances, which you have brought to me, M. Bourgaud has written to me to say that he had sent to his brother and obtained them for the purpose of presenting them to me. I have therefore ordered 4,000 dollars to be paid to him by the Nagadrás of Tigré.

"You told me that Mr. Munzinger entertained a sincere regard for me; and, consequently, when you go I wish to send him by you a token of my esteem. Let me know what will be acceptable, in order that I may prepare it."

(Without date.)

A case containing the arms above alluded to was consigned to me by Padre Delmonte, on our departure from Massowah, for the French armourer, M. Bourgaud. Not to excite suspicion in the King's mind, I had preferred taking the arms to him—stating at the same time how I became possessed of them—instead of sending them direct from Chálga to the consignee. His Majesty was highly gratified by this mark of deference, and, instead of leaving me to forward the case, he undertook to take charge of it himself for his "son"—the name whereby he invariably designated his European artisans.

The reference to Mr. Munzinger arose out of the following circumstance. On my arrival at the Court, the King had particularly requested me to tell him who were his friends and who his enemies at Massowah. I replied that his enemies were too many to be enumerated; but that, to the best of my belief, Mr. Munzinger, now British Consular Agent at Massowah, and the Náyib Mohammed, of Harkiko, were well-disposed towards him. This answer highly amused him, and was to him—so he said—a proof of my sincerity, inasmuch as he knew full well that all the Turks hated him. On that occasion he had promised to send the Nâyib, through me, a fine mule, richly caparisoned; the present for Mr. Munzinger was left for future consideration.

I received two verbal messages from the King, together with the foregoing letter: one was to the effect that, before our departure out of the country, he wished to decorate with the Royal Shirt all those of my followers who had contributed to bring about our meeting, and had served as messengers between us; in the other, his Majesty apprised me that he had directed his European artisans at Gâffàt to build him some wooden boats to ply on the Lake, instead of the ordinary native canoes made of bulrushes; and that having been told that fresh and salt water possessed different qualities which affected the floating, he wished me to enlighten him on the subject. In consequence of this message, a rumour was circulated among the Europeans that the King had requested me and my companions to build boats for him—an idea which I am certain he never entertained, neither was it his policy to lower our dignity by supposing us capable of doing the work of artificers or mechanics. Besides, if such a thought had ever occurred to him, he would certainly not have hesitated to broach it to me.

On referring to Agafâri Gôlam, who was said to have originated the report, he assured me that he must have been misunderstood, as he had only mentioned the inquiry which the King had made of me, through Lij Abitu, that same day.

To my infinite delight Agafâri Gôlam started for Mágdala this morning. In accordance with the King's request, I sent with him Mohammed Sa'id, one of my messengers, to see that Consul Cameron and his party were well attended to on the road.

19*th.*—I dispatched the following to the King in reply to his last letter and its accompanying verbal messages:—

"*Koráta, 19th February*, 1866.

" Most Gracious Sovereign,

"I had the honour of receiving your letter yesterday by Lij Abítu and Hailo, and I was greatly pleased to learn therefrom of your well-being; for which I offer my humble thanks to our Lord, the Most High. Thank God, both my companions and I are well, and by your Majesty's favour we are all happy. Dr. Blanc and Mr. Prideaux send their respectful compliments to your Majesty.

"I beg to return you my most grateful thanks for sending Agafári Gólam to Mágdala for the purpose of releasing the European prisoners of their fetters, and bringing them at once to me; and I also thank you for the liberal payment you have made to M. Bourgaud for the guns and pistols which I brought from Massowah.

"With regard to the present which your Majesty wishes to send to Mr. Munzinger, in consequence of what I had mentioned about his regard for you, I beg to inform your Majesty that that gentleman, I am sure, will appreciate any little token of esteem which you may be pleased to send him, were it only a few friendly lines to assure him of your good-will. I need not assure your Majesty that I shall be delighted to convey it to him.

"With respect to the wooden boat which you wish to build to ply on the Lake Tána, I beg to say that such a vessel would answer very well. The only difference between the Lake water and that of the sea to be taken into consideration in this case is, that the latter, being salt, is more buoyant.

"I feel greatly obliged to your Majesty for the honour you intend to confer on some of my followers by decorating them with the Royal Shirt, for the good and faithful service they have rendered to your Majesty and myself in our communications with each other. The men most deserving of this royal favour are Hailo, Wald-Taklu, Mohammed Sa'id, and Mohammed Siháwy. The two latter are absent at present: one I had to send with our animals from Wandígé round the Lake, through Dámběa; and the other I have sent to Mágdala with Agafári Gólam, according to your desire. Mohammed Sihâwy having committed a fault, I feel it incumbent upon me to report it to your Majesty, and shall leave it to you, after you learn his offence, to confer the royal distinction on him or not."

Mohammed Sihâwy, as the reader will remember, was the individual who had told me the falsehood about Cameron's release. I was compelled to include his name as a candidate for the royal honour, because he was unquestionably the man who had brought about my meeting with the King, his Majesty having entrusted him with his letter of invitation to me. Moreover, as I had reason to suspect that Theodore himself was cognizant of the deception which had been practised upon me, I did not deem it advisable to manifest any animosity towards his accomplice. The messenger himself reported that the Nâyib of Harkîko had instigated him to fabricate the story, which I believe to be another falsehood. However, I was determined that his Majesty should know what I had to complain of in the man before he was decorated; hence my reference to his misconduct in the preceding letter, but I also sent him a full account of the case by verbal message.

We were so tortured by vermin that we were obliged to leave the houses of our hospitable hosts, Aito Kâsa and Aito Wandé, and take to our tents, which we pitched in a line on an eligible piece of ground near the Lake, just above the spot where the priests met us on our first landing. The fresh breeze from the Lake, and the clear open sky, were luxuries after our sojourn in the filthy town. This side of the Lake being rocky, with a gravelly soil, is much healthier than the opposite or north-western side, where the ground is low and covered with marshes. There are some marshes also to the south-west of Korâta, but they are too distant to affect the atmosphere here. We could plainly distinguish the church of Zagê, situated on the top of the promontory, as we looked westward from our tents. The smoke also of the royal camp was discernible behind the lofty peninsula, but the camp itself was hid by the neck of high land whereon the scattered town of Zagê is built.

21st.—Hailo, one of the messengers who carried my second and fifth letter from Massowah to the King, and who had been sent by his Majesty to meet me at Matámma, returned to-day in high glee, decorated with the Royal Shirt. This man was the most upright of all the messengers who had been employed between the King and myself, and he often served me subsequently, in the same capacity, when I was a prisoner at Mágdala. On these latter occasions he generally looked as if he did not altogether relish the task; nevertheless, his sense of duty always prevailed over his scruples. The last time I employed him was in May, 1867, from which journey he was doomed never to return. When he reached Debra Tábor, on his way back, the whole country between that place and Mágdala had risen in rebellion, which effectually prevented his progress as a bearer of a message from the King. He then fell sick, but was brought on when the royal army began to move towards Mágdala, his Majesty intending to forward him to me as soon as he approached near enough to send him in safety. He expired one day before the dispatch of the royal messengers whom he had hoped to accompany, and who were the first to make their way to us after a lapse of nine months. On his return from Zagê to-day, accompanied by Lij Kâsa and Lij Abítu, he brought me the following polite but extraordinary letter from the King, wherein his Majesty unequivocally expresses his satisfaction at the fraud of which

Mohammed Sihâwy had been guilty, on the ground that it had been perpetrated with a good intention :—

(After compliments.)

"I wish to decorate these servants [messengers] of yours, who are present, with the Royal Shirt. Be not angry with the servant who informed you of the release of Mr. Cameron. I thought that you [i. e., the English] hated me because I delayed answering your letter, O sons of the English; and in order that you might not fear, but come to me from that great Queen, he tried in this way to bring about the interview between me and you, Aito Hormuzd Rassam, who are a great man and my friend. It is necessary that this man should be brought to the notice of the Queen, and you yourself must love him for my sake. I, on my part, on hearing of what he had done, by the power of God, entertained great affection for him. If you had not come, who would have been able to release the prisoners? And if I had not met you, how could I have obtained your [i. e., the English] friendship? May our Creator from above love, for our sake, him who brought about our interview and made us friends, and those who are His creatures below will love him also. Please God, I shall reward him. I have sent Lij Abitu to Debra Tábor to bring to you my European friends, in order that they might come and see you."

(Without date.)

Lij Abitu left me to go to Gáffat, near Debra Tábor, in order to bring all the European artisans to keep me company—so he stated—until the arrival of the captives. I received another message from the King to-day, expressing a wish that I should send my interpreters to him to be decorated with the Royal Shirt.

23rd.—Dispatched the subjoined letter by 'Omar 'Ali and Mohammed Sihâwy, together with Hailo, whom the King has appointed a confidential medium of intercourse between him and myself:—

"*Korâta, 23rd February*, 1866.

"Most Gracious Sovereign,

"I had the pleasure to receive your kind letter the day before yesterday through Lij Abitu and Hailo, and I was exceedingly gratified to learn that your Majesty was quite well, and thinking of me and my companions. The latter desire to be respectfully remembered.

"With regard to Mohammed Sihâwy, he was doubtless the one who tried his best to bring about our meeting, which I was so anxious for, and on that account I forgave him the deception which he practised upon me. I was not a little gratified also on learning that your Majesty had also extended to him your mercy, and pardoned his offence on account of his good intention of pleasing me.

"I have also to thank your Majesty for the honour you intend to confer on my interpreters by presenting them with the Royal Shirt, and no one can be more worthy of your kindness than 'Omar 'Ali, whom I send to you with Mohammed Sihâwy. The reason I am not able to send all those whom you wish to honour is, because I do not like to be left without interpreters, whose services are constantly required."

To this I received a complimentary answer the following day, brought to me by 'Omar 'Ali and his companions.

Having been given to understand that the King, subsequent to its seizure by his orders, had restored part of the property belonging to Consul Cameron and the Missionaries, but had kept back all the books, watches, rings and other small articles, such as keepsakes, &c., which were of little or no value to his Majesty but might be highly prized by the owners, I had determined to make an attempt to recover them. I did not venture to write to the King on the subject, lest my letter might reach him when he was in an angry mood. I therefore decided to employ Samuel in the matter, and in reply to a request on my part to that effect I received the King's permission to-day, through 'Omar 'Ali, to dispatch him on a message to his Majesty. I accordingly held a long consultation with Samuel as to the terms which he should use about the confiscated property, which was said to be partly deposited in the house of Nagadrâs Gabra-Mádhan, at Góndar, and partly at Mágdala. Samuel's advice and conduct on this occasion convinced me that he was a perfect master of diplomacy, and, moreover, that he was sincerely desirous of serving me to the extent of his ability. He left this afternoon with Dasta, my young interpreter, in charge of the following letter. Dasta's mission was to ask the King, from me, how he fared, and to receive the decoration of the Royal Shirt.

"*Koráta, 24th February*, 1866.

"Most Gracious Sovereign,

" I have the honour to acknowledge the receipt of your Majesty's letter of yesterday's date, by 'Omar 'Ali, Mohammed Siháwy and Hailo, and I beg to return you my sincere thanks for the honour you conferred upon them by investing them with the Royal Shirt.

" Both my companions and myself are well, and we are glad to find that your Majesty is in perfect health.

" Your Majesty has conferred a great favour upon me by ordering Aito Samuel to your Court, agreeably with my desire. His confidential position with your Majesty, and my reliance in him, have induced me to intrust him with a communication which I have asked him to make to you. I hope you will not consider it amiss in me for having craved the boon which I have requested him to ask of you. After your great kindness and attention to me, I cannot but hope that you will extend your gracious favour in that behalf."

In accordance with my request, Mr. Flad came to me from Gáffat this afternoon. After the King had ordered the release of Consul Cameron and the other captives, and directed that they should be made over to me to take with me on my departure from Abyssinia, I had begged his Majesty to allow

Mr. and Mrs. Flad and their children, and Messrs. Brandeis, Staiger, Schiller and Essler—who were, in fact, prisoners on parole at Gáffat, and who had begged me to urge the request on their behalf—to leave the country at the same time. The King had acceded to my solicitation at once, and told me that I was at liberty to take any persons away with me— even native Abyssinians—who wished to depart out of his territories. I accordingly sent for Mr. Flad to consult with him about the preparations for the journey, and also regarding the reception of the liberated captives who were expected to reach Debra Tábor shortly.

26th.—Aito Samuel and Dasta returned from the royal camp, the latter greatly elated with his decoration, and the former intensely happy at having executed the commission with which I had entrusted him to my entire satisfaction. He handed me the following characteristic reply from his Majesty:—

(After compliments.)

"I acted formerly erroneously, through the devil, without consideration; and now I have ordered Aito Samuel to see if there is any property [belonging to the prisoners] which he can bring to you; and if anything has been lost or spoilt, I shall make it good, not merely for the sake of my friendship for the great Queen, but for the friendship which I entertain for you three, and which is sufficient for me. If I can make compensation from my property to you at all, by the help of the Lord, I will do it; if not, I offer my body. When the people [prisoners] reach you in safety, ask them if what they had done was not true; it will be proved to you from their mouth.

"I apprehended that I had lost all hopes of your [the English] friendship; otherwise, I would not have acted so badly.

"Dated 16th of Yekâtit."

The King also ordered Aito Samuel to proceed to Mágdala as soon as the captives joined me, for the purpose of collecting and consigning over to me all their remaining property. They were then expected to arrive within four or five days, but unfortunately, owing to the inability of most of them to travel fast after their long and painful confinement, they did not join us till the 12th of March, by which time, as the sequel will show, the aspect of things had undergone a change.

27th.—Dispatched the following reply to the King this morning by 'Omar 'Ali and Wald-Gabriêl—the latter the suspended interpreter, whom his Majesty has been pleased to decorate with the Royal Shirt, although at the outset he had objected to him as a translator of our intercommunications:—

"*Korâta, 27th February,* 1866.

"Most Gracious Sovereign,

"Yesterday I had the honour of receiving your letter by Aito Samuel, and I was glad to learn from him that he left your Majesty in perfect health.

"Both my companions, Dr. Blanc and Mr. Prideaux, and myself are extremely obliged to your Majesty for your gracious inquiries, and we all send you our respectful regards.

"I have to return you my best and grateful thanks for having granted the favour which I asked of you through Aito Samuel, and I pray our merciful Lord to reward you for all your kindness.

"I beg to inform your Majesty that in consequence of Aito Samuel's second communication to Kántiba Hailo, Mr. Flad came to me from Gáffat, agreeably with my request. That gentleman begs me to present you with his respectful compliments."

The foregoing allusion to Kántiba Hailo refers to a report which had reached Theodore, that that officer had refused to allow Mr. Flad to come to me without a special order to that effect. His Majesty, it appears, had got into a great rage on hearing this, and would have visited the Kántiba with severe chastisement, had not Samuel pleaded that there had probably been some mistake in the matter.

The King sent his valet, Wald-Gâbir, to me this afternoon with a most polite message, inquiring whether I had expended the money which he had given me, as in that case he wished to present me with another similar sum. I replied that through the bounty of our gracious Sovereign and his Majesty's munificence, I was amply provided with funds, and that in the event of needing any I should not hesitate to apply to him.

28th.—The King's European artisans arrived at Korâta from Gâffat this morning. They comprised Messrs. Moritz Hall, Schimper, Waldmeier, Salmüller, Bender, Bourgaud—the remaining two, namely, Messrs. Zander and Mayer, did not come with them. In accordance with orders from the King they all called upon me, clad in their silk shirts. Mr. Schimper began to narrate to me, in Arabic, his experience of Abyssinia and the Abyssinians since his arrival in the country, warning me not to trust present appearances, however favourable they might be. Placing the palm of his hand upwards, and then reversing it, he said, "Abyssinia is like that; but I must say no more, as the walls have ears." After the artisans had stayed a short time with me, they went and pitched their tents, as they had been ordered, beyond the fence of our encampment.

Wald-Gâbir came again this afternoon, bringing me the subjoined letter from the King; also two monkeys and a baboon, which I was to take to England for the Zoological Society, together with the lion cubs and antelope:—

(After compliments.)

"Yashálaka Wald-Gâbir has informed me that you wished my permission to make the messenger a present. You are the servant of her whom God has exalted and honoured—the Queen of England, and you are also, by the power of God, my friend; consequently, you are not restrained from giving remuneration, except in a way unpleasing to God. Do as you please."

" Dated 22nd of Yekatit " (28th February).

When Wald-Gâbir came to me on the 27th with the message from the King inquiring whether I was out of money, I had expressed a wish that his Majesty would allow me to give a gratuity to the royal couriers and others, in requital of their services, as it was judged that he would like me to act liberally with his people. The messenger had mentioned this desire on my part to the King; hence this letter. He sent me the monkeys to replace a pretty one which had been presented to me while passing through Agówmĕdĕr, and which he heard I had recently lost. Wald-Gâbir was also instructed on the part of his Majesty to say, that if I wanted silks, or arms, or any other articles, I must not hesitate to apply to him for them, as he considered me in the light of a brother. I returned my best thanks for the kind offer, stating at the same time that at present I was not in want of anything.

1st March.—I had not hitherto received the five thousand dollars which the King had presented me with on the 4th of February, when I left him in Agówmĕdĕr, hoping all along to leave the country without taking any portion of it; but it having been strongly urged upon me to-day that his Majesty might be highly offended if it came to his notice that I had deferred accepting his gift, I was constrained to write and acknowledge its receipt, which I did in the following terms:—

" *Koráta, 1st March*, 1866.

" MOST GRACIOUS SOVEREIGN,

" I have the honour to acknowledge the receipt of your Majesty's letter on the 22nd day of the month Yekatit, from which I was glad to learn that you were in perfect health.

"Allow me to thank your Majesty for the present of monkeys you so graciously sent me by Yasháłaka Wald-Gâbir, and also for the handsome gift of five thousand dollars you so kindly sent me through Aito Samuel, and which I have duly received. May the Lord reward you out of His bountiful mercies for all your favours; and, with respectful salutations from my companions and myself, I remain," &c.

The sum above alluded to was paid out of the revenues of Bagámĕdĕr. That district comprises five chieftainships, each paying 70,000 dollars annually to the Sovereign. All the other districts are sub-divided in a similar manner, for fiscal purposes. In addition to that impost, the peasantry generally have to contribute one-fifth of their sheep and cattle. The tolls established throughout the country are another source of royal revenue. Those collected in Chálga—on the high road to the Soodân—averaged 100,000 dollars per annum.

2*nd*.—The King ordered his artisans to send for their wives from Gáffat, who were to remain with them until the Mission left the country with the released captives. In his message to me on the same subject he stated that, knowing how much Europeans appreciated the society of ladies, he had directed his European servants to send for their families, in order that I might have a little agreeable company at Koráta. He also dispatched orders to Agafári Gôlam to bring the released captives to me without delay.

I received a visit in the course of the day from Kántiba Hailo, the ex-Mayor of Góndar. He was considered a very good Christian, and exceedingly pious withal. During our interview, when not addressing me, he was wholly engaged in muttering prayers. The King reposed such confidence in his loyalty that he appointed him overseer of his European artisans, or their Báldárábâ. When Theodore, then Dajjáj

Kâsa, began to acquire political power, he was warmly supported by Kántiba Hailo, who had great influence at Góndar, and who espoused his cause mainly owing to his distrust of Râs 'Ali, whom he regarded as a questionable convert, and as having embraced Christianity merely for the sake of extending his sway over the Christians. Theodore, who was naturally of a most suspicious disposition, had accepted the Kántiba's aid with some reserve at first, but eventually he adopted him as his foster-father by sucking his thumb, in accordance with the Abyssinian usage on such occasions. Thenceforward Theodore always addressed him as "father;" but when his power began to decline, his distrust of every one around him increased. Even up to the time of which I am writing, Kántiba Hailo considered Theodore as the best man living; but soon after my consignment to Mágdala, together with my companions, matters assumed another aspect, and he began to regard his adopted royal son in a different light. His zeal for Christianity bordered on fanaticism, and being a native of Góndar he held the churches there almost in idolatrous veneration. When, in November, 1866, the King utterly destroyed that capital, he did not spare one of the forty-eight churches which it contained. This sacrilegious act drew a flood of tears from the mortified Kántiba, who dared not remonstrate at the time, knowing that his life might have been the penalty for any such interference. His grief was duly reported to the King by ill-disposed persons; but as it was contrary to Theodore's nature to bring a straightforward charge against any one, he had given out on the occasion that he had destroyed the old capital because its inhabitants had harboured the rebels, and, more especially, because they had not protected the messenger of his "friend" Rassam, and had allowed him to be plundered not far from the city. Soon after the King's return to Debra Tábor, he had the Kántiba arrested and brought two separate charges against him. The first was, that he had sent him a present of grain, which the accused had declined to accept; the second, that one of the royal female bakers, who had been dismissed by the King, had been received by the Kántiba into his service. The old man's defence was, that owing to his Majesty's bounty he had more grain than sufficed for his requirements, and that being a disinterested and faithful subject he had ventured to suggest that the royal bounty, in this instance, might be bestowed on some more needy follower. With respect to the female domestic, that she had been brought up in his house from childhood, and he had made her over to the King in consequence of his Majesty's desire to have her, she being considered a good hand at making *tèf* bread; that when his Majesty had turned her adrift, having no further need of her services, it was quite natural that the woman should revert for a livelihood to her old master, and he could not condemn himself for charitably receiving her again into his house. This most reasonable defence, however, failed to satisfy the King, who forthwith sentenced him to be put in chains until he could adduce some better excuses for his misbehaviour. Thereupon the degraded functionary lost his temper, and claimed to be tried by the laws of the realm as contained in the *Fètèh-Negúst*, declaring that he was ready to be hanged, if found guilty by the statutes. This unexpected retort somewhat excited the King who, turning to the guard, said, "Take the old woman away! Who or what is the law but myself? Am I not the fountain of it?" To aggravate the Kántiba's misery, the inexorable judge ordered his grandson to be imprisoned with him, simply because he knew him to be very fond of him, the lad having lost his father—the Kántiba's son-in-law—when he was a child. After they were both put into chains, the King demanded that the old man should refund all the money which he had paid him for many years. To this the Kántiba replied, that not having been given to understand that the money was advanced as a loan, and considering that it was nothing more than the regular pay from a master to his servant, he had spent it all. The two victims were then put to the dreadful torture of having their hands tied tightly by a rope, wound several times round the body, until the blood spirted out. This fiendish punishment was persisted in for several weeks until the King, finding that nothing more could be squeezed out of the Kántiba, sent him and his grandson to Mágdala, where they were retained in chains until the 8th of April, 1868, when they were released together with other incarcerated Chiefs two days before the engagement with the British army. Kántiba Hailo was uniformly kind to me and friendly to the Mission; on one occasion he received a severe reprimand from the King for having recommended him to permit me to leave the country. Theodore had an idea that the Kántiba was conversant with the black art, and in former times, when he was credulous in such matters, he had a superstitious dread of his occult powers, but of late he appears to have disregarded them altogether; for one day, while the Kántiba was under torture, he sent to tell the King that his power over him would soon be at an end, inasmuch as it was decreed that his rule would terminate in the fourteenth year of his reign, which was not far off. To this Theodore sent the following reply:—"If your prediction be true, you may live long; but if I survive the fourteenth year, your life shall be forfeited." "Be it so," was the Kántiba's answer. It is a singular coincidence that Theodore terminated his existence in the fourteenth year of his reign.

3rd.—I received the subjoined note from the King this morning by Wald-Gâbir and my messenger Hailo:—

(After compliments.)

"The people [prisoners] whom you want, may the Lord bring to you, and may He cause you to reach your country in safety. May the Lord plant my friendship and goodwill in your hearts, and may He cause you to open my blind eyes.

"Dated 24th of Yekâtît."

The messengers ought to have reached me yesterday, but owing to a storm they were driven to a place called Zanzalima, to the north of the Abai outlet. A lady who was on her way to the royal camp was so terrified when she got near the coast that, fancying the canoe to be in shallow water, she threw herself into the Lake. Fortunately, the canoe-men, who were on the alert, rescued her from drowning.

4th.—Dispatched the following answer to the King this morning by Wald-Gâbir and Hailo:—

"*Koráta, 4th March,* 1866.

"MOST GRACIOUS SOVEREIGN,

"I have received, with much pleasure, your gracious and kind letter by Wald-Gâbir and Hailo, who only arrived here yesterday morning, owing to the winds and heavy sea they encountered after leaving your coast the day before yesterday. They were driven to the coast of Zanzalima, where they had to spend the night. I offer my humble thanks to Almighty God for their safety.

"I trust that this letter will find your Majesty in perfect health, in which happy condition both my companions and myself are at present. Dr. Blanc and Mr. Prideaux beg to be respectfully remembered to your Majesty.

"I return you my best thanks for the good wishes conveyed in your letter under reply, and I hope that by your favour and through your prayers we shall all reach our destinations safely. I need not assure your Majesty that I am ready to leave Abyssinia for England as soon as I shall obtain your leave, which I hope you will grant me before long, because I am most anxious that we should quit the Soodân country before the unhealthy season sets in.

"News has reached this place of the arrival of Agafâri Gôlam and his companions near Debra Tâbor, and I doubt not that through your kindness they will soon join me here."

In the afternoon I received two notes from the captives—one from Consul Cameron and the other from Mr. Stern—informing me that they were released from their fetters on the 24th ultimo, and were on the way to join me, but that in consequence of physical debility they were obliged to travel very slowly.

5th.—Dispatched messengers to Consul Cameron with a supply of money.

6th.—Received a startling letter from his Majesty to-day, wherein, for the first time since my arrival in Abyssinia, he expressed a wish to "consult" with me when the released captives joined me. It was as follows:—

(After compliments.)

"When the people [prisoners] reach you, we will consult. I have tried to find some nice silk amongst my property, and also in the market in this country, but did not succeed; but of the silks with which you presented me, I have sent three pieces, with their lining. If they will suit you, make shirts of them, and wear them for me; but if you think they will bring any obloquy on me—because what hurts my reputation hurts yours—send me an answer.

"Dated 28th of Yekâtit."

In this communication he also, for the first time, proposed to decorate my companions and myself with silk shirts. The letter, however, was accompanied by a message invoking God as a witness between his Majesty and myself that I was not to do what would tend to degrade either of us in the eyes of his people; that he had merely sent the three pieces of silk in order to know which we preferred, in the event of our consenting to have shirts made of them. I found out, on inquiry, that if I accepted the shirts, we should be obliged to wear them when we met the King; and considering that such an exhibition would have been degrading to our position as British officers, as well as ridiculous, I determined at once to decline them. Fortunately, the King himself had helped me out of my embarrassment by not sending ready-made shirts, which he certainly would have done had he fully resolved that we should wear them. It seemed also very odd that after what he had stated some time before, when he decorated my servants with royal shirts—namely, that he could not think of putting us on the same footing with his own people or any of the Europeans who had preceded us, but that he intended to institute a new Order specially for us—I say, it seems strange that he should so suddenly alter his mind in this respect, and propose placing us on an equality with our own messengers and interpreters.

I date the change in the King's conduct towards me, and the misfortunes which eventually befell the members of the Mission and the old captives, from this day. Everything, as the reader may judge for himself, had gone on most prosperously up to this time. Whence, then, this unexpected alteration in his tone? I fully believe that his Majesty had then heard, as I did two days after, of the arrival of another person at Massowah to intercede for the liberation of the captives. This is by no means improbable, seeing that Dr. Beke reached that place towards the end of January.

How that gentleman's ill-timed intervention militated against the interests of the Mission will be made obvious in the course of this narrative.

7*th*.—Having, as already stated, declined to wear the proffered shirts, I addressed the following letter to the King on the subject:—

"*Koráta, 7th March*, 1866.

"Most Gracious Sovereign,

"I have had the honour of receiving your Majesty's kind letter of the 28th of the month Yekâtit, and was glad to learn therefrom that you were quite well.

"Dr. Blanc and Mr. Prideaux return you their respectful compliments.

"Pray accept my most grateful thanks for the honour which your Majesty intends to confer upon me and my companions, and also for the things which you were so good as to send me by Yashálaka Wald-Gâbir to select from.

"Be assured that the meanest token of friendship and goodwill coming from your Majesty will always be appreciated and considered by me a great honour.

"When the above-named Yashálaka Wald-Gâbir brought me your gracious message the other day concerning the same subject, I had intrusted your confidant, Aito Samuel, with some matters which I hoped he would have had an opportunity before now of communicating in person to your Majesty. I trust, however, that when Agafâri Gôlam and his companions arrive here, he will be able, with your Majesty's permission, to come to you.

"Commending you to the protection of our Heavenly Father, I remain," &c.

Having left my explanation to be made by Samuel, I deemed it discreet to retain the silks until I received his Majesty's permission to return them. My instructions to Samuel were to this effect: that if we had the shirts made, and did not wear them before the King, such a course would hardly be becoming; that it was not usual in the Courts of Christian Powers for the representative of a foreign State to appear before a Sovereign in any other than the uniform of his own Government; that had we been in his Majesty's service the case would have been different, but that as matters stood it would be derogatory to the King if we appeared before him in an uniform different from that which we were bound to wear before our own Queen.

Dr. Schimper called on me this morning with some geological specimens; also a sketch-map of the district of Bagáměděr, which he requested me to convey to the Royal Geographical Society. As the map was not completed as far as Koráta, I got Samuel's permission for him to go up to the hills and make the necessary survey. I also obtained the King's sanction to his proposal to make a collection of the fish in the Lake to send to England. I heard subsequently that he wrote himself to his Majesty, soliciting pecuniary aid to enable him to carry out his project—an application which surprised the King not a little, as he could not conceive why he should take any interest in Dr. Schimper's ichthyological researches.

8*th*.—Mr. Mayer arrived this morning with four brass cannons which had been made at Gáfflat by the King's European artisans. They were drawn by horses, and were mounted on the carriages of the guns that had been brought to the King by 'Abd-ur-Rahmán Bey from Egypt, the guns of which had been left at Mágdala. As his Majesty is a great hand at making roads by forced labour exacted from the peasantry, these pieces of ordnance were transported through the mountains to Koráta without much difficulty.

Dábterá Dusta, the messenger I sent down to Massowah

on the 12th of January with dispatches from Chálga, returned to-day with letters from Colonel Merewether and Mr. Munzinger. He was the first to inform me of Dr. Beke's arrival at Massowah, and of the object of his visit. The messenger declared that he had entreated that gentleman to keep quiet, and not to allow any intimation of his mission to reach the King, otherwise harm might befall us all; that he had taken special care to inform him of the preparations which his Majesty had made to give us a favourable reception, and that it was the general opinion in Abyssinia that the captives would certainly be released, and be allowed to leave the country with me; but the only response he could elicit from the gentleman referred to was, that I had no chance of succeeding, and that he was the only person likely to effect the desired object.

When the King heard of the arrival of my messenger from the coast, he sent for him immediately, and kept him at the Court four days, treating him very well, and decorating him with the Royal Shirt. On his return, I inquired whether the King had questioned him respecting Dr. Beke's mission. He replied in the negative; nevertheless, I fully believe that he related everything he knew of the subject, but was afraid to confess to me that he had done so. It will be noticed that in the following note which he brought me on the 15th from the King, his Majesty says that Dasta had acquainted him with "other matters" besides the state of affairs in Tigré:—

(After compliments.)

"Your servant Dasta, who came from Massowah, has informed me of the re-establishment of order in Tigré, and other matters. By the power of God, I have rejoiced greatly. I am glad to hear of their [the prisoners] safe arrival, and of the good health of you all.

"Dated Monday, the 4th of Magâbit."

9th.—Gave a dinner-party to all the King's European artisans to-day. Just as we had taken our seats at the table, Kántiba Hailo came in from the royal camp, bringing me the following letter from his Majesty:—

After compliments—

"Agafári Gólam has sent to inform me that your people [prisoners] had arrived, by the power of God [at Debra Tábor]. I have greatly rejoiced, and I wish you also to be glad. Wald-Gábir informed me that you had wished the doctor to go to him [Consul Cameron]. Very well; let Aito Samuel go with him at once. When they reach you safely, let me at once know of their arrival, by the power of God, in order that we may have a chat together.

"Dated Friday, the 1st of Magâbit."

It was now becoming clear to me, to my great disappointment, as well from the tenor of the message with which Kántiba Hailo was charged as from the foregoing note, that the King had determined to subject Consul Cameron and his companions to another trial. I had also been questioned whether, after conveying the released captives out of the country, it was my intention to return to Abyssinia as British Agent, his Majesty having expressed a strong wish that I should represent the British Government at his Court. My reply to this was, that I was only a servant and must obey orders. This answer, it appears, did not satisfy the King, for when it was repeated to him he remarked, "What have I in my hands to ensure Mr. Rassam's return to me?"

Having been informed to-day that his Majesty was

particularly anxious to know the import of the crown and star embroidered on the collar of Dr. Blanc and Lieutenant Prideaux's uniform, I sent to tell him that they were symbols indicating the rank of officers in the British army.

It having been frequently represented to me that the King hated the Mágdala captives so intensely that it might result in the failure of the Mission if the latter were brought face to face with him, I was strongly advised to try and prevent a meeting between them. As I was not in a position, however, to protest against any such proceeding on the part of his Majesty—notwithstanding that he had already forgiven the prisoners and virtually made them over to me in accordance with his letter to her Majesty of the 29th of January—I had intrusted Samuel with a message to induce the King to dispense with their attendance upon him; but that if he were bent on preferring charges against them before me, to allow the case to be proceeded with at Koráta. I also urged the trouble which it would give to convey so large a party by water to Zagé, and adduced Consul Cameron's indisposition as another consideration to lead him to forego his intention of having the released captives brought before him, requesting his Majesty at the same time to allow me to send Dr. Blanc to the Consul—a request which, as will be seen from the foregoing note, he readily granted.

10*th*.—All the ladies of the King's European artisans who arrived from Gáffat yesterday assembled in Mr. Waldmeier's tent this morning to receive a formal visit from me. They were all in gorgeous Abyssinian attire, with the exception of Madame Bourgaud, a French lady, who was dressed in the European style. Two of the ladies were the daughters of the late Mr. Bell by an Abyssinian mother; one was married to Mr. Waldmeier, and the other to Mr. Salmüller. There were present besides, two daughters of Dr. Schimper—also by an Abyssinian mother: one of these was the wife of Mr. Bender, the other the widow of a German named Kunzlin, who had died at Gáffat a few months before. The wives of Messrs. Mayer and Zander were converted Gallas, who had made them excellent helpmates; and Mrs. Moritz Hall was an Armenian on the father's and an Abyssinian on the mother's side. As they all spoke Amharic only, and Madame Bourgaud knew no other language except her native French, I was obliged to address them through an interpreter.

11*th*.—I was glad to hear from Consul Cameron to-day that he was a little better, and that we might expect him and his party to-morrow.

12*th*.—At 1 P.M. the gratifying intelligence reached us that Consul Cameron and his companions had arrived in the vicinity of Korâta; but as Agafâri Gôlam had received instructions from the King to hand them over to me in a particular form and order, he kept the poor fellows outside the town nearly an hour, until he had ascertained that he was not approaching me without due notice. Even when, an hour later, he entered our inclosure, there was endless running in and out of my tent on some frivolous errand or other: first, he wanted Samuel, the King's Bâldărâbâ, to be ready to see the released captives correctly counted; then he wished to know whether my tent was large enough to receive them, or if I would not have them counted before me outside. However, I soon brought this farce to an end, and was at length rejoiced to welcome the unfortunate sufferers. The following is the list of those who joined us on this occasion:—

Names	Occupation.	Country.	County, &c.	Inhabitant of.
', D. Cameron ..	Her Britannic Majesty's Consul at Massowah.			
.. Kerans	Late Secretary of Consul Cameron	Ireland ..	.. Galway ..	Southpark, Abascragh.
'. McKelvie ..	Late servant of Consul Cameron	Ireland ..	.. Down ..	.. Downpatrick.
I. Macraire ..	Servant of Consul Cameron	France ..	.. Department of Haute Rhin	Vhiran-val.
). Pietro	Late servant of Consul Cameron	Italy ..	.. Turin ..	.. Tavcia.
\. Bardel	Painter, and late teacher of languages	France ..	.. Department Meuse	Sampigny.
ev. H. A. Stern	Missionary	Cur-Hessen ..	.. .. ..	.. London.
I. Rosenthal ..	Missionary	Mecklenburg ..	Furstenberg	.. London.
Irs. E. Rosenthal	.. ..	England ..	.. London ..	.. London.
Ir. T. M. Flad ..	Missionary	Wurtemburg ..	Reutlingen	.. Unlingen.
Irs. P. Flad	.. ..	Rhenish Prussia	Trèves ..	.. Saarbrück.
\. Flad				
'r. Flad } children	.. ..	.. ..	.. ..
'. Flad				
V. Staiger	.. Missionary	Grand Duchy of Baden	Lahr ..	.. Langenwinkel.
'. Brandeis	.. Missionary	Ditto	Wiesloch ..	.. Baierthal.
\. Schiller	} Natural history collectors {	Prussia	Posen ..	.. Posen.
'. Essler ..		Hungary	Odenburg ..	.. Neustadthal.

After a little chat, I showed each party where to take up their quarters, and then returned to my tent to write the following letter to the King, which I dispatched forthwith by Aito Samuel and two of my messengers:—

"*Koráta, 12th March,* 1866.

" MOST GRACIOUS SOVEREIGN,

" I have had the honour of receiving your Majesty's kind letter of the 1st Magábit by Kántiba Hailo, and I was rejoiced to learn from its bearer that he left you in perfect health and prosperity. May the Lord continue to keep you in the same happy condition.

" I have the pleasure to inform your Majesty that Consul Cameron and his European companions, who have been brought from Mágdala by Agafári Gólam, reached this place this afternoon; and I return you my best thanks for the kindness and attention shown them on the road by your Majesty's servants, in accordance with your orders.

"Mr. Flad and his companions who were at Gáffat have also joined me here.

"The rest of the news will be given to your Majesty by your servant, Aito Samuel, who is going to your Court with some communications which I have desired him to make to you.

"My companions join me in presenting your Majesty with my respectful salutations."

The reader will probably have remarked that my reception of the captives was cold and formal. It was so undoubtedly in outward appearance, as it was also designedly, for I had been specially warned against any cordial demonstration of friendship towards them, lest the King might take umbrage thereat, and suspect me of siding with his "enemies." "If you desire to leave the country with them," was the advice of those who knew the King's disposition well, "keep aloof from them for the present." It was extremely painful to me to act with such reserve, even for a time, more especially towards Consul Cameron and the Rev. Mr. Stern, with whom I had been formerly acquainted, and above all when they had just been released from a long and horrible confinement; but the safety of all, the members of the Mission included, obliged me to repress my own feelings in the matter. However, I directed my servants to supply them with every requisite; and I hardly need add that when the Mission was disgraced, and there was no longer any object to be gained by humouring the King, I gladly threw off the assumed disguise, feeling that then we were all in the same plight, and must escape or perish together.

CHAPTER XIV.

TRIAL OF THE CAPTIVES.

Theodore decides on the trial of the Captives — His charges against them — His object — The Captives plead culpable — Mistranslation of Earl Russell's and her Majesty's letters — A dilemma — Arrival of a messenger from Dr. Beke — The Petition from the relatives of the Captives — The Order of "the Cross and Solomon's Seal" — Another present from Theodore — Dr. Beke's mission injudicious — Ôna Mohammed invested with the "Royal Shirt" — Dâbterâ Dasta in the royal garments — Visit to Theodore at Zagê postponed — Alâkâ I'ngâdâ, the royal Scribe — Reception of the Mission at Zagê — Theodore's courtesy — Consults with his Chiefs about the departure of the Mission and Captives — His grievances against M. Lejean, the Coptic Patriarch, a German, and Mr. Speedy — His opinion of his own subjects — Our return to Korâta.

IT took the King two days to decide how to act, for he evidently wavered between a desire to gratify me by acceding to my request, and an inclination to refuse what I had asked, and thereby to break with me at once. The course he eventually took was this:—he sent Alâkâ I'ngâdâ and Agafâri Gôlam with Aito Samuel to say, that he wished me to hold a Court in my tent, and that in the presence of his European artisans and some Abyssinian officials the charges which he had preferred against the released captives should be read over to them, and they be asked whether they were true or not.

On delivering the King's letter, Alâkâ I'ngâdâ told me, in the presence of the assembly and his colleagues, that his royal master felt happy that the Court, which was to all intents and purposes his Court, was to be held in my tent, where I should represent his Majesty; that what the King wanted was to convince me that he had been badly treated by the released captives, and to obtain for him from them a "Fĕkĕr-Kâsâ," or friendly indemnity; that, on the other hand, if I found him to be in fault, he would indemnify them in any way I judged right. The following are the documents which were read on the occasion:—

(After compliments.)

"By the power of God, and the fortune of Queen Victoria and myself, those people [prisoners] whom my friend [the Queen] asked me to release have reached you safely, and when I heard of it I was glad. What my friend, the Queen, asked me to do I have, by the power of God, performed. In the letter which my friend the Queen sent, it is thus said: 'We have sent to you Mr. Hormuzd Rassam, who was Governor at Aden, and whom we esteem and trust; consult with him concerning what you require of us, and he will do it for you.' She says that I am blind now, and what I require is a remedy, to give light to my eyes. As I have gladdened your heart, I wish you to gladden mine by sending and obtaining for me [such a remedy]. Of the translation of the Queen's communication which you gave me, I send you a copy, in order that you may hear it. I wish you to ask the people [prisoners] whom you have, by the power of God, released, before your brothers and Mr. Waldmeier's party, whether it be true that they had abused me or not.

"Dated A.M. 7358, and A.D. 1858, in the year of St. Mark, on the 6th of Magâbit."

(I may mention here that the translation of the Queen's letter to Theodore, of which I was the bearer, was made at the request of his Majesty with the assistance of Mr. Prideaux, the royal Chief Scribe, Samuel, and one of my Abyssinian interpreters.)

Charges against the Prisoners.

After compliments:—

"The charges against Cameron, who calls himself Consul, are these:—This gentleman and his agent Bardel sent to tell me that they had come as messengers from the Queen, and wished me to receive them. By the power of God, I sent an escort to Massowah and brought him up. I was then at Debra Mäi, in the district of Métcha. When he arrived, I sent my nobles to meet him, and had a salute fired for him. According to the custom of my country, I decorated my house for his reception, and welcomed him therein, by the power of God. He then gave me a letter, which he said was from the Queen; after I had read the letter, he presented me with a double-barrelled gun and a pair of double-barrelled pistols, which he said were presents from the Queen. I bowed on receiving them, and thanked her Majesty for them. In the letter the Queen said that she wishes to be my friend and relation, and that she heard that I loved and befriended her on account of what I had done for Plowden and his party against the people of my country; that formerly England and Abyssinia had an interest; and now she wished that her Consul should remain with me, and that sportsmen and merchants should be allowed to follow their avocations. He [the Consul] said to me that a Consul from me should go to England, and my sportsmen and merchants also, and that, by the power of God, we [the English] would protect them. I was glad at hearing this, and said, 'Very well.'

"In accordance with the rules of my country, I treated him and Bardel well.

"I told the Consul that the Turks had taken my country, and were my enemies; nor had I a ship to do my work, by the power of God, and I said that I wished that the Mission and presents which I intended to send to the Queen should be conveyed safely. I gave him a friendly letter to the Queen and sent him away. The letter which he brought me, and the consultation which we had together, he abandoned, and went to the Turks, who do not love me, and before whom he insulted and lowered me. He stayed with them some time, and returned to me. I asked him, 'Where is the answer to the friendly letter I intrusted you with; what have you come for?' He said to me, 'I do not know.' So I said to him, 'You are not the servant of my friend, the Queen, as you had represented yourself to be;' and, by the power of my Creator, I imprisoned him. Ask him if he can deny this.

"The charge against Bardel is this: that he told me that he wished to make me acquainted with the Emperor of the French. I said to him, 'Very well;' and sent him. He came back and said that the Emperor refused to see him. I answered, 'Never mind; I have my God.' After keeping silence, he asked me to release Macraire, a Frenchman. I replied that he had formerly told me that he wished to make me acquainted with the Emperor of the French, and on his return [from France] he had told me that he had been ignored. I said then, 'For whose sake shall I release him?' and I refused to do so. He was angry at what I said; and in my Court he ungirt himself and covered his head with the cloth.* I was annoyed at this, and, by the power of my Lord, I imprisoned him. Ask him if he can deny this."

Charges against the Rest of the Prisoners.

"The other prisoners have abused me, I am well aware. I used to love and honour them. A friend ought to be a shield to his friend, and they ought to have shielded me. Why did they not defend me? On this account I disliked them.

"Now, by the power of God, for the sake of the Queen and the British people and yourselves, I cannot continue my dislike towards them. I wish you to make between us a reconciliation from the heart. If I am in fault, do you tell me, and I will requite them; but if you find that I am wronged, I wish you to get them to requite me."

When the letter was read I noticed that the King had only sent charges against Consul Cameron and M. Bardel, and as the latter had introduced himself to Theodore—so the King

* A mark of insult in Abyssinia, especially before a Sovereign.

asserted—as a servant of the British Queen, it was quite evident that his Majesty was intent on making political capital out of his present proceedings; since even Mr. Stern, whom he had always accused of having abused him, was not mentioned by name in the list now sent of his grievances. Towards the end of the document, however, an implied charge, which caused me no little uneasiness, was made against all the released captives, together with a hint—given for the first time—that he wished them to give him a friendly indemnity, or, in plainer terms, substantial damages. I had hitherto laboured under the mistaken notion that the King simply wanted them to forgive and forget, and to promise him their lasting friendship in future; but Messrs. Flad and Waldmeier disabused me of that idea, by explaining that *Fëkër-Kâsâ* meant something more substantial. Money, of course, the King would not demand, as that would be beneath his dignity to receive; still he might insist on their sending to Europe for any articles he might fancy, and the chances were that he would detain them until they arrived, and when they came that he would ask for more. I deemed it advisable, therefore, to make no allusion whatever to the *Fëkër-Kâsâ* in my reply, but put myself forward as answerable for the whole party, wishing, if possible, to prevent his Majesty from bullying the old captives again, which he was evidently aiming at.

The Court was convened in my tent at eleven o'clock, when I caused the charges to be read out. As Consul Cameron was rather weak, I took upon myself to permit him to be seated during the trial, telling the Commissioners that I felt sure the King would not object; if he did, that I would take the blame. They replied at once that they were certain what pleased me would please his Majesty. But the whole thing was a farce, as there was neither judge nor jury present, and none of the captives would have dared to dispute the King's assertions, even if he had accused them of the most inconceivable criminality; consequently, it was unanimously agreed that they should all admit having done wrong and beg his Majesty's forgiveness. Mons. Bardel had come into my tent before the opening of the proceedings, and on the arrival of the King's Commissioners seemed disposed to create a disturbance, by calling upon his fellow released captives and the Gáffat Europeans to prove the charges which they had always alleged against him. On my pointing out to him, however, that it was unbecoming to moot such questions then, begging him at the same time to postpone all these and similar matters of discussion until we were fairly out of the country, he at once desisted.

We discovered now that the letter which Consul Cameron had brought from Earl Russell, as also the letter from her Majesty which I had the honour to convey to the King, both of which were quoted in the foregoing communications from his Majesty, had been sadly garbled in the Amharic version, and made to state things which were contrary to fact. For my own part, I felt certain that the additions and alterations were made after the royal letter was translated; but as I was told that it would be useless, and might perhaps do mischief, if I brought the matter to the King's notice, I was constrained to hold my peace.

It was not true, moreover, that her Majesty the Queen had sent a letter to Theodore by Consul Cameron. The letter of which he was the bearer was written by Earl Russell, and the following copy of the original will show how strangely its contents had been mistranslated or perverted to suit the King's views:—

Earl Russell to King Theodore of Abyssinia.

"SIR, "*Foreign Office, London, Feb.* 20, 1862.

"The Queen my Sovereign has been informed by her servants in the East of the exertions which your Highness kindly made to recover the remains of her late Consul, Mr. Plowden, and of your generosity in declining to accept repayment of the sum of money which you paid for that purpose. Her Majesty commands me to assure your Highness that she views your conduct in regard to this affair as a proof of friendship towards herself and the British nation, of which she is duly sensible.

"In order more particularly to manifest her Majesty's thankfulness for these your Highness's services, and to show her regard and friendship for you personally, her Majesty requests your acceptance of a rifle and a pair of revolver pistols, as a present from herself. Her Majesty has intrusted these articles to Captain Charles Duncan Cameron, whom she has appointed her Consul in Abyssinia, as the successor of the late Mr. Plowden, and who has lately taken his departure for his post; and I take this opportunity of introducing him to your Highness, and of requesting your protection and favour in his behalf. He is well acquainted with all that concerns the interests of both countries, and will, I am confident, do all in his power to make himself acceptable to your Highness, and to promote your welfare.

"I thank your Highness for the letter which you addressed to me, informing me of the steps which you had taken to punish the men who murdered Mr. Plowden and Mr. Bell; and with my best wishes for your uninterrupted health and happiness, I recommend you to the protection of the Almighty.

"Your faithful friend,

(Signed) "RUSSELL."

(L.S. The large Signet.)

That similar liberties had been taken with her Majesty's letter to Theodore, of which I was the honoured bearer, will be evident on comparing the subjoined transcript with the interpretation which the King, either wilfully or otherwise, had put upon it:—

Her Majesty the Queen to the King of Abyssinia.

"*May* 26, 1864.

" VICTORIA, by the grace of God, Queen of the United Kingdom of Great Britain and Ireland, Defender of the Faith, &c., &c., &c., to Theodore, King of Abyssinia, sendeth greeting. We have duly received the letter which your Majesty delivered to Our servant Cameron, and We have read with pleasure the friendly expressions which it conveys. We learn with satisfaction that Your Majesty has successfully established your authority in the country over which you rule, and We trust that you may long continue to administer its affairs in peace and prosperity. Our servant Cameron has no doubt conveyed to you the assurance of Our friendship and goodwill, and We are glad to learn by your letter that he had been duly received by your Majesty. Accounts have indeed reached Us of late that your Majesty had withdrawn your favour from Our servant, We trust however that these accounts have originated in false representations on the part of persons ill-disposed to your Majesty, and who may desire to produce an alteration in Our feelings towards you. But your Majesty can give no better proof of the sincerity of the sentiments which you profess towards Us, nor ensure more effectually a continuance of Our friendship and goodwill, than by dismissing Our servant Cameron, and any other Europeans who may desire it, from your Court, and by affording them every assistance and protection on their journey to the destination to which they desire to proceed. With the view of renewing to you the expression of Our friendship, and of explaining to you our wishes respecting Our servant Cameron, We have directed Our servant Hormuzd Rassam, First Assistant to the Political Resident at Aden, to proceed to your residence, and to deliver to you this Our Royal letter. We have instructed him to inform your Majesty that if, notwithstanding the long distance which separates Our dominions from those of your Majesty, you should, after having permitted Our servant Cameron and the other Europeans to take their leave and depart, desire to send an Embassy to this country, that Embassy will be very well received by Us. And so, not doubting that you will receive Our servant Rassam in a favourable manner, and give entire credit to all that he shall say to you on Our part, as well as comply with the requests which he is instructed to make to you, We recommend you to the protection of the Almighty.

"Given at Our Court at Balmoral, the Twenty-sixth day of May, in the year of Our Lord 1864, and in the Twenty-seventh year of Our reign.

" Your good Friend,
(Signed) " Victoria R."

(L.S. The large Signet.)
(Not countersigned.)

Superscribed:
" To Our Good Friend Theodore,
" King of Abyssinia."

Towards evening, Messrs. Flad and Waldmeier as well as Samuel expressed their unanimous opinion that as they understood the King's letter received during the day, it was evidently his Majesty's intention to get me to write to England for artisans to be employed in his service, and in the mean time to detain us in the country. What was to be done under this unlooked-for dilemma? Was I to refuse the request at once and stand the consequences, even to the risk of our all being consigned in chains to Mágdala? Or, was I to consent? in which case, we should all have to remain in the country as hostages. Either alternative was objectionable; however, as I was told that the King intended to invite me to spend a day or two with him at Zagê, when I should have an opportunity of explaining to him verbally how important it was that I should leave Abyssinia, together with all the European party, as soon as possible, and might then manage to elicit his consent to our speedy departure. I made but slight allusion to this subject in my next communication. The letter was written on the 16th, but owing to a violent storm which raged over the Lake the messengers who conveyed it were unable to proceed to Zagé till the day following:—

"*Koráta, 16th March*, 1866.

"Most Gracious Sovereign,

"I have had the honour of receiving your Majesty's letter dated the 6th of Magábit, and I was glad to learn from your servants, Aláká I'ngádá and Aito Samuel, that you were enjoying perfect health.

"In accordance with your Majesty's request, I summoned to my tent yesterday morning Mr. Cameron and the rest of the Europeans who came from Mágdala, and had the charges which you had preferred against them read to them before your servants Kántiba Hailo, Aito Samuel, Nagadrás Gabra-Mádhen, Aláká I'ngádá and others, and also in the presence of your European servants of Gáffat. They all confessed that they had done wrong, and hoped that, as your Majesty had been good enough to release them for the sake of your friendship to our Queen, you would extend to them the forgiveness due from one Christian to another.

"With regard to your Majesty's wish that I should gladden your heart, as you have done mine, by writing to England and obtaining for you a scientific person to teach your people the arts, be assured that nothing would please me better than to be of service to you, especially after the great kindness I have received from your Majesty. I should consider myself ungrateful and unfriendly were I not to be honest in all my dealings with you, and acquaint you with what would strengthen your friendship with my Queen, and prove of material service to your Majesty's benefit and happiness hereafter.

"My Queen sent you a most friendly letter, which your Majesty received in a cordial and honourable manner. To that letter you have written a most courteous answer, showing the friendly sentiments with which your heart was inspired. That letter shall be conveyed by me to her Majesty.

"Whatever service you wish me to render you, I could not do it better than for myself to be on the spot, and aid you in everything which my Queen can do for you; but if your Majesty desire otherwise, I shall be happy to comply with your wishes."

I dispatched this letter by Aito Samuel, Aláká I'ngádá,

Agafári Gôlam and one of my messengers. I requested them all to speak to the King about the dangerous course he was pursuing, because, although he intended to keep me in his country, as a friend, until the arrival of the "scientific man," yet that such a step would in Europe be construed to mean that he kept me as a hostage. I begged that he would trust me, and abandon the idea that I should forget him after I had left Abyssinia.

As will be seen from the contents of the letter, I was very guarded in the expressions which I used respecting the admission which the captives had made when the King's charges were read over to them. I merely reported that all had confessed that they had done wrong, and begged his Majesty to forgive them, as one Christian ought to forgive another; and not that they had confessed themselves to be guilty, and begged him - as a King sitting in judgment to pardon them. But the whole thing was a pretext got up by the wily Monarch to veil his real object. The die was about to be cast, and whether it was to be favourable to us or the contrary depended entirely on the whim of the royal gamester.

On the day of the mock trial a messenger came to me with a letter, which he said was from Dr. Beke, addressed to the King. I asked the messenger if there was with it any letter for me; he replied in the negative, saying that Dr. Beke had not intended him to come to me, but had told him to go straight to the King. He said he had not done so, because he was afraid to take the letter to the King, and thought it would be better to bring it to me. He told me that he had been obliged to remain four days at Góndar, having been too tired to come on at once. When this letter came to hand, I was asked by some of my fellow-Europeans to suppress it, as it was apprehended that its receipt might prove a stumbling-block to our departure from Abyssinia. This, of course, I refused to do, and accordingly sent it on to the King.

18th.—Aito Samuel, accompanied by two of the royal deputies, returned from Zagê this morning, bringing me the following satisfactory answer from the King:—

(After compliments.)

"With regard to the affair of Cameron and his party, I used to reckon them as my friends, and honoured them, and it has been proved to you that they have wronged me. For the sake of our Lord, and, below him, for the sake of the great Queen, my friend, Victoria, I have forgiven them. The contents of your letter have made me glad, by the power of God; I wish to bow my head and kiss your hand and foot. I want you to come to me, in order that we may consult together.

"The relations of Cameron and his imprisoned companions have written to me in sorrow about them. By the power of God, and for the sake of my friend, the great Queen Victoria, I have been reconciled to them, and by the power of our Creator we will consult on all matters when we meet.

"Dated Sunday, the 10th of Magâbit."

When the King dictated the last paragraph in the foregoing communication, he had, of course, perused the petition of the relatives of the captives, and also Dr. Beke's letter which accompanied it; nevertheless, he does not mention that he was moved by either to the announced reconciliation. It is by no means improbable, however, that when he read the petition, wherein the petitioners " humbly, at the feet of your Majesty, plead for mercy and pardon for the wretched Europeans," and understood from Dr. Beke himself, "the Englishman," that he was commissioned on the part of the petitioners to " supplicate your Majesty in their names for their [the captives'] pardon and release"—in fact, that the said " Englishman" proposed to come up to him with a verdict of guilty in his hand against those whom the King designated his "enemies"—that his Majesty began to think he had let the captives off too cheaply, and was more than ever disposed to exact satisfaction in some shape or other. That the King, as he states in his letter, had intended to "consult" me on this matter, there can be no doubt. That he never did so was in all probability owing to an after-suspicion that I was cognizant of Dr. Beke's mission, and that it was a trick to overreach him.

The success of the Mission up to this point is thus described by Mr. Waldmeier, in a letter addressed to Bishop Gobat, dated Korâta, 20th March, 1866, and published in the London *Record* of the 11th July of the same year:—

"Mr. Rassam has so far perfectly succeeded. The King has delivered all the liberated prisoners into his hands, saying that he did it for the sake of friendship between England and Abyssinia; to which he added, 'the friendship between Abyssinia and England has been disturbed by the Europeans who came to my land with the devil in their hearts, who abused me, speaking all kinds of evil against me; but now the great Queen of England having sent a great man, Mr. Rassam, to me with a friendly letter, I have set Mr. Cameron and all the Europeans at liberty, desiring a cordial and solid reconciliation.' . . . The King has invited us (the Scripture Readers), together with Mr. Rassam, to go to him at Zagé, to consult together about several particulars. . . . We expect that in about three weeks Mr. Rassam will take his departure, together with the liberated Europeans. At any rate, it would be a dangerous thing if they were obliged to spend the rainy season in this country. I fear, in that case, that the peace and friendship which have been so wisely restored by Mr. Rassam might suffer, which would be most painful to us. We shall, therefore, do our utmost to forward Mr. Rassam's departure, together with those to whom he has been a saviour, with all possible speed. . . . Three days ago the King received several petitions in favour of the captives, sent to him by Dr. and Mrs. Beke from Massowah. These petitions, especially that from Mr. Stern's family, are written in very good terms, and are exceedingly touching; they deeply moved the heart of the King, though they were too late. The short answer of the King was: 'I have delivered all these persons to Mr. Rassam out of friendship to the Queen; they are all free.' With respect to the presents about which Dr. Beke has written to the King, his Majesty was most displeased, and expressed strongly his dissatisfaction that people should think that he loves presents, whilst friendship and love is all that he desires."

I was informed by the messengers that the King was vacillating, and that he had not quite made up his mind whether to permit me to leave for England, or keep me until his object was attained. They hoped, however, that as the King had expressed a wish to have an interview with me, he would allow me to go with all the Europeans that were with me. Wednesday, the 21st of March, was the day appointed for "consulting" me.

Samuel informed me that his Majesty was much pleased with the message I had sent him about the Shirts intended for the members of the Mission, and that he had been directed to take the silk back to Zagê. The King, however, had expressed a wish to institute an Order, to be called "the Cross and Solomon's Seal," for the special purpose of decorating the members of the Mission, in token of his esteem, and he asked me to show his Abyssinian goldsmiths — he sent no less than four to our camp — how to make them. They worked for nearly a fortnight, but could not succeed in making the Orders according to pattern; so the King ordered Mr. Zander, one of the artisans, to undertake them. The new Order was to be of three classes:—the first, wholly of gold; the second, a gold cross and silver seal; the third, wholly of silver. The King insisted that three of each should be got ready before our departure, in order that some of his Abyssinian Chiefs might share in the honour which he intended to confer on us. The first Order was to be presented to Râs Mashisha, the King's eldest son, Râs I'ngădă, the chief minister, and myself; the second was

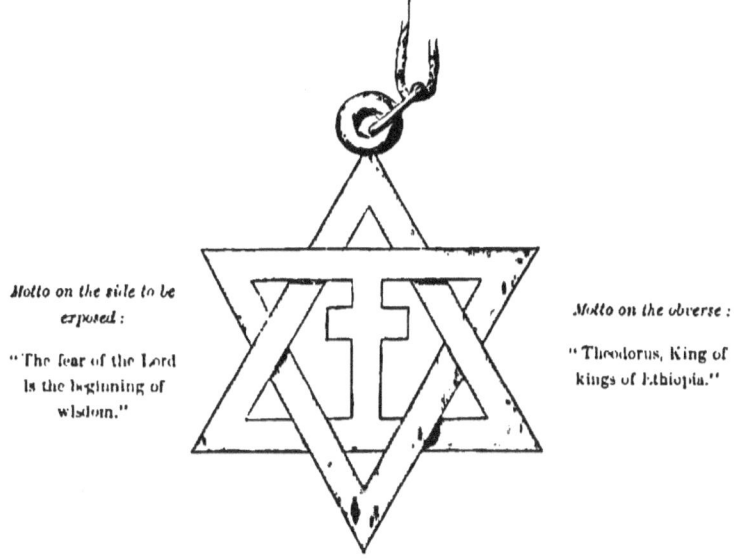

Motto on the side to be exposed:

"The fear of the Lord is the beginning of wisdom."

Motto on the obverse:

"Theodorus, King of kings of Ethiopia."

ORDER OF THE CROSS AND SOLOMON'S SEAL.

to be conferred on Râs Túgga, the Commander-in-Chief of all the Musketeers, Dr. Blanc and Lieutenant Prideaux. Who was to be invested with the third Order had not been decided on.

So anxious was the King to decorate my companions and myself before we left, that he sent daily to Mr. Zander to hurry on the work.

On the same day his Majesty sent me, from the royal Treasury, another present of 5,000 dollars through the Kántiba, which I reluctantly accepted; not that I was in want of the money, but because, under existing circumstances, I deemed it advisable to give the King no excuse for carping at my conduct. He also sent fifty milch cows, with their keepers, it having been reported to him that I found great difficulty in providing milk for our large party. I did not actually receive the money either on this or the previous occasion, but I told Aito Samuel that I should draw on him from time to time for whatever sums I required. As far as the expenses of the Mission were concerned, I had more than enough money remaining of the sum which I took with me into Abyssinia for all purposes—quite sufficient to take us to Matámma; but as I was told that if the King heard that I had not spent any of the present he gave me, he would be greatly offended, I drew sometimes on his agent.

The King also sent me Dr. Beke's letter, which he asked me to peruse, together with a petition which had been forwarded by Dr. Beke from the families of Messrs. Cameron, Stern, Rosenthal and Kerans. The King said that he did not wish to answer it until he had seen me, and when we met he would consult me about it. The letter was headed, "From the Englishman"—a style which is neither English nor Oriental, and must have seemed as strange to an Abyssinian as it would be to an European. It did not allude to me or the Mission; and from the effect which the letter appeared to me likely to produce upon a mind like the King's, as well as from what afterwards took place, I could not help thinking, that from the day the King heard of Dr. Beke's arrival at Massowah, he began to suspect that the British Government was not sincere towards him.

As far back as the 8th of March, 1866, I wrote to a friend in England in these terms of Dr. Beke's enterprise:—"It is feared that his mission will do a good deal of harm; and should any interruption take place in the good understanding now existing between his Majesty of Abyssinia and myself, those who were instrumental in getting up that job ought to be blamed for it." The Europeans generally on the spot, as well as the native officials of rank who were favourably disposed to our Mission, concurred in this opinion. The same view was taken by men eminent for their political experience in the East, who did all in their power to arrest the rash undertaking. Colonel Stanton, her Britannic Majesty's Consul-General in Egypt, in his dispatch to the Under-Secretary of State for Foreign Affairs, dated 13th December, 1865, writes:—

"Dr. Beke, who arrived in Egypt some time since, is still here; he has informed me his intention is to proceed to Massowah, and from thence try to reach Adowa; he talks of proceeding in about a week. I informed him I feared his journey might interfere with Rassam's mission, but I hope the latter will have accomplished his task before Dr. Beke can reach the country."

Colonel Merewether, also, took special pains to point out the mischief which he foresaw would almost certainly arise out of this independent attempt on the part of Dr. Beke. In his official communication to that gentleman, he enters so fully into the then critical state of our relations with Theodore, and draws so correct a portrait of that intractable monarch, that I shall make no apology for quoting it *in extenso* from the Blue Book :—

"*Aden, February* 8, 1866.

"Sir,—Her Majesty's ship 'Lyra' will leave this for Massowah in a few days, and I take the opportunity of communicating to you the latest intelligence I have received from Abyssinia, both from the captives and Mr. Rassam.

"The letters from the former were up to the 28th September only, the messengers bringing them down having delayed in Tigré from dread of the cholera, said to be raging on the coast. On the above date Captain Cameron and his fellow-prisoners were still at Mágdala and all well, having got through the winter better than they had expected to do.

"Mr. Rassam had reached Cásala on the 6th November, and

left it again on the 9th, expecting to arrive at Matámma on the 20th *idem*. From there he would immediately communicate with King Theodorus, and it was hoped would either meet or speedily be joined by an escort to take him to the King. Of the latter's movements it was said that he had entered Gójjam, so as to be nearer to Matámma, and that he had the captives with him. The first part of this report was supposed to be true, the latter not to be strictly relied on.

"My object in mentioning the above is to show you exactly the position of affairs now, and while desirous of not in the least trammelling you in the execution of the kindly object you have in view, to suggest to you the unquestionable expediency of your deferring your entry into Abyssinia until something more decisive is heard of the result of Mr. Rassam's mission to Matámma. That gentleman has progressed as favourably and as rapidly as could under the circumstances be expected; he is proceeding to the King by the route selected by that potentate, and at this moment, if not actually with him, will be in direct communication, and engaged in negotiations regarding the release of the unfortunate captives whose safety and freedom is your chief point of solicitude.

"With your knowledge of Abyssinia, its present ruler and its people, I need not enter at length into the difficulties and complications that are likely to be raised, if, while these negotiations are going on, and before they have been brought to any issue, the King should hear that another Mission (for your retinue will of course be greatly magnified) has entered Abyssinia, headed by an English gentleman of repute in the country itself, and having professedly the same object, viz., the liberation of the captives; it will also be pointed out to him that this second Mission is entering the country not at his invitation—a point on which, as you know, he is particularly sensitive—and, further, that it is proceeding through the territory of those who are rebels to his authority, and that it is enabled to do so only by entering into friendly communication and association with those who are in arms against him. In any person's mind such a mode of procedure would naturally raise doubts; how much more so will it in a person of such a notoriously suspicious and hasty nature as the Emperor of Abyssinia? In the understanding of himself and those around him, it will be impossible to dissever you from the British Government, or to induce them to believe that you are acting separately, and entirely in a private capacity; it will therefore seem as if Government was acting on two different plans, one of which would personally be most objectionable to him, and would immediately lead him to question the other. The confidence in Mr. Rassam's mission, which has been brought about by careful management and long patient waiting, would be at once withdrawn, and the position of the captives rendered more critical than ever.

"As far as we are able to judge, Mr. Rassam's mission has every chance of success: he is proceeding to join the King's Court at the invitation of that Monarch. On the 20th of November he was to have reached the place appointed, and if the King was in Gójjam, there would not be above fourteen days' march between them; and, further, he is the bearer of a letter from her Majesty the Queen of England, which cannot fail to prove most satisfactory to his wounded dignity; but the receipt thereof—so all are agreed—is the point on which he has always laid the greatest stress, as the one essential before the question of the condition of the captives, or any other, could be entertained.

"Under these circumstances I would strongly recommend your deferring your advance from Massowah until further tidings have been received of Mr. Rassam's movements. Such cannot be long delayed now; they may indeed be at Massowah at this moment; and to save time I shall by this opportunity write and request M. Munzinger, who is in charge of the British Consulate, to be good enough to communicate to you any authentic intelligence he may receive, that you may be the better able to judge how you can act with advantage to the cause you have undertaken.

"I have, &c.,
(Signed) "W. L. MEREWETHER.
"To Dr. Beke."

Kindly remonstrances like these would have induced any ordinary philanthropist to hesitate before he placed in jeopardy the liberty, and perhaps the lives, of those whose release it was his avowed object to effect. But Dr. Beke's overweening estimate of his own abilities and of his knowledge of the customs of the country—a knowledge which the tenor of his letter to the King goes far to disprove—led him to persist at all risks—not to himself, but to the captives generally and the members of the Mission—in his most injudicious scheme. Even Samuel laughed when he handed me that gentleman's letter, and said, "Do you know that man Beke, sir? He is a queer man. I travelled with him for some time in Abyssinia. He coming to release the captives, indeed! He had better remain where he is; for from what I know of him he will not be two days with the King before he is sent to Mágdala in chains." Fortunately, when the ill-timed letter arrived I was on the best terms with his Majesty, otherwise we should all have been condemned to that fate at once; but the King's suspicions had been aroused, and the consequence was not long delayed in the disgrace of our Mission and the re-incarceration of the captives.

Mohammed Sihâwy, the false reporter, was presented by the King to-day with a small district in Tigrê, called Wêna, together with the title of "Ôna," and by royal order he was in future to be styled "Ôna Mohammed." He was inordinately puffed up with his new title, and assumed at once an overbearing demeanour towards his late comrades. Dâbtĕrâ Dasta, who had just returned from Massowah, took offence at his assumption of superiority, and on receiving some directions from him given in the tone of a command, he asked him who or what he was to think so much of himself. The new Ôna adjured him, by the death of the King, to hold his tongue, which merely added fuel to fire, for Dasta thereupon abused him roundly, and then, stripping off his Royal Shirt, threw it on the ground, saying, "Here are the few ells of silk; give them back to the King." As Samuel and other of the King's officers, who were witnesses of this scene, expressed their fears that if a report of what had occurred should reach his Majesty, the rash man might lose his life, I ordered him to be arrested forthwith, as well with the hope of saving the poor fellow, as to show the officials that I disapproved of his conduct. During the night a consultation took place between Samuel and his colleagues, Ôna Mohammed among the number, when it was unanimously agreed that the matter should be hushed up, and they all came to me in a body to solicit forgiveness for the culprit. I accordingly sent for him and made him receive the Shirt, with a stone on the back of his neck, in accordance with the Abyssinian custom in such cases. After kissing the Shirt thrice, he put it on, not a little delighted to find that he had got out of the scrape so easily. I sent this man again to Massowah with letters in May, 1866, and on his return in August he was plundered and imprisoned by the rebels near Gondar. (That, as I have already mentioned, was the King's alleged reason for destroying the capital.) He eventually effected his escape, and on the way back to me, *viâ* Debra Tábor, he thought he might as well pay his respects to the Sovereign—in the hope, of course, of getting something from him. He was clad in rags at the time, and on seeing him in that plight the King bade him approach, saying: "What is the matter with you, Dâbtĕrâ Dasta? Why are you so ragged?" He then narrated all that had befallen him, whereupon his Majesty remarked, "So you have been plundered and imprisoned by those vicious rebels! Come here, and put on these clothes, and when you have rested I will send you to your master;" the King simultaneously divesting himself of his drawers and *shámma*, and giving them to the man, who came to me shortly after, at Mágdala, clad in these royal garments. I subsequently employed this Dâbtêrâ Dasta as a courier between Mágdala and the coast, and when Dajjâj Kâsa took possession of Tigrê he was the confidential messenger between me and that Chief. I also sent him once charged with an important communication to the Wakshum Gobazê, Dajjâj Kâsa's rival; but although he was so engaged on my behalf with contending parties, and that at a most critical time, he never once failed to keep his counsel.

19*th*.—I wrote the following letter to the King to-day, but the messengers were unable to proceed with it till next morning:—

"*Korâta*, 19*th March*, 1866.
"MOST GRACIOUS SOVEREIGN,

"I have the honour to acknowledge the receipt of your kind and welcome letter of the 10th of the month of Magâbit, which was brought to me by Aito Samuel and his companions, and I am not a little rejoiced to learn that you are in perfect health and prosperity.

"The five thousand dollars with which you have kindly presented me, through Kántiba Hailo, have reached me in full, and now I beg to return you my best thanks for them. I pray God to reward you for all your kindness to me.

"With reference to your Majesty's desire that I should come and see you, doubtless it is a pleasure for which my heart has been longing ever since we separated; and by God's help I hope to repair to you with my companions, Dr. Blanc and Mr. Prideaux, on Wednesday morning next, as those gentlemen are also glad of the opportunity of being honoured once more by seeing your Majesty.

"I pray God to show us the light of your countenance in gladness and joy.

"My companions join me in respectful compliments."

I must remark on the above that his Majesty had expressed a desire to see me "alone;" for what object, probably none but that inscrutable Monarch himself knew. However, I was determined not to be separated from my colleagues, who had thus far shared the fortunes of the Mission.

20*th*.—This morning I received the following note from the King:—

(After compliments.)

"Unavoidable business has called me hence, and I wish you to remain where you are until I return, when I will send for you.

"Dated the 12th of Magâbit."

The reason for this postponement of my visit was, because he thought fit to go in person to escort his horses, which he had ordered from Debra Tâbor. As they were to be conducted to Zagé round the south-eastern side of the Lake, he feared that in reaching the Abai they might be pounced upon by the rebels of Gójjam. A detachment headed by a Râs would have sufficed for the duty, but he evidently distrusted placing even a small body of troops, under independent command, any distance out of his sight. All his female establishment also came from Debra Tâbor on the same occasion; but they were sent to Zagé in canoes, together with all the ladies of rank who were going to join their husbands at the royal camp.

21*st*.—Received the subjoined from the King just as he was starting for the Abai:—

(After compliments.)

"I have been desirous and anxious to have an interview with you, but now I intend to be absent from this place for a day or two. When I return, by the power of God, I will send for you, as I am longing for your friendship. May our Creator cause us to meet in peace, and may He give you and me health.

"Dated Wednesday, the 13th of Magâbit."

He sent no reply either verbally or by letter to my

intimation that I should take my companions with me to Zagê. I did not answer the foregoing, because I was told that his Majesty would send for me on his return.

As I was uncertain what would be the upshot of the projected interview, I deemed it advisable to dispatch a post to the coast, in order to give the captives an opportunity of communicating with their friends at home. I enjoined them to be very careful to write nothing which might compromise us, having been given to understand that the King was very fond of prying into other people's secrets, and that he would not scruple to have all the correspondence seized. I am bound, on the other hand, to state that my own experience wholly absolves his late Majesty from any such propensity; for during our detention in Abyssinia he had possession of all our papers for some time, and on two occasions when my letters fell into his hands he sent them to me unopened. Nor have I the least reason to believe that he surreptitiously caused any single document belonging to us to be read to him. Judging that it would be better to make no secret of the proposed transmission of letters to Massowah, I instructed Samuel to obtain a couple of messengers for me from the Chief of Korâta, and they started on their journey on the morning of the 23rd. On the same day I received the following letter from the King by Alâkâ I'ngâdâ, who brought also a number of canoes with him for the transport of all the European artisans to Zagê:—

(After compliments.)

"By the power of God, I have returned in safety to my home. I had gone to escort my horses, which were coming to me, and now may He cause me to meet with you, my friend, in safety.

"I used to pray to our Creator that the people [prisoners] whom I disliked and imprisoned might reach you in health and safety. Now, firstly, I pray that God may give peace and prosperity to my friend, the Queen; and, secondly, that He may give you, who are the flower of my gladness, health and long life. I also crave from our Creator that He will cause you to concede me your love. With regard to myself, whether I dislike you or love you, oh English! you can discover from my conduct in the affair of Plowden and Yuhannés [Mr. Bell]. According to the rules of my country and my ability, I used to love and honour them [the English]. My love and honour towards them was for the purpose of obtaining the regard of the Queen and yourselves. That love of yours which I was longing for, I feel convinced I have obtained, and, by the power of God, it has given me joy. I send you, by Aläkâ I'ngädä, boats. Come yourself and the party of Kántiba Hailo [the European artisans].

"Dated Friday, the 15th of Magábit."

Aläkâ I'ngädä was chief Amharic scribe to the King, and the only servant he implicitly trusted. He always carried the royal seal, had possession of the King's papers, and was his Majesty's constant companion. He was, in fact, his public and private secretary, and one of the few men about the Court who could boast that he had never been abused or beaten by the Sovereign. He was a man of undoubted integrity, and I never heard him utter a disparaging word of any one. His remarks touching his master's subsequent treachery and ill-treatment of me were generally confined to the following:—"Trust in God, sir, and He will yet deliver you; for He will not forsake you after having implanted such strong affection for you in the heart of the King." Eventually, however, when his Majesty reached Mágdala, at the end of March, 1868, and the lives of all were in imminent danger, he applied to me to provide him with guides to enable him to effect his escape from the royal camp and through the intervening rebels to the invading British army. But I advised him to wait until the arrival of our troops, when matters might assume a more favourable aspect; whereas, if detected in his attempt to escape, his life and that of the guides would be forfeited, and the safety of myself and party compromised. This man was dispatched by the King with a letter to Sir Robert Napier on Easter Sunday, the 12th of April, and was fortunate enough to remain in the British camp until after the attack on Mágdala. He was always friendly towards me, and if he was scrupulously cautious not to reveal his master's secrets, he was equally careful never to betray me. The King allowed me to present him with a silver inkstand, made after an English pattern, which one of the Koráta silversmiths managed to copy remarkably well. He was also one of those whom the King allowed to wear a silk shirt of my presentation, and he and other courtiers who were similarly privileged made it a point of wearing these shirts whenever I was well received by his Majesty, or whenever they came to me on business from the royal Court.

25th.—Dr. Blanc, Lieutenant Prideaux and all the European artisans, with Kántiba Hailo, accompanied me to Zagé early this morning. We landed about two miles from the bottom of the bay, where the King's residence stood, to put on our uniforms. On reaching the beach we found Rás I'ngádá and other Chiefs in waiting. Mules with rich trappings had been prepared for us, and when all were mounted we followed the Prime Minister at a brisk trot towards the royal dwelling. Three new silk tents had been prepared for the Mission, and Dr. Blanc, Lieutenant Prideaux and myself were ushered into them by Rás I'ngádá. Two other red-cloth tents were pitched for our followers, besides a black one for our kitchen. Our camp had been pitched in a corner of the King's inclosure, partitioned off by a fence, which to make it look neater was covered with white native calico. Immediately after, a plentiful supply of live stock, honey, butter, *téj* and curry-stuff were sent to the kitchen, with a polite message from the King, that although it was then the fast of Lent in Abyssinia, yet his English friends must not scruple to eat meat. To show his joy on the occasion, he allowed my Mohammedan servants to slaughter their sheep within the royal inclosure—a privilege which Mussulmans had never been allowed before.

In the course of a couple of hours the King sent to say that he wanted to come and pay me a visit, in order to show all his people how he respected me. As he had never, to my knowledge, visited any one since his accession to the throne, I sent and begged him not to trouble himself, but hoped he would grant me an interview where he was. He answered, "Are you not my brother, and the servant of my friend, the great Queen of England, and shall it be below my dignity to enter the tent of the Queen, which I have pitched expressly for her? No, my friend, I will not listen to you in this matter." Accordingly, he came to see me soon afterwards; and on entering my tent, as a mark of respect, he put his right arm out of his robe, and said, "I feel as happy as if I were visiting the Queen." After remaining about ten minutes in my tent, he rose, took me by the hand, and said to Dr. Blanc, Lieutenant Prideaux and me, "Come along, and let us have a chat."

The King and I walked hand in hand until we reached the audience-hall, where we found carpets had been spread for all the Europeans. My companions and I sat near the King, but the artisans occupied places at some distance on our left. After some friendly conversation, in which the King could not help alluding to his old grievances, Râs Mashisha, the eldest illegitimate son of Theodore, came in, wearing a shirt of the Lyons silk that I had presented to his father. As soon as we saw him come in we stood up, and the King said, "Mashisha, draw near, and shake hands with my English friends in the English fashion, as I want you to become one of them." After he had shaken hands with my companions and myself, he sat down next to us, by his father's directions. The King then turned round to me, and said, "Mr. Rassam, I wish this son of mine, and another at Mágdala (Dajjáj 'Alamâyo), to be adopted children of the English; and when you go back to your country, I want you to recommend them to your Queen, in order that, when I die, they may be looked after by the English, and not be allowed to govern badly."

When this ceremony was over, different kinds of muskets and pistols were shown us, the King exhibiting them to us singly, relating the history of each weapon—from that which had been presented to him by Mr. Plowden, to those which I had brought from Massowah for M. Bourgaud, the French gunsmith, for the King's use.

We sat together about two hours discussing different topics, Theodore making casual allusions to the Bishop, Consul Cameron and Mr. Stern in the course of the conversation. We were then dismissed, the King ordering Râs Mashisha, Râs I'ngădă, and all the European artisans to escort us to our tents.

Early next morning, 26th of March, it was reported to me that the King had summoned all the great Chiefs to consult them about our departure for the coast, and that the European artisans were also ordered to attend. First, he consulted Aito Samuel and Wald-Gâbir, the valet and constant attendant on the King, and when they advised him to send me to my country with joy, he told them that they were asses and blockheads, and did not know what they were saying. The European artisans were called next, and on their unanimously advising him to send me away, the King said, "But what surety have I in my hand?" Mr. Zander now came forward, and taking up her Majesty's letter of the 26th May, 1864, which was before the King, he first opened it, and then placing his hand on the royal signature and seal, exclaimed, "Trust to these, your Majesty; they are a true voucher to the word of the English Queen, who never breaks her word." Thereupon the Europeans were told to go out of the room and wait outside.

The King had now only the native Chiefs to depend upon for the decision which he desired. They were, I believe, about eighty-five in number, and of the highest rank. When they had all assembled, the King asked them whether he ought to allow me to return to England, or keep me until the friendship of my Government had been proved to him by external evidence. They all, without a dissenting voice, answered, "Let Mr. Rassam go." "But what have I in my hands?" was the rejoinder. One of the Râses, named Tágga, replied, "We beg your Majesty to let Mr. Rassam depart in peace; and if he behaves falsely to you, let God be judge between him and you. Trust in God; He is enough for us." Another Chief said, "If your Majesty does not trust the English, make Mr. Rassam swear on the Bible, before you permit him to go, that he will not prove false to you; because the English are very scrupulous in keeping an oath taken on the Bible." These arguments silenced the King for a time, but they did not satisfy him.

After all the counsellors were dismissed, the King sent for me by Râs I'ngadâ and Kántiba Hailu, the ex-Mayor of Góndar, to communicate to me the result of that morning's council. As usual, I repaired to the audience-chamber with my companions, and found that all the native Chiefs had gone, but the European artisans were standing outside the door. As soon as we entered, the King called out to them to join us. This time they sat in front of us.

On going in I noticed that the King was not in the best of moods, and the first thing he said, after we had sat down, was: "I have this morning called all those people in whom I trust, Europeans as well as Abyssinians, and I inquired of them whether it would be better to let you go back to your country at once, or keep you with me until I obtained a token of friendship from England. They all said that I ought to send you away, and you shall depart as soon as our Easter is over; but," he continued, "how can I trust any European now after the ill-behaviour of those whom I have treated like brothers?" He then proceeded to relate his grievances against different Europeans, the names of some of whom I had never heard before. He began to inveigh against the Bishop, whom he accused of having taken liberties with the Queen, and who had given him trouble both in political and domestic affairs. M. Lejean was the next subject of the royal displeasure. He said, "A man came to me riding on a donkey, and said that he was a servant of the great Emperor of the French, and that he had come to my country for the sole purpose of establishing friendship between me and his Sovereign. I said, 'I do not object to making friends with great Christian Kings; you are welcome.' The next day he said he wished to see me on business, and I assented; but to my astonishment he came to me with a bundle of rags [patterns of silk]. I asked him what those were. He replied that the French had a large town in their country where they made silks, and that the merchants of that place had commissioned him to bring them to me for the sake of barter. I said to myself, 'what have I done that these people insult me thus by treating me like a shopkeeper?' I bore the insult then, and said nothing. Another day, while I was out on a war expedition, this Frenchman sent to say that he wished to see me. I told the messenger that I was very busy just then and could not see him. On receiving my message he rushed out of his tent, dressed in his uniform, and said, that as he was wearing his King's robes, he could not disgrace them by taking them off before he had had an interview, and that I must see him. On hearing this I said, 'Who is his father? seize him!' and I put him in chains in the very dress of his King. After a short time I had pity on him, as I thought the man was not in his right senses; so I ordered him to be unfettered and sent out of the country. All the time he was with me I treated him kindly and hospitably; and when he reached Massowah he rewarded my kindness by sending me an insulting letter, in which he abused me most grossly." I afterwards learned from the late Mr. Dufton that it was he, and not his fellow-traveller M. Lejean, who came to the royal camp riding on a donkey.

It appears that when M. Lejean arrived at Massowah, after his disgrace, he wrote what he called "a protest" to the King, in which he commented very strongly upon his Majesty's conduct towards him. It was very well for M. Lejean to say what he liked to a crazy monarch while he was safe out of his reach; he ought to have known, however, that such a letter could do no good, but might endanger the safety of the Europeans who were still in the power of the despot. I believe that letter did a good deal of harm.

The King then commenced his complaints against the

Egyptian Government, and said that they had sent him a man who called himself a Patriarch, to whom, as the head of the Abyssinian Church, he had accorded a good reception, and had condescended so far as to carry his chair in public. The King concluded by saying, "This did not content the man, because the next day he asked me to give him the crown." 'What,' said I, 'do you want to take my crown and give it to the Turks? Is this the mission on which you have come?' After that, I was compelled to watch his movements; and, for a few days, I did not allow him to leave his house."

I heard through a reliable authority that the Patriarch of the Copts had never presumed to ask Theodore for the crown, but only begged for a bishop's mitre, thinking it would look well when he went back to Egypt if he wore a mitre, which he could say had been given to him by a Christian King, who was one of his flock. In Amharic, there is only one word for mitre and crown; and as the King wished to have a case against the Patriarch, he accused him of having come to Abyssinia to give his country to the Turks. He thought it was very hard that one bishop should take possession of his wife, and another covet his crown. Although these charges were utterly unfounded, the King seems to have worked himself up into believing them.

The King then continued the statement of his grievances, saying that after the Patriarch had left, the Egyptian Government sent him a Turk, named 'Abd-ur-Rahmân Bey, to establish good friendship between him and the Egyptian Government, and that this Mohammedan had scarcely been a year in the country before he began to play all kinds of tricks, and plunder the inhabitants; that one day, while the Ambassador was at Góndar, the King gave a feast to his soldiers, and, in accordance with Abyssinian custom, the Chiefs commenced a war-dance after the entertainment was over; that thereupon the Turkish Envoy came out of his tent and ridiculed the royal troops before thousands of people; that when the King heard of this, he sent to tell 'Abd-ur-Rahmân Bey that he could not put up with his impertinence any longer, and that he must pack up and leave the country at once; that when the Turkish Envoy reached Chálga, on the western frontier of Abyssinia, he began his old pranks again, ordering his people to plunder; that he even went so far as to carry off some girls, but that the villagers fell upon him and his people and took the girls and the other spoil away from them.

The King then spoke of what he called the ingratitude of a German and an Englishman. The former, he said, who was the Austrian Consul at Khartûm, had come to Abyssinia and made a treaty with him, which, on his return, he tried to turn to the benefit of the Turks. The latter, whose name was Falláké (Mr. Speedy), had stayed some months with him, and he had in every respect treated him well; but when he went down to Massowah he had abused him before the Turks, and called the Abyssinians "asses."

The King finished by saying, "You see how I have been treated by people who ought to have requited me differently. How am I to know that you will act differently? You may not abuse me when you leave my country, but still you may forget me." I replied that it would not be becoming in me to praise myself by saying that I should behave better than others. I only begged him to try me, and judge from my future conduct what kind of a person I was. He said, "Very well, I will try you; and may you reach your country safely."

After this, he reverted to the rebellion, and asked me to advise him how to stop it. As I did not wish to meddle in such a delicate affair, and yet did not deem it advisable to vex him by telling him that it was not my business to mix myself up in matters which did not concern me, I related to him the history of the Indian mutiny, and how her Majesty the Queen had ultimately granted an amnesty to all those who had been implicated in it. On saying this the King smiled, and said, "Do you think the Abyssinians are like other people? They are bad and will not listen to reason. To show you that I am right, I will instantly proclaim a general amnesty to all the rebels, and you will find that no one will give heed to me." He then asked me to send my interpreter to hear the proclamation by the herald. The crier was accordingly ordered to announce the amnesty, and one of my interpreters had to witness the ceremony.

On this day the King did not refer to Dr. Beke's letter, but that gentleman's messenger received orders that he was to return with me to Massowah, without an answer. I began then to hope that the King had put Dr. Beke's mission out of his mind.

Our interview lasted more than two hours, and on dismissing us the King said he wished me to return to Korâta that evening, and that I was to prepare myself to start from Abyssinia with my companions and the released captives. He said he would see me again, because he wanted me to come and bid him good-bye before I finally left Abyssinia. Towards evening, the European artisans came to ask me to remain until the following morning, as it was hardly pleasant to cross the Lake at night; or, if I did not like to do so on my own responsibility, to request his Majesty's permission to that effect. As I was given to understand that the King was not in the best of moods, I declined to alter the original plan, unless the proposal came from the King himself. Kántiba Hailo repaired accordingly to the royal presence to request permission to depart, and on his rejoining us we started, Râs I'ngădă, as usual, escorting us as far as the boats. He said, on wishing me good-bye, "I hope to escort you much farther next time;" meaning, that when I went again to Zagê, according to appointment, to take leave of the King, he would have to travel with me some distance from the royal camp. I truly believe that he meant what he said.

CHAPTER XV.

OUR EXODUS SANCTIONED.

Fresh difficulties — M. Bardel and I'ngădă Wark — Intestine troubles — The European artisans — Dr. Beke's mission — Theodore's suspicions aroused — Favourable prognostications — Theodore and his Shirts — Men-milliners — The King's Dispatch box — Directions given for homeward route — Reasons for preventing a final meeting between the King and the Captives — Theodore dispenses with the interview — Orders our immediate departure — Arrangements made to re-arrest the Captives.

Two or three days after my return to Koráta, I found fresh troubles looming in the distance. Every day messengers from I'ngădă Wark were going to and fro between Zagê and Koráta, visiting M. Bardel. I also heard that the latter had a document in his possession, by the use of which he threatened to prevent Consul Cameron from leaving the country. It appears that when Consul Cameron was a prisoner at Mágdala, before I went to Abyssinia, he had given a kind of passport to a number of rebel Chiefs who were then confined in the same place with the Europeans, promising them British protection and rewards in case of war with England. Afterwards, however, it was feared that the existence of such papers involved great risk, for if the King heard of them, the safety of Consul Cameron and his fellow-prisoners would be compromised. The passports were therefore recalled and destroyed; but M. Bardel managed to obtain a copy through Consul Cameron's secretary, and kept it concealed, in order that he might use it against us when it suited him. The said copy was eventually burnt at Korâta, which relieved us from any further anxiety on that score.

Soon after the return of the Mission from Zagê, one of the courtiers sent to apprise me of a report having reached the Court that some of my party had requested Messrs. Schimper and Waldmeier to furnish them with an outline of the former sufferings of the captives, as they had forgotten several of the incidents and dates. I was accordingly advised by my Abyssinian informants to put a stop to such a dangerous proceeding, otherwise the King might get wind of it and conclude that other "abusive" accounts of him were being prepared for publication on our return to Europe, to the certain jeopardy of the Mission and the released captives. "Let those who want 'to write books," was the wise and friendly injunction conveyed to me, "wait until they are safe out of the country; then let them write whatever they please." On receiving this intelligence I immediately sent for Messrs. Schimper and Waldmeier, and was glad to hear from them that they had refused the solicited assistance. They also kindly promised to give no countenance whatever to a proposition so fraught with hazard to all concerned; in fact, the Gáffat artisans were always avowedly friendly to the Mission.

These were some of the difficulties which beset the Mission at this time. Jealousy, and envy, and self-interest seemed at work around us, and there is no knowing how far their united influence was brought to bear, directly or indirectly, on the mind of the King. Then, again, there can be no doubt that Dr. Beke's intervention excited the misgivings of the mistrustful Monarch. Thus much is certain, that at the end of January, 1866, Theodore had no thought of detaining us, and that he began to change his mind when he heard of the arrival at Massowah of another person whose ostensible object was to procure the liberation of the Mágdala captives. Ignorant as he was of the liberty of the subject in England, it is not surprising that, at a loss to comprehend how a private Englishman dared to interfere in an important matter which had already been taken in hand by his Sovereign, Theodore was led to question whether we were dealing with him in a straightforward manner; and, of course, his suspicions would be confirmed on hearing that the agent referred to had been conveyed to and from Massowah in a Government steamer.

Another circumstance which seems to have aroused the suspicion of Theodore at this juncture was a rumour, set on foot at Korâta, that I had been sent by the British Government to obtain the release of Consul Cameron only. If so, it seemed inconsistent in me, in his estimation, that I should make such strenuous efforts to secure the liberation of all the captives.

The foregoing are some of the causes to which I attribute the King's altered tone towards the Mission. Indications of the unfavourable change were already evident, but I thought then that the symptoms would prove merely transitory.

I reached Korâta about midnight, and next morning dispatched the following letter to the King:—

"*Korâta, 27th March,* 1866.
"Most Gracious Sovereign,

"I have the honour to inform your Majesty that, by God's mercy and your favour, I arrived here safely last night, with Kántiba Hailo and our respective parties. I trust that this letter will find you in perfect health and prosperity.

"Allow me to return you my grateful thanks for the kindness and favour I received at your hands, which I trust, by the help of God, I shall never forget; and may He who knows our hearts enable me to do always what is pleasing to Him and agreeable to your Majesty.

"In presenting you with my respectful compliments, in which my companions join, I remain," &c.

His Majesty had written me a complimentary letter the same day, begging me to report my safe arrival at Korâta. In fact, we seemed to be trying which should outvie the other in courtesy. Three days later I received the following note, to my intense gratification, inasmuch as it reassured me that our departure was in contemplation :—

(After compliments.)

"Before this I sent to inquire after your safe arrival, and afterwards Lij Abitu and his party came and informed me of it. By the power of God, I was greatly delighted. I had ordered the party of Kántiba Hailo [the European artisans] to do certain work [to make saddles, shields, &c.]; if it is completed, I wish you to hold yourselves in readiness to start [for Europe], by the power of God.

"Dated Friday, the 22nd of Magábit."

I certainly believed at this time that the clouds had blown over, and that we might now hope for uninterrupted fair weather; this confidence, however, did not restrain me from wishing all shields and saddles at the bottom of the sea. Even a few days' delay, or some malicious report brought to his notice, might suffice to change the fickle mind of the King. However, it was useless, in our position, to kick against the pricks: his Majesty had directed the presents to be prepared for us, and we might not leave without them. They had been ordered as far back as the beginning of February, but his Majesty had only just heard that the golden saddle destined for me could not be got ready before the end of April. In consequence of that intimation, his Majesty gave instructions to-day that the best gold saddle available among his Gáffat servants—European and native—should be taken up for me; all the filigree work was to be regilt, and the leather and velvet renewed. To expedite the completion of the Orders of the Cross and Solomon's Seal, he directed six additional silversmiths to assist Mr. Zander to have a certain number prepared by the Abyssinian Easter, which fell on the 8th of April.

To-day I wrote to the King as follows:—

"*Koráta*, 31*st March*, 1866.
"MOST GRACIOUS SOVEREIGN,—

"I have had the honour to receive your welcome epistles, dated respectively the 20th and 22nd of the month of Magâbit, from which I was glad to learn that your Majesty was in the enjoyment of perfect health.

"Thank God, we are all well here, and, by your favour, in good spirits.

"With regard to our departure, we are ready to start as soon as your Majesty shall give us leave to do so. I trust ere long to behold the light of your countenance again.

"Dr. Blanc and Mr. Prideaux present you with their respectful compliments."

1*st April*, 1866.—This being our Easter Sunday, all the Protestant community met together to offer up our united thanks to Almighty God for His care over us. Twenty-two persons, including the wives of the European artisans, assembled in my tent for solemn worship. The Rev. Mr. Stern officiated on the occasion, and administered the Lord's Supper.

2*nd*.—I gave a party this afternoon to all the European artisans and their families. As we had not tables sufficient to accommodate all the guests, the dinner was served on the floor. Received the following from the King:—

(After compliments.)

"The shirts which you sent me by Ôna Mohammed have

reached me, and I return you my thanks for them. Why do you give yourself such trouble and such thought for me? You are my guest, and it is for me to inconvenience myself for you. If God assist you, I wish you to trouble yourself about what I require; but, oh my brother! do not incommode yourself by parting with your property.

"At Amba Chára, in the province of Wággárá, my toll-keepers seized some messengers who were coming this way with letters. They imprisoned them and sent the packet on to me. I found it directed in an European language, and as I thought it might belong to you, I send it to you unopened. If you should find it to be yours, I have directed that your messengers should be released; if not, return the packet to me, and I shall order the messengers to be brought to me.

"I have ordered some cows to be given to you, in order that you may have a merry feast. I did not know that your Easter fell before ours, but thought that both corresponded in date, otherwise I would have sent them before. Why did you not inform me, since my house is yours, and the house of your brothers and friends?

"Dated Monday, the 25th of Magábit."

On first reaching the King's Court I had presented him with a dozen of my own shirts, which were made at Aden, of fine calico, with loose wristbands, and without buttons. These he admired very much, but with his usual liberality he had given most of them to his favourite Chiefs. I sent him another dozen on the 31st of March, the receipt of which he acknowledges in the above. Subsequently, he sent two pieces of longcloth, with which I had also presented him, begging me to have them made into shirts like mine, which I was enabled to do through the joint kindness of Mrs. Flad and Mrs. Rosenthal. The most amusing part of this shirt business was, that mine were made for studs, of which I gave his Majesty a set. These, however, he lost the first time of using them, and was obliged afterwards to call in a tailor, whenever he donned his shirt, to put in a few stitches to keep the front together. This expedient was the more troublesome because it is considered disgraceful for an Abyssinian, male or female, to sleep in any kind of garment; consequently his Majesty was under the necessity of sending for a tailor whenever he retired for the night. One day he became so impatient that he tore his shirt open, and resorted to me to remedy the inconvenience. This I did by sending him a supply of buttons, directing the tailor to affix them to one side after he had sewn up the button-holes. It may sound somewhat strange to English ears that a tailor, rather than his wife or one of his female domestics should have been called in by his Majesty to put a few stitches to his shirts; but the reason is, that few if any Abyssinian women can sew; and, even if they could, it would be deemed highly unbecoming in them to ply the needle in public. Sewing and laundry-work are left to the males; spinning and carrying wood and water are tasks apportioned to the weaker sex.

I was extremely surprised to see the packet which I had dispatched to the coast on the 23rd of March brought back to me to-day. It appears that the guards at the toll-gate near Amba Chára had been ordered to arrest all persons carrying letters either up or down, and that my messengers had accordingly been seized, bound with cords, and put into prison until the King's pleasure was known. The packet which was taken from them was brought to his Majesty simultaneously with Ôna Mohammed's arrival at Court with my letter of the 31st March, and the guard who delivered it stated that the messengers from whom it had been seized said that it came from the Franchotsh (Europeans). On being asked by the King if he knew to whom the packet belonged, Ôna Mohammed, with his usual assurance, replied that it belonged to me. Thereupon Lij Abitu was ordered to bring it to me for identification, and to direct the release of the messengers, should it prove to be mine. Fortunately, no inhibition had been given against their resuming the journey, and Lij Abitu kindly undertook to forward the packet to the detained messengers, who, on their release, were to proceed with it at once to the coast. The Aitos Kâsa and Wandé had sent a letter with the packet to their agent at Massowah, which the King caused to be opened and read. On finding that it related solely to mercantile matters, he took no further notice of it; but he did not return it to the owners.

3rd.—I addressed the subjoined letter to the King to-day:—

"*Koráta, 3rd April,* 1866.
"Most Gracious Sovereign,

"I have received with much pleasure your Majesty's gracious letter by Lij Abitu and Ôna Mohammed, dated the 25th of Magâbit, and was glad to learn from them that they had left you in perfect health.

"With regard to the packet of letters which your Majesty kindly sent me, I found it to be mine—one which I forwarded a few days ago to Mr. Munzinger at Massowah. It contains several communications from myself and my companions, and the other Europeans who are with me at Koráta, addressed to different friends at Aden and in Europe, reporting my good reception by your Majesty, and the safe arrival of the released prisoners at our camp.

"In accordance with your orders, Lij Abitu, immediately on finding that the messengers who were detained at Amba Chára, in Wággárá, were those whom I had sent to Massowah, sent orders to have them released, and forwarded the packet also to be given to them to take on to Mr. Munzinger.

"I am extremely obliged to your Majesty for your continual acts of kindness to me, and for your thought of us at the commemoration of our Saviour's Resurrection, by sending us a token of your good-will. It is quite impossible for me to requite your favours in this country, but I trust I shall have it in my power when I go to England to show my sincere gratitude for all your kindness.

"In presenting your Majesty with my salutations, in which my companions join, I remain," &c.

On the 5th I received the following note from the King, acquainting me with his rigid fast, and his joy at the approach of Easter:—

(After compliments.)

"I have been long fasting, and have abstained from eating meat, and I am anxious to see the light of Easter. Pray that I may see it in health. By the power of God, I will also offer up to Him the same supplication for you.

"Dated Wednesday, the 27th of Magâbit."

On the same day his Majesty sent me twenty jars of honey, half of which contained honeycomb perfectly transparent. What led to this gift was my having asked Samuel to procure some good honey for me. Samuel, accordingly, having heard that it was procurable in the market near the royal camp, directed his friend Balambarâs Gabra-Mâdhanê 'Âlam, the Governor of Wandígê, to purchase a few jars. By some means or other, these facts were reported to the King, who forthwith sent for the Chief and reprimanded him most severely for having presumed to resort to the market for me, instead of applying to the royal store-house, where he might have obtained as many jars of honey as he pleased. Samuel also got a similar rebuke from his Majesty the day following; and both were not a little delighted to have got off so easily.

6th.—Wrote as follows to the King, in reply to his last:—

"*Koráta, 6th April*, 1866.

"Most Gracious Sovereign,

"I have had the honour of receiving your Majesty's welcome letter of the 27th of Magábit, by Lij Abitu and Ôna Mohammed, together with your acceptable present of honey. Pray accept my best thanks for all your kindness and favours.

"May the Almighty who, as on this Holy Friday [Abyssinian reckoning] gave His Only-begotten Son, Jesus Christ, to suffer death upon the Cross for our redemption, grant that your fasting and prayers may be registered in heaven; and that through our Saviour's suffering we may rise with Him to endless salvation.

"I pray our Heavenly Father to enable you to commemorate the day of His Son's resurrection in good health and prosperity, and may He grant you a long and happy life to celebrate that blessed day for many years to come.

"In presenting you with my respectful congratulations on the anniversary of our Lord's rising from the dead, in which my companions join, I remain," &c.

I gave the foregoing to Samuel, who had been summoned to Zagê to receive instructions about our departure. By the same opportunity I sent his Majesty a tin dispatch-box, which, I was told, he would appreciate very much. He certainly did, for he afterwards used it as the receptacle for what he called his important papers, and always kept it by him. On several occasions he was heard to say, placing his hand the while on the box, "When the English troops come, I shall show them some astonishing letters that I have here." Unfortunately, this box was found open in the Treasury at Mágdala, rifled of its contents, when that place was captured by the British Army.

8th.—Samuel returned with Lij Abitu and Ôna Mohammed, bringing me the following from the King:—

"May God grant me a meeting with you, my friend, after the light of Easter. The token of friendship, namely, the tin box which you sent me, I have received with much pleasure, and I return you my best thanks for it. I have ordered Lij Abitu to take your mules through Dámbëa; and Kántiba Hailo and Aito Samuel to bring you to me."

In this letter the King did not mention the released captives; but he sent me a verbal message that I was to take all the Europeans with me, including the artisans, and all the baggage; the mules, he said, were to go round the northern side of the Lake, but no place was named where we were to meet them. No reason was assigned for the change in the former more definite arrangement, which was, that the released captives should proceed to Gójja, on the north-western corner of the Lake, where Dr. Blanc, Lieutenant Prideaux and I were to join them, after we had taken leave of the King at Zagê. We were told at first that we (the Mission) were not to carry any tents with us when we went to take leave of the King, or more luggage than was necessary for three or four days; but on the 8th of April the old plan was wholly set aside. I was also told that the King had inclosed a large space outside his camp at Zagê, within which we were to pitch our tents on our arrival there. These proceedings perplexed me, and I asked Aito Samuel and Lij Abitu what they meant. They answered that they were as much in the dark as I was, and did not know what the King intended to do. The inclosure seemed to every one most suspicious.

Up to that day I had been repeatedly advised to try all I could to prevent the King from seeing Consul Cameron and Messrs. Stern and Rosenthal; and when Aito Samuel and Lij Abitu came with the message from their master that I was to take the released captives with me to Zagê, it was thought that we should be inevitably detained if I did so—

so intense was his Majesty's hatred towards them. Taking all these objections into consideration, I deemed it advisable to try to induce the King to dispense with the attendance of the released captives.

Had he written to me in a straightforward manner and told me that he wished to see the released captives before they left, or even that he wished to be reconciled to them— though a reconciliation had been effected twice before—I should certainly have taken them to him; but all that he did was to write, directing me to go to him, without even mentioning the name of any released captive in the letter, sending me a verbal message only to take all the Europeans with me, some of whom he detested, and whose faces he had been heard very often to say he hoped never to see again. In fact, I was told that had I taken them with me to Zagê, he would have had me and my companions arrested, on the plea that I had insulted him by taking his enemies to the royal camp, without his having written to me to do so.

M. Bardel and I'ngädä Wark were all this time in constant communication, and it was rumoured that the former was about to be reconciled to the King, and to remain in his service as formerly.

After careful deliberation, I resolved to ask the King's permission to allow the released captives to proceed straight on their way to Matámma, round the eastern side of the Lake, and Lij Abitu, who always befriended me, undertook to return to the King with my communication—though it was hazardous for him to do so, after the previous order which he had received from his Majesty, directing him to take our mules round the Lake. I therefore entrusted him with the following letter, directing him to tell the King that what I was proposing was for the welfare of all, and to ask his Majesty's forgiveness, if he did not approve of the suggestion:—

"Most Gracious Sovereign,
"I have had much pleasure in receiving your Majesty's letter of the 30th Magâbit, by Aito Samuel, Lij Abitu and Ôna Mohammed, and I was greatly rejoiced to learn therefrom that you are quite well.

"Dr. Blanc and Mr. Prideaux beg to present their respectful compliments to your Majesty.

"I am taking the liberty of sending Lij Abitu to you, with a message from me; and I trust your Majesty will pardon me for having done so."

Before Lij Abitu started I received the following note from the King, which I acknowledged with suitable compliments in a postscript to the above:—

"I send you good tidings of my having passed Easter. How have my friends passed it? Let me know if you have spent it happily and prosperously, by the power of God.
"Dated Monday, the 2nd of Miyâzëya."

On the 10th of April, Lij Abitu returned with the following answer, and he also gave me the joyful intelligence that the King had made no objection to the released captives proceeding on their way round the eastern side of the Lake, as had been formerly arranged:—

"When I heard of your good health and prosperity, by the power of God, I was greatly delighted. Very well; as you say, Lij Abitu shall take them by the lower road, and your baggage will cross to any spot which you may choose. I have directed Agafâri Gôlam and the party of Aito Kâsa to convey it for you."

I had hoped that we were certain of being allowed to leave, especially as arrangements were made for the transport of our baggage across the Lake to Gójja, where we were all to meet before our departure. Lij Abítu was formally appointed by the King to escort the released captives to Gójja; and the two principal merchants of Koráta, Aito Kâsa and Aito Wandé, with Agafári Gôlam, were to transport the baggage in boats across the Lake, while Kántiba Hailo, with all the European artisans, were to escort the Mission to Zagé on the same day.

There is no doubt that, on the 8th of April, the King really intended that I should leave Abyssinia with the released captives, although he had previously thought of keeping us a few months longer; but everything depended upon the whim of the moment. It was a mere chance how long he would keep to his word, as he could not be depended upon for an hour. A mere suspicion, or a mischievous report while he was heated with drink, was quite sufficient to make him order hundreds of men to be executed for whom, perhaps a few minutes before, he had professed great friendship. I was also told, on good authority, that the King had even given orders on the 11th of the month directing the silk tents to be pitched for the Mission within his inclosure, as on a former occasion, and that he had actually indicated the mules and horses which were to be presented to us; also, that Râs l'ngádă was told that he was to escort us as far as Wandígé, while Aito Samuel, with Lij Abítu and Agafári Gôlam, were to go with us to Chálga, where we were to be handed over to the old escort who had brought us to the King from the frontier. There is no doubt, moreover, that these Chiefs of Chálga were ordered to be ready to receive us after the Abyssinian Easter-week, and directed to collect carriers to transport our baggage as far as Matámma.

On the morning of the 12th it was reported to the King, from Korâta, that the Orders of the Cross and Solomon's Seal could not be got ready by the time his Majesty wished us to leave Abyssinia, and that the saddle and shields, which had been ordered for my companions and myself, were not quite completed. He had been told, also, that I had supplied his enemies, the released captives, with arms; and as he knew I had not brought any spare muskets and pistols with me, and that those he had himself given me I had long since disposed of, he wondered how I had got them, and began to suspect that I had them concealed, and might have more to give to his other enemies, the rebels, when I went down to Chálga. He had also, probably, just then heard of Dr. Beke's visit to the rebels of Tigrê. At all events, on the morning of Thursday, the 12th of April, 1866, the King was in a fearful mood, and sent orders to Korâta that we were to start, without fail, early next morning, according to previous arrangement. In the evening he began to waver, and asked Wald-Gâbir and I'ngădă Wark whether he should let me go. The former informed me that he had advised the King to let me depart in peace; but he did not know what answer the latter gave, as they were asked separately. The King could not sleep that night, and towards the morning he sent for Bitwáddad Tadla, and in a private interview commanded him to take the soldiers under his command and cross at once to Korâta, but to take care to land at Zanzalima, about four miles from our encampment, towards Zagê; that he was to go on to a certain village about a day's march on the other side of Korâta, and stay there till the arrival of the released captives, whom he was ordered to arrest and bring back in chains to Korâta, and await further orders. One of Bitwáddad Tadla's soldiers was directed to remain at Korâta to give orders as to the disposal of our baggage. About 10 o'clock A.M., on that day, the silk tents, which had been pitched for the Mission, were ordered to be struck and packed up, and all the Chiefs in camp were summoned to attend. The King had been drinking a great deal for three days, and that day he was very much excited. While the Chiefs were assembling, the King called for an Amharic writer, and got him to write down the different charges he had against me—not omitting, of course, to include his genealogy in full. I was told that the King did not think of having us arrested until after Rûs I'ngädä had been sent to meet me; and when that Chief saw us arrested he was as much surprised as we were. The King ordered nine colonels to arrest me and my companions—three officers for each—as soon as we entered the reception-hall; and they were to guard us against any attempt at suicide, until they received further orders.

I have been obliged to digress from the main narrative because I wished to show what took place at Zagê from the time the King got into a rage on the morning of the 12th until the afternoon of the next day.

CHAPTER XVI.

DISGRACE OF THE MISSION.

The released Captives start homewards — The Mission repairs to Zagê and is arrested there — Charges made against the Author — Theodore apologizes — The Mission placed under surveillance — Our baggage ransacked — Present from the King — We destroy all our papers — The Captives arrested and brought to Zagê — A fresh trial — The King's charges against the Captives and against the Author — He determines to retain the Mission — Theodore unchains the Captives — Craves forgiveness of all the Europeans — The Petition from the relatives of the Captives read — Theodore's letter to the Queen — We are to be kept as hostages — Theodore's request for artificers from England — The Author's letter to the British Government — Mr. Flad selected to go to England — A native matricide — Theodore and Abyssinian law — Charges against Samuel and two other Aitos — Sympathy for the Mission.

ABOUT 10 o'clock on Friday, the 13th of April, the released captives started from Korâta on their way to the north-western corner of the Lake, and Dr. Blanc, Lieutenant Prideaux and I embarked on board the canoes provided for us by the Chiefs of Korâta and went on to Zagê, accompanied by the European artisans, Aito Samuel and Kántiba Hailo. About two miles before we reached the landing-place at Zagê, we were told to land and put on our uniforms under some trees on the beach, that we might appear in due trim before his Majesty. We landed at Zagê at about one o'clock in the afternoon, and, as usual, Râs I'ngădă met us on the beach below the King's house, with mules for the members of the Mission. The first thing that struck me on entering the royal courtyard was, that there were no tents pitched for us; but as Râs I'ngădă took us straight to the audience-hall, I thought that, owing to the heat of the weather, the King was going to locate us in houses. When we reached the door of the hall I was surprised to find it crowded with Chiefs, all dressed in their silk shirts. Even this I thought nothing of, as I knew it was still the feast of Easter, and imagined that the King was only entertaining his troops, as was his wont. On going into the room I looked towards the throne, intending to salute the King, when suddenly three strapping Chiefs fell on me, two of whom held my arms and the other the tail of my coat; meanwhile they all searched me to see if I carried any arms. The arrest took place so abruptly that I thought at first I had passed the King without noticing him, and that these Chiefs were only keeping me back. Râs I'ngâdâ then glanced round, and said, "Do not fear." It now struck me that there was something wrong; and on looking behind for my companions I found that they also had been arrested and were being roughly handled by the soldiers. We were then pushed up towards the throne, but held so tightly by the soldiers that we could scarcely move our arms. After reaching the throne we were made to wait, standing, for further orders from the King, who was sitting and listening behind the door at the back of the room, not more than ten yards from us. Even in our disgrace the King ordered that we should have the highest seat amongst the Chiefs, for we were placed at the foot of the throne, and on our right and left were the Râses, all dressed in Royal Shirts made of the silks I had brought. The first message sent to me was, " Where are the Mágdala European prisoners?" I replied, that the King knew better than I did where they were. He then sent to say that we ought not to fear, as the present was only a misunderstanding which would soon vanish. I replied, " What have we to fear? Have we not come into this country depending

G 2

upon the word of a King, and one who calls himself a Christian? And where are we now but in the house of the very person who ought to afford us protection? But why this insult and disgrace? Is this the way to receive the messengers of a friendly Sovereign, who came for the sole purpose of establishing friendship?" No sooner were these words translated to the King's Commissioners, Râs I'ngădă and Kántiba Hailo, who were appointed by the King to carry our messages backwards and forwards, than all the Râses cried out, "Malcam! Malcam!"—well said!

Kántiba Hailo, who was the spokesman, then returned with Râs I'ngădă and told me that the Chief Scribe had a paper which contained some charges against me, and that the King's order was that they should be read over to me, and I must answer each charge separately. The scribes were also ordered to put down in writing what I said.

The Chief Scribe then produced the document and began to read, first, the pedigree of Theodore, who was the offspring of Solomon and David by the Queen of Sheba. To this I made no objection, but said I was delighted to learn that he was descended from so wise a King. After this the history of my Mission was read: how I had arrived at Massowah and had come to Abyssinia on the invitation of the King, who had received me graciously and released his enemies, the European captives, for my sake. I replied that I fully admitted all that had been said on that point, and had already proclaimed our good reception to the world.

Now came the charge that, while I knew that the King hated the European captives, I had sent them towards Matámma without reconciling him to them. I replied, that I did not understand why the King made such a charge against me, when he himself, in a letter to me, had given the released captives permission to depart, which letter, if his Majesty would allow me, I would produce; and, besides, Lij Abitu had been sent to escort them by order of the King. "As for the reconciliation," I continued, "I took it for granted when the King wrote to me that he had forgiven the European captives, that he really meant what he said; and the only reason why I preferred their going away from Korâta instead of coming to Zagê was, because I had heard from different people, one of whom was Aito Samuel, that the King disliked the released captives, and did not wish to see them. But if his Majesty really wished to have them here, why did he not write to me to say so? I had always been honest in my transactions with the King, and his Majesty ought also to have dealt with me in the same manner." Aito Samuel broke down before I had half finished, and obtained permission to be seated. A native of Adwa was then brought to translate, and before he had acted as dragoman five minutes he also had to retire, after disputing with the writers as to the way of recording my words. When this man sat down, it was found that even the writers had got somewhat frightened, and could not proceed with their occupation. At last the King, who must have understood every word I said, as he knew Arabic well, sent to say that the scribes might dispense with writing what I said, but that the Commissioners should communicate to him all my answers. The King now ordered two other interpreters to come forward—one a native of Tigrê and the other a Copt. In the beginning of the sham trial the European artisans were closeted with the King, and while the mock Court was being held they came in and sat down below the Râses.

The document, which was in charge of the Chief Scribe, not half of which had been read, was now ordered to be folded up and placed in the tin box which I had given to the King.

The last charge was, that I had sent letters to the coast without the King's permission, and that his Majesty had not been told what I had written. I said, first, I did not know it was against the rules in Abyssinia to communicate with one's friends without the sanction of the King. Secondly, that I had dispatched the letters through the Governor of Koráta, with the sanction of Aito Samuel, whom he had given me as Báldárábâ, and that none of his officials had objected to my having done so. Moreover, the letters were from myself and fellow-Europeans, wherein we gave our friends an account of the good reception of the Mission by the King and the release of the Mágdala captives. This I had already communicated to his Majesty.

Aito Samuel was first interrogated whether he had assisted me in sending letters to the coast; and on his answering in the affirmative, the King sent to say that he did not remember my having written to him about these letters. I referred him to the Chief Scribe, who, after a long hesitation, corroborated my statement. Then I concluded by saying, "But supposing I had really committed an unintentional error, was it right of the King to insult my companions and myself as he had done that afternoon? Did I not ask him the first day I met him to forgive any mistake my companions or I might commit during our stay in his country, and did he not promise to do so? Is this the way that he keeps his word?" No sooner had I finished this sentence than some of the Râses cried out again "Malcam!" Even Mr. Zander joined this time in expressing his approval of what I had said.

After this the King thought it best not to proceed with

the other charges—two of which, I was told afterwards, were, first, that I had supplied arms to Consul Cameron and the Missionaries; and, secondly, that after he had warned me against using the money he gave me in any way "unpleasing to the Lord," I had given large sums to his enemies, the captives. (He discovered afterwards that the arms were purchased from his European artisans, and that the money which I had given to the released captives was from my own funds, and not from the sum with which he had presented me.)

Thereupon the King began to change his tactics and apologized for his misbehaviour towards us. After the last answer had been delivered to him he sent to say, that he hoped I would not take to heart his treatment of us that afternoon, because he had always loved me and held me in high esteem, and that he was very much vexed with those Europeans who had always abused him and treated him with contempt; that he could not allow them to leave the country before they had been tried before me, therefore he had sent for them, and they would be at Zagê in a day or two; until then we were to remain with him, and his European artisans were to act as our Bâldârâbâs. The latter arrangement, however, was subsequently cancelled. With regard to our arrest and the disarming of Dr. Blanc and Lieutenant Prideaux, the King said that he had ordered it because he was afraid that we might kill ourselves from vexation when the charges were read to us, as he had heard that Europeans very often committed suicide when they got into difficulty. On hearing this I exclaimed, "What! Does the King think that we do not believe in eternal salvation, that we should put an end to our lives in that un-Christian manner?" The Tigrê interpreter was afraid to translate my answer, but the others came forward, including Aito Samuel, and said that the Assembly ought to know what I had said, and the Copt recommended that I should add that I was not so wicked and impure as the Mágdala captives. I objected to this addition, and at last my former answer was translated. On this occasion only two Râses and Mr. Zander showed their approbation by saying "Malcam."

By this time the King had got over his angry mood and began to look somewhat placid. He sent and dismissed all the officers in attendance, but kept two Râses, Wald-Máryam and Gabrîê, with a few followers to watch us. They were to be our jailors while we remained at Zagê. They behaved very civilly to us all the time we were in their charge. These two Râses were afterwards chained and imprisoned by the King, merely because he was afraid to trust them at large. They were ultimately released by Sir Robert Napier, after the taking of Mágdala.

At the end of the trial we found that all the baggage had been brought to Zagê and submitted to the King's inspection. His Majesty sent to say that, as he could not trust his soldiers, he was obliged to see if all our things were right; and he asked us to send him the keys of our boxes in order that he might not be obliged to break them open. At the same time he promised to return everything to us in perfect order. I began to fear that he was going to search our papers, as in the case of the Missionaries. After a while we were informed that he was looking for concealed arms, as he was afraid that we should kill ourselves in case we had any with us. He took possession of every article of defence that he could lay his eye upon, even to the kitchen-knives; but he overlooked Dr. Blanc's formidable case of dissecting instruments, which he returned. One of my interpreters was called to witness the overhauling of our kit, and the King said to him jocosely, " 'Omar 'Ali, come and see that I do not steal any of your master's things." All the European artisans also were ordered by the King to attend the examination, and had to note down everything the King chose to keep. He told them they were to act as witnesses between him and me.

The King at first wished to imprison my companions and myself in the inclosure which had been constructed for us about ten days before; but when he had cooled down he thought he could not send his friends out of his sight, so he ordered one single white tent to be pitched for us at some distance from the hall, and a black one for a kitchen, and as soon as ours was erected we were ordered into it, escorted by the two Râses. A strong guard was appointed to watch us, and we could not move a yard, either within or without the tent, without a soldier scrutinizing our movements. Afterwards, all our things were sent back to us, excepting the arms, silver trinkets and money. We were glad to find that none of our books or papers had been retained. This was satisfactory proof that the King's suspicions were not directed to anything which we had written.

Dr. Blanc's and my servants were detained in the mean time by the soldiers in a corner of the audience-hall; and when the King went in, after we had left, and found them there, he asked them what they were about. On their replying that they were confined by the soldiers, he said, " What! who has dared to imprison the servants of my friend, Rassam? Do not think that I am angry with him. There is only a little disagreement between us, which will soon be got over." That evening he sent us ten jars of mead, and the same number of sheep, with butter and red-pepper sauce. The soldiers had strict orders not to interfere with our servants, who were allowed to visit us and go out of the inclosure whenever they liked.

We had no idea what was to befall us next, but fearing that our property might be seized again, and memoranda capable of being misconstrued to our greater risk found therein, we deemed it advisable to destroy every scrap of written paper we had. Some we attempted to chew, others we soaked in wash-basins, but were obliged to abandon both expedients, for the former was rather an unpalatable and the latter a slow process. The kitchen fire was finally resorted to as the best alternative, and by filling our butlers' pockets with them every time they were called to wait upon us, we soon got rid of all our written documents.

The King sent us no compliments either that evening or the next morning, as had been his wont; and Aito Samuel was kept at a distance from his master after the trial. The European artisans, as well as our Abyssinian acquaintances, were afraid to approach us, or even to send us their compliments. The only persons who ventured to communicate with us during our disgrace and rigorous confinement were, the lady—an old friend of the late Consul Plowden—to whom I had shown some slight attention on our journey through Agówmĕdĕr, and the Balambarâs Gabra-Mâdhanê 'Âlam. When this lady heard that I was going to Zagê to take a final leave of the King, she came to the royal camp to bid me farewell, and on finding that I had been imprisoned she sent me a present of eggs and fowls, and tried to encourage me. The other, the Governor of Wandigê, who had been severely reprimanded by the King for purchasing honey for me, sent to tell me to-day that he had it still in his possession, and asked if he should send it to me, offering at the same time to procure any other supplies that I might require.

In the afternoon of the 14th the King sent us some fowls and eggs, but no message came with them; so I asked Aito Samuel if he could go and thank the King for his present. He said it was dangerous for him to do so without having first obtained the royal permission; nevertheless, he would go at all hazards. Theodore at the time occupied a raised seat, near the audience-hall, hearing a case judicially; so Samuel went and stood before him. The King asked him, through his spokesman, what he wanted; and on Samuel answering that he had a message from me, he commanded him to approach and communicate what he had to say. After my message was delivered he said, "Ah! my friend, Aito Rassam, why have I ill-treated you thus?" Thereupon he called his valet, Wald-Gâbir, and directed him to accompany Aito Samuel and convey his compliments to my companions and myself. I was also told that I might send one of my interpreters every day with compliments to the King, as I had done heretofore.

On the morning of the 15th we were allowed to pitch our tents, and the guard was ordered not to intrude upon our privacy, but to watch a short distance off. In the afternoon the King sent to inform me that Consul Cameron and his party had arrived from Korâta, and, as he did not wish them to be with the Mission, he had ordered them to be placed in the inclosure, some distance from us. As the day was very hot, and I knew that Consul Cameron and the ladies must be very tired after what they had undergone, I sent and asked the King if he would allow them to ride as far as the inclosure. He immediately gave his consent, and ordered three mules to be supplied from his stable. He afterwards sent, through me, a cow, a basket of *téf* bread, and a jar of mead, for each of the European prisoners, with some butter and red-pepper sauce. After a while, when I heard that they had been allowed only one tent, I sent and requested his Majesty to permit me to send them another— one belonging to the Mission. As he made no objection, I sent it to them, with a few skins for bedding.

Early on Monday, the 16th, all the Chiefs were ordered to attend the Court which his Majesty had intended to hold on the European prisoners. About eight o'clock everything was in readiness for our reception, and the King sent to us to say that as he wished to receive my companions and myself as friends, we were to go to him in uniform, at once, before he sent for the prisoners; so we dressed and repaired to his presence. We found the King sitting on a couch, on the left of the throne, at the door of the audience-chamber, and about 1,000 officers standing on the right and left, while the Râses were sitting below him, on the left, with their backs turned to him, in accordance with court etiquette. The European artisans occupied a place about ten feet behind us. As soon as my companions and I appeared, he welcomed us, and asked us to sit at the foot of the throne, on his right hand. He said he had sent for us before the captives came, in order to assure us of his unceasing friendship, and that we must not think he was going to place us on a par with them; for it was quite impossible for him to have any ill-feeling against us. Referring to our arrest on the 13th, he said he was sorry for what had taken place, but he never meant that we should be roughly handled; it was true that he had given his soldiers orders to search us, but they had greatly exceeded their duty; that my

companions ought not to have worn swords; and that it was
only through the stupidity of Samuel that they were allowed
to appear with them on our first visit to him in Dâmôt.

As the morning was very hot, and we were sitting in the
sun, the King provided us with umbrellas. In the mean
time the imprisoned Europeans were sent for, and I was
glad to find that Mrs. Rosenthal and Mrs. Flad were not
summoned with their husbands. Samuel having intimated
that Consul Cameron was not well enough to walk, the
King ordered him a mule from his own stable. After we had
been more than an hour talking to the King upon different
subjects, Consul Cameron and his party made their appearance, chained arm to arm, in couples. After the usual compliments, they were told to approach, and directed to stand
about twenty yards in front of the King. Consul Cameron
was then called to come forward, and the King ordered him
to be unfettered. When freed from his chains, he was
told to sit with my companions and myself, the King
turning towards me, saying, "He is one of you; let him
sit down with you." M. Bardel was then called forward;
and after his chain had been removed, he was told to take
a seat next to us. I was not at all surprised to see this last
act of clemency on the part of the King; my only wonder
was that M. Bardel had not been released before.

After this the King told me that some of the Europeans
who were present had abused him and said that he was
of low origin; whereas he was ready to prove before me
that he was descended from noble families both on the father
and mother's side. A number of old men were called and
asked different questions about the King's pedigree; of course,
they all declared, on oath, that what the King had said
about his forefathers was true. All the witnesses had to

swear by the death of the Bishop—the most binding oath in Abyssinia—that the King was descended from the first King of Judah; and even the puppet Emperor, Hatsê Yuhannês, who was sick and could not come to the assembly, was referred to. The King was so anxious that I should believe all this, that he insisted upon my sending a representative with Râs I'ngădă and two other Chiefs to hear, in my behalf, the testimony from the mouth of the ex-Emperor.

When the King was satisfied that I was convinced of his noble descent, he said that he had some charges against the Europeans who were then standing before him, and he requested that all questions and answers should pass through me. I had no other alternative but to assent. As the King spoke in Amharic, Aito Samuel had to translate what his Majesty said into Arabic; and as some of the prisoners did not understand English, Mr. Flad had to render what I said into German. So both questions and answers had to pass through three different mouths before they were disposed of. The King did not choose on that occasion to speak Amharic either to Mr. Flad or to any of his fellow-captives; and as they were standing a good distance off, I had sometimes to repeat his Majesty's words twice before they could hear them.

The first thing the King asked the prisoners was, why they had left without coming to see him? Whereupon I interposed and remarked that, if allowed to do so, I would answer that question myself. The King replied, "Wait: I want to see what Mr. Stern and his party say."

When this question was put to them, Mr. Flad replied on the part of his fellow-prisoners, that they had nothing to say on the subject, as the King had made them all over to me, and they had only to listen to my orders; that I was the only one who was responsible to his Majesty, and that through me they had acted as they had done. The King then told them they ought to have begged me to bring them to him. I then told the King that if any one was to blame for the released captives not having gone to him it was myself, and I trusted that he would not lay the fault to their charge. He then began the old complaints against the prisoners individually; even Mr. Flad, who had never before been accused of having abused the King, did not escape on that occasion.

When the King had finished with the prisoners, he ordered me to stand before him, with Dr. Blanc and Lieutenant Prideaux, to answer certain questions which he wished to put to me. I was asked why I had not taken the Mágdala European prisoners to him to beg his Majesty's pardon before they left the country. I replied, that he had never intimated to me, either by letter or otherwise, that he wished me to do so; but, on the contrary, I had always heard that he did not wish to see them. He then asked, why I had allowed the released captives to leave Korâta instead of bringing them to Zagé? I replied, that I had done so with his sanction, which I could prove by his Majesty's letter, and also through his own officer, Lij Abitu. Whereupon the King called Lij Abitu to come forward, and asked him if it was true that he had received his Majesty's permission to take the released captives away from Korâta. He answered in the affirmative; and he even went so far as to tell the King that when he had delivered my message to him about dispensing with the attendance of the released captives, his Majesty had received my suggestion with great approbation.

After this, the King looked at me and said, "Do you consider yourself a King?" I replied in the negative, but said that I was his friend, and begged to know what I had done to lead him to ask me such a question. He said that I had taken away the European released captives without reconciling them to him, in order that I might boast, on my return to England, that I had conducted them out of Abyssinia by my own power and skill;* that, had I brought them to Zagê, he would have given them mules and money, whereas they were now in chains.

We were then asked to sit down, as formerly, at the foot of the throne—reckoned the most honourable post—and he recommenced his grievances against the rebels and the Turks, and said that he hoped one day to show me how he could thrash the unbelievers. "Ah!" he said, "if the English would only assist me, we could build a fence round Sennaar." (Sennaar is a large district in the possession of the Egyptian Government, on the western frontier of Abyssinia.) He then concluded by saying, "Is this your friendship, Mr. Rassam, that you wish to leave me and take away those who have abused me? Wherever I am, there you shall be." He then became all smiles, rose, and told us to go back to our tents. I thought that as I had taken the blame upon myself for the departure of the prisoners from Korâta, he would now release them from their fetters; but, on seeing that he did not do so, I asked him to oblige me by ordering their chains to be removed. He replied, "We have had enough for to-day; I will see to the rest to-morrow." Thereupon, Dr. Blanc, Lieutenant Prideaux and I returned to our tents, Consul

---

* From some invidious remarks which have recently been published on the Continent, wherein the writer assumes to have been cognizant of my feelings when the success of the Mission seemed certain, and ventures, moreover, to dilate on the anticipation which I then entertained of a handsome reward in store for me from the Government, I have no doubt that this idea was suggested to the King, indirectly, by some of the European artisans.

Cameron accompanying us, the King having given him permission to that effect. His Majesty left in company with M. Bardel.

Never before, since my arrival in Abyssinia, had Theodore manifested such bitter animosity against the prisoners as he did on this occasion; and although I took all the blame upon myself for their not having gone in person to be reconciled to him, nevertheless he declined to accede to my earnest appeal for their release, and it was not until I had engaged to become surety for them that he allowed their fetters to be removed. On the other hand, M. Bardel, against whom so much has been said, as having been at the bottom of all the mischief which created the breach between the King and his European captives, underwent no questioning whatever, and was directed to sit by our side. That the whole thing was a solemn farce, there cannot be the shadow of a doubt; even Theodore himself could not restrain a smile when he blamed me for having tried to smuggle a large party of Europeans out of his territories, just as if they were a bale of cotton, knowing at the same time that I had acted throughout with his special sanction. If I, personally, had been the object of the King's displeasure, why, before the arrival of the captives on the day of the trial, did he ask me to sit by his side and have a friendly chat? And how comes it, if such had been the case, that he did not tell me to hold my peace, when I afterwards begged him to unfetter the captives? Why, moreover, if he entertained any distrust of me, did he shortly after grant my request, on condition that I became security for them? And why, lastly, if he really had been offended with me, did he never again, for a whole year, allude to the charge he had preferred against me on that occasion? The whole affair had been got up—as he himself afterwards told me on several occasions, and as the tenor of his subsequent letters to me will prove—as a mere pretext to detain me in the country for the furtherance of his own indefinite views. But I am anticipating.

At sunrise next morning, the 17th, we saw the King busily engaged in marking out a piece of ground within the royal inclosure, which was to be fenced in, and we were told that it was intended for us, as his Majesty had resolved to place us there, together with all the Europeans for whom I stood security. When the soldiers began to construct the fence, the King sent me this message—that for my sake he would release the prisoners from their chains, provided I became surety for their good behaviour. I replied, that I could not give him an answer before I had spoken to them, as none of them were servants of our Government, nor were they all British subjects. The King then ordered them all to repair to my tent. When they had expressed their willingness that I should be surety for them, I sent and informed his Majesty of the fact. After a while, the King's consent was obtained for striking off the chains, and when his Majesty heard that all had been unfettered, he sent me this message: "Mind, Mr. Rassam, although you have become surety for all the Europeans, and I hold you alone responsible for their acts, yet I shall always be at your service to assist you in case any of them become refractory or troublesome. Only tell me to chain this man or imprison the other, and I will do as you bid me. Do not fear; I will take care of them for you."

Shortly after, all the Europeans were summoned to appear before the King that we might have a private "cháwata" (chat) together. We all went to the same audience-hall in a body, and, after the usual salutations were over, Dr. Blanc, Lieutenant Prideaux, Consul Cameron and I were invited by the King to sit next to him, on his left hand, while the artisans were told to occupy a place between the door and the King's right. His Majesty placed a pillow for me to lean upon, near him. When we had sat down, the released captives were called in, and after prostrating themselves they were directed to sit on our left, near another entrance. The King on that occasion put on a most humble countenance, and asked us all to forgive and to forget. He then bowed his head and said, "For Christ's sake, forgive me." All of us, including myself and companions, were obliged to stoop, following his example. So intent were we on showing our respect, that we forgot the royal head was still bent, till one of the European artisans called out, "You have forgotten the King's head; tell his Majesty to sit up." I then apologized to the King, and begged him to raise his head.

When this ceremony was over, the King told Consul Cameron that he had received a petition from his (the Consul's) relatives and the relatives of his late fellow-captives, which he characterized as "touching," and asked him to read it for the edification of all those who understood English. Accordingly, Consul Cameron read it in full. This done, the King looked towards Mr. Stern and his party, and said that they ought to be very grateful to me for the great trouble I had undergone for them. They were all dismissed, but my companions, the European artisans and myself were told to remain a little while longer. Dr. Beke's letter was not produced, neither did the King make any allusion to it.

I had hoped that after this formal reconciliation there would be no further hindrance to our departure; but I was sadly disappointed. As soon as we were left alone, the King called the Chief Scribe and directed him to write what he should dictate. Aito Samuel was ordered to translate to me word by word as they went on; and after a great deal of disputing about certain phrases and titles, between the Monarch, the scribes, Aito Samuel and Wald-Gâbir, the valet, the following letter to our Queen was decided upon:—

"In the name of the Father, Son, and Holy Ghost—One God.

"From God's slave and His created being, the son of David, the son of Solomon, the King of kings, Theodorus.

"To her whom God has exalted above all people, the Defender of the Christian Faith, the Protector of the poor and oppressed, the Queen of England, Victoria.

"Had not your servant Mr. Hormuzd Rassam, whom you said that you had sent in the affair of Mr. Cameron, come, but the lowest of your slaves, I would have welcomed him. By the power of God, I have released Mr. Cameron and made him over to your servant, Mr. Rassam; and, by the power of God, I have also released the other prisoners and all other Europeans who might wish to leave the country, and made them over to him; and I have kept your servant Mr. Hormuzd Rassam for the sake of consulting together upon the extension of our friendship. We, the people of Ethiopia, are blind, and we beg of your Majesty that you would give light to our eyes, and so may you receive light in the kingdom of Heaven."

My feelings may well be conceived when I understood that I was to be retained as a hostage; for such, undoubtedly, was the case, although the King had expressed it differently. We were then in his power, and it was useless to protest against his double-dealing, or to refuse sending the letter. Good advice he would not take, and any opposition to his will on my part might have led him to treat all the Europeans with still greater severity.

It has been asserted that the King had asked me to remain with him as a hostage, leaving Consul Cameron and the other released captives to depart out of the country, and that I had refused my consent. How this absurd story originated I cannot tell; all I can say is that Theodore never once hinted any such proposal to me. Besides, the story itself is preposterous, since if the King really entertained a desire to send the captives away, retaining me in his power, he unquestionably might have done so without asking my sanction to the arrangement. Having once made them over to me, to be taken by me out of Abyssinia, I am convinced that, ill-disposed as he was towards them, the thought never occurred to him to let them go without me. The fact is, from the time he informed her Majesty that he had released the captives and consigned them to me, he never considered them in any way apart from me as the head of the Mission. In his letter to Dr. Beke, in answer to the petition forwarded by the relatives of the captives, he says, " the prisoners, from whose families you brought a petition, I have released for the sake of my friend, the Queen, and have made them over to Mr. Rassam *to take out with him* when he leaves Abyssinia." In like manner, whereas the King had sent all my fellow-captives with me to the British camp on the 11th of April, 1868, when referring to that circumstance on the following day, in his letter to Sir Robert Napier, he merely says, " I sent to you Mr. Rassam the same evening, that your heart might be made easy."

After we left, Theodore sent me the following note, with a message that he wished me to write a letter to accompany his own. He also asked me to select one of the Europeans to take it to England and bring an answer:—

" From God's slave and His created being, the son of David, the son of Solomon, the King of kings, Theodorus.

" To my friend and counsellor, the servant of the Queen of England, Aito Hormuzd Rassam.

" My desire is that you should send to her Majesty, the Queen, and obtain for me a man who can make cannons and muskets, and one who can smelt iron; also an instructor of artillery. I want these people to come here with their implements and everything necessary for their work, and then they shall teach us and return. By the power of God, forward this my request to England."

He said, further, that he would like to see the letter before I sent it. This led me to draw it up in terms which might please him, in case he had it read. The following is a copy of the letter which I addressed on the occasion to her Majesty's Principal Secretary of State for Foreign Affairs:—

"*Emperor's Court at Zagé, April* 18, 1866.
"MY LORD,

"I HAVE the honour to report to your Lordship that my companions, Dr. Blanc and Mr. Prideaux, and I reached the Court of the Emperor of Abyssinia on the 28th of January, and his Majesty gave us a most magnificent reception, and treated us with great kindness and civility.

"He received her Majesty's letter graciously; in answer to which he wrote a very friendly and courteous reply.

"I had the first interview with his Majesty on the very afternoon of my arrival at his Court, when he related to me all his grievances with regard to Consul Cameron and the other European prisoners. Early the next morning he ordered the release of all the prisoners, a nominal list of whom is herewith inclosed for your Lordship's information. All the released prisoners have been made over to me by his Majesty, and are now with me, enjoying good health.

"All the prisoners presented themselves before the Emperor on the 16th instant, and after the charges were read to them, they all confessed that they were wrong in what they had written and spoken against his Majesty. The Emperor then forgave them for all that they had done, and said that he would be as friendly towards them henceforth as he is towards myself and my companions.

"His Majesty has been good enough to present me with 10,000 dollars for my expenditure, and has in every respect been very kind and hospitable. The other day he did me the honour of coming in person to see me in my tent, and said that he held me dear on account of my being the servant of his friend, the British Queen. He has also presented me with a royal saddle, shield, sword, spear and armlet, and has given each of my companions a shield, spear and armlet, in addition to five mules. He is about to create an Order, with which he intends to invest us.

"His Majesty has had for some years a desire to procure some scientific men from England, and yesterday he spoke to me about obtaining for him two or three men who could teach his people how to make cannons, muskets and shot, and how to melt iron; also an instructor of artillery. He said he wished these persons to come here with their instruments and everything necessary for their work, and after they had taught his people they should be allowed to return.

"His Majesty would be much obliged to her Majesty's Government if his request could be complied with, and from his second letter to the Queen, which I inclose herewith, your Lordship will perceive that we are all detained in this country for the present, for friendship's sake.

"I should be obliged if her Majesty's Government could send me 100,000 percussion-caps of different sizes, a few double-barrelled rifles and pistols, some gunpowder, a boat, if practicable, for the use of his Majesty on the Lake, and any other thing which Mr. Flad, who is the bearer of this letter, may suggest.

"If her Majesty's Government are able to send the persons required, it is necessary that they should be informed that they will be required to remain in the service of the Emperor at least one year, and that no European articles are obtainable here."

With regard to the messenger, I left the selection to the King, and I was glad to find that he chose Mr. Flad, as I knew he would report honestly and truthfully all that had taken place between me and the King since my first reception at Court. I did not omit to request Mr. Flad to inform her Majesty's Government of the restraint under which I wrote the foregoing letter.

Before writing the letter, however, I asked Aito Samuel to speak to the King about the unfriendly course he was pursuing, and to advise him to allow us all to leave the country; to say, also, that everything he wanted would be attended to. His answer was, that I ought by that time to know the King well enough to be convinced that he was not a man to listen to advice, or to be diverted from doing what he had decided upon, whether good or bad. I also applied to Mr. Waldmeier and Mr. Moritz Hall, who were then in great favour with his Majesty, on the same subject; but they agreed with Samuel that no intervention would be of any avail.

In the course of the day the King sent me an Abyssinian criminal in chains, a young man about twenty years of age, who had killed his own mother for the sake of plunder. His Majesty wished me to hear the murderer's confession of guilt, in order that I might see what a bad set of people he had to deal with. "Were I to order this wicked man to be executed according to law"— such was the conclusion of Theodore's message—" some of the Europeans whom I have made over to you would denounce me as a murderer." By the Abyssinian code, this matricide would have been mutilated and his remains left to rot above ground; but the King ordered him to be shot, and his body to be interred. Notwithstanding all the cruelties practised by Theodore, he was far more lenient in his judgments than the *Fettch-Negúst*, or the common law in Abyssinia. It is undeniable that he occasionally sacrificed human life wholesale; nevertheless he was not guilty of half the barbarities of Dajjàj Oobê or Sáhéla Salassê, the old king of Shoa. Prior to Theodore's reign, men were deprived of their eyes, tongues, hands, and other members—to say nothing of still more horrible tortures to which they were liable—for slight misdemeanours; whereas I believe a traveller might go through the length and breadth of the country without finding a single instance of such mutilation caused by Theodore.

In the afternoon we moved our tents within the fence which had been erected for us in the morning, and then the rest of the Europeans were brought to the same place. The artisans were allowed to occupy a spot at the outskirts.

After we had returned to our tents, the Aitos Samuel, Kása and Wandé were summoned before the King to be tried for having assisted me in sending letters to the coast. The two last were the first to be arraigned. Their simple answer was, that having received a written order from his Majesty to attend to my wants and to obey any instructions which they might receive from me through Aito Samuel, they had conformed strictly to the directions of his Majesty's confidential Báldărăbâ.

Samuel's turn came next, and on being asked whether it was true that he had told those merchants to find messengers for me, and, if so, how he dared to do so without his Majesty's permission, he replied in the affirmative, alleging that he did not think there was any harm in my writing to inform my friends in England of the release of the captives, and of his Majesty's kindness towards me, which I had assured him formed the contents of the letters. He pleaded, moreover, that when we left the King in Agówmědĕr, his Majesty had given him stringent orders to obey me in everything, and to serve me as a slave.

The merchants were then charged with having supplied the rebels of Gójjam with muskets. This they indignantly denied, as being two of his Majesty's most loyal subjects; whereupon he ordered them to be chained by the hand to a couple of his soldiers, and imposed a fine upon them of 20,000 dollars. They managed to scrape together a moiety of that sum by the sale of their property, but the King insisted that it should be paid in full, and, to that end, had them subjected to torture. By borrowing and begging they collected a little more. As even that did not satisfy the inexorable tyrant, he resorted to the rope. Finding, after subjecting them to every species of cruelty for several months, that nothing more could be extorted from 'them, he left them in chains, and ultimately sent them to Mágdala. Aito Kâsa, who was really a good man and respected by all who knew him, was upwards of sixty years old.

As soon as Kántiba Hailo heard that I was to be detained, he went to the King and advised him to send me away, telling him that ten thousand men would be a less formidable array for him to contend against than my tongue. The only rejoinder he received was this :—" Aha ! I know now that you are my enemy and that Mr. Rassam is my friend. You had better hold your tongue, you old fool, and go away." The kind man came to me afterwards, and recommended me to put the best face upon my misfortunes ; " for," said he, " you can do no good by appearing gloomy." In the course of the evening, Itamanyo, the favourite Queen, sent me a similar message, with this addition :—" If you take matters cheerily, you have nothing to fear ; everything will come right at last, for the King really loves you." The disgrace of the Mission was also, I believe, sincerely deplored by the European artisans, especially by Mr. Waldmeier and Mr. Moritz Hall— two upright men, who I am sure would have done their best to assist us. Unfortunately, they were powerless in this instance to influence the perverse Monarch.

CHAPTER XVII.

UNDER ARREST AT ZAGÊ.

Presents from the King — He restores our confiscated property — His studied courtesy — Theodore not a good marksman — " Who is your father ?" — Our Queen's birthday commemorated by the King — Another letter from Dr. Beke — Theodore kills a man at a blow — Artillery practice — Theodore's account of his strategy and exploits — His nimbleness — His cruelties at this time — A case of high treason — " Shrimps " and " Bob " — The Itégé's *Márgaf* — The peninsula and town of Zagê — Theodore's " imitation of a steamer " — A native Tournament.

On the 18th of April the King sent the presents which he had intended to give us on leaving Abyssinia, namely, to me, a royal saddle, shield, sword, spear and armlet; and a shield, spear and armlet to each of my companions, Dr. Blanc and Lieutenant Prideaux; also a first-rate mule for each of us. (When we were sent to Mágdala as prisoners, all these presents were taken from us, excepting the armlets.) That day my companions and I went out for a ride, as we were told it would please the King. The Master of the Horse and two other officers accompanied us.

On the morning of the 21st, the day Mr. Flad left for England, the King restored all our arms and silver trinkets; and of the money he took on the 13th of April he sent me back 1,000 dollars, with a promise that he would soon give me back the whole, and present my companions and myself with the Order of the " Cross and Solomon's Seal," the decorations of which were not quite ready. Of the cash which was taken from the other captives when they were arrested and chained near Korâta, amounting nearly to 800 dollars, he only sent them back, through me, 550 dollars, which, he said, was all the money that had reached him. It appears that the soldiers who carried out the confiscation had not forgotten to help themselves on the occasion.

As the King wished to show Mr. Flad, before he left for Europe, that his Majesty and I were on the best terms, he came to pay me a visit just before that gentleman started; and, on seeing the floor of my tent bare, he fetched some carpets, and spread them himself on the ground, with the assistance of Râs I'ngădă and Aito Samuel. He afterwards sent the chief minister to carpet the tents of Dr. Blanc and Lieutenant Prideaux. On his rising to depart, I asked him if he would allow me to escort him as far as his house. He immediately advanced, took me by the hand, and said, " Come on." We walked together, hand in hand, all the way, and the Abyssinians could not help smiling to see the Great Emperor walking as a bosom friend with his prisoner. On going out of the inclosure the King saw one of the Chiefs of our guard, Râs Wald-Máryam, standing at attention; his Majesty stopped and asked him what business he had there. The Chief answering that he was keeping guard, he said to him, " What! you are watching my friend Rassam? Go away at once. I have nothing to fear from him;" and then, pointing to his mouth, he added, " not if he were to put the muzzle of a pistol here."

After that day every one was able to go out when he liked, either walking or riding; but I was not allowed to move a yard without some officers to attend me, whom the King called a "guard of honour." Ultimately, my protectors were reduced to the Bâldărăbâ and the Master of the Horse.

Soon after Mr. Flad's departure, the King presented

Dr. Blanc, Lieutenant Prideaux and myself with a thoroughbred Galla horse each.

The King became more affectionate in his manner towards me every day, taking me with him on several occasions to shoot hippopotami at one of their favourite haunts on the northern extremity of the Zagê peninsula, where the southern side of the Lake takes the form of a spacious bay. Twice he left me alone with his followers to try my luck, while he retired into the thick wood to pray, as, starting from home as he always did before sunrise, it was too early for him to repair to the church. He was by no means a good shot, and whenever he missed he always abused the rifle, saying, "Who is your father?" This, one of the most offensive epithets in Abyssinia, consists of two words, both Semitic,— "Man abât?"—and is addressed indiscriminately to animate and inanimate objects. A native almost instinctively uses it to a stone which has tripped him, or to a troublesome fly. Thus, on the great day of the trial at Zagê, there were so many flies near the door of the audience-hall where the King was seated, that one entered the royal mouth and nearly choked him. On ejecting it, he vilified the hapless insect by the usual reflection on its paternity. Whenever the question is asked, no abuse being intended, the words are transposed—the noun being made to precede the pronoun, thus: "Abâteh, mánnû?"—"Your father, who is he?" Twice, at Mágdala, I inadvertently used the wrong phrase when asking whose child my visitor was. The Abyssinians, who are generally good-natured, knowing that I did so from ignorance of their language, could not help bursting out into laughter at my mistake.

The King, having heard from Samuel that the 24th of May was our Queen's birthday, sent to me in the morning to say he was going to make a holiday in honour of Her Majesty, and that he had ordered all his people to be merry. He asked me to give him permission to entertain all the servants of the Europeans who were with me, Indians as well as Abyssinians. There was nothing but feasting the whole day in our establishment, as well as in that of the King. His Majesty having learnt also that it was customary in our country to fire a salute on this anniversary, ordered that the same form should be observed. He requested me to take all my fellow-Europeans down to the shore of the Lake to witness the firing. At noon precisely we were ready on the spot, and witnessed the salute of twenty-one guns fired "in honour of the birthday of the great Queen of England."

On the 27th, another messenger arrived with a letter from Dr. Beke, dated from Halai, to the address of the King. His Majesty forwarded the letter to me after he had read it, and asked me to reply to it. I sent him back word that it was not customary in our country to answer a letter which was not addressed to one's self. Next day he sent to say that as I objected to answer Dr. Beke myself, he hoped that I would get his Amharic version translated into English for him. Not wishing to annoy the King by refusing, I asked Lieutenant Prideaux to do so.

Dr. Beke told the King in his letter that, as he had heard that his Majesty had graciously released the captives, he was coming up to thank him for his act of clemency. He also informed the King that the rebels of Tigré had imprisoned him, and demanded from him as many dollars as there were stones at Halai, and as much powder as there was dust. He asked his Majesty to send and have him released. In his answer Theodore told Dr. Beke that he had no business to penetrate into Abyssinia without his (the King's) permission, and he directed him to go down to Massowah and await there until further orders. He would not see either Dr. Beke's first or second messenger, and both were told to remain in our encampment until they were dismissed.

The King was reported to be very much out of temper this morning, and while in that mood he had caused the death of a poor peasant who had applied to him for justice in the matter of a field which was in dispute between him and one of his neighbours. The appellant, it appears, not hearing distinctly what the King had said, repeated his question, whereupon his Majesty, who was then standing in the courtyard, stooping down, seized a piece of a rafter about six inches long and five in diameter and felled him with it to the ground with one fatal blow. Mr. Bender and Mr. Moritz Hall, two of the royal artisans, who were just then paying some visits within our fence, were summoned before his Majesty, who abruptly asked where they had been prowling. They replied that they had been to see me, which was not the case, as they had not entered my tent. Mr. Moritz Hall told me the story laughingly, stating that they were in too great dread of a severe rebuke to say at the time that they had been calling on any one else.

It had previously been arranged by the King that I should accompany him this same morning to witness some practice from a three-pounder gun which had been cast at Gáffat. When, in pursuance of this arrangement, Samuel came to take me and my companions to follow his Majesty, he could scarcely walk from fear of meeting his royal master in his present dangerous mood; but as neither he nor I dared to refuse, Blanc, Prideaux and I donned our uniforms and set off. Two of the released captives, named Kerans and McKelvie, both Irishmen, who had formerly been in Consul Cameron's employ, the former as secretary and the latter as a servant, had already volunteered to enter the royal service, but for some reason or other, known only to the King, his Majesty had declined their offer. On this occasion, however, he sent to say that McKelvie, who had informed him that he was an artilleryman, was to accompany us. When we were yet full half a mile from the royal cavalcade, Samuel advised us to dismount. We did so, and marched slowly onward, no one venturing to utter a word—not unlike a funeral procession. The King, who had an eye like a hawk, on seeing that we had arrived, sent to bid us mount and follow him, and in less than five minutes we were by his side. After the usual inquiries about our health, which he uttered in a most lugubrious style, as if he had just been bereft of both his parents, he asked me where he should post the gun for practice towards the Lake. Being altogether ignorant of gunnery, I referred him to Messrs. Moritz Hall and McKelvie, who were walking near me. Thereat he looked as black as thunder—his bare reply made many a man quake behind me—and said peevishly to me, "Never mind Moritz and McKelvie: I want *you* to indicate the site." As soon as Samuel translated these words to me, I pointed out a slight rise in the ground a little in advance of us, where the King immediately ordered the gun, which had been brought on the back of one mule and the carriage on another, to be put together. His Majesty then retired to the wood to pray for about half an hour; on his return he looked much more placid, and began to relate to me his exploits against "those infidel Mohammedans, the Turks and Gallas." He told me that from childhood he had been fond of artillery practice, and that the first cannon he made was constructed out of the trunk of a tree, bored, and bound round with rings of iron. To charge it, he had the butt-end fixed in the ground, and after it was filled with powder and stone, and well rammed down, he fired it against the infidels by means of a train. He said, also, that he had been addicted to using mines in his engagements with the Gallas, believing that all Mohammedans deserved to be killed and sent to Gehenna wholesale. One day he made a formidable mine, which he intended to spring when the Galla horse advanced to the attack, but one of his disaffected subjects had apprised the enemy of the design, which caused them to change their tactics. He had also employed looking-glasses to dazzle the eyes of man and beast, and by these and other stratagems he had concluded an honourable peace with the Gallas, after having obliged them to pay the tribute which they had refused to his forefathers for centuries. While on the expedition referred to, a Turk of high rank was seized by his soldiers and taken before him, and on seeing the wretched man, he said to him, "So you have come thus far to fight against me! But, never mind; as you are a stranger and know no better, I will do you no harm. Thereupon," continued his Majesty, "I sent him safely to the border, telling him to go home, and not to let me behold his face again." The King was highly excited while relating these adventures to me, and every one was delighted that he seemed so fully absorbed by his subject.

Although McKelvie had offered his services to his Majesty as a skilled artilleryman, and he had been specially ordered to attend on this occasion, he was not called upon to assist in any way, the entire management of the gun being left to Mr. Moritz Hall. His practice was so successful that the King rushed upon him in an ecstasy of delight, kissing his head and calling him his "pet son." '(In less than a year afterwards this same Moritz Hall, than whom none of the other Europeans served Theodore more faithfully, was, out of sheer caprice on the part of his ungrateful employer, dragged in foot- and hand- chains for nearly six months between Debra Tâbor and Mágdala.) The artillery practice ended, his Majesty asked me to follow him to a rocky part near the Lake, to shoot at the ducks and geese which frequent the beach, presenting me at the same time with a fowling-piece, which he thought better than my own. We had not proceeded more than a hundred yards when he called my attention to a flying goose. I accordingly fired, and must have winged the bird, for it could not fly, but was swimming as fast as it was able towards the open Lake. Not wishing to lose the prize, I commenced running over the rough ground, and, on placing my foot on a smooth rock, slipped and fell. The King was by my side in a moment, and raising me by one arm said, in Arabic, "Rise, my son, and take heart; may your enemies die in your stead!" It was marvellous to see with what dexterity his Majesty jumped from one rock to another, never tripping and never seemingly deterred by the sharp stones, though he was barefooted. He then proceeded to shoot vultures—a sure sign, so Samuel informed me, that he was out of temper. Betaking himself to "sleep," or scourging and ruthlessly shedding of blood, were other well-known symptoms of his being in an angry mood. In fact, during this period, the King perpetrated some fearful deeds of cruelty, causing several Chiefs and also a lady of rank to be flogged to death a few yards from our inclosure. I was generally out riding when these tragedies were performed, and only heard of them on my return. The fence round our camp was so loosely constructed that everything which took place on the opposite side could be distinctly seen through it. Unfortunately for her, Mrs. Rosenthal's tent was nearest to the spot where these horrible scenes occurred, so that she could hear every lash as it descended on the body of the writhing sufferers. When the King was about to commit one of these outrages, the Master of the Horse generally came to me beforehand and suggested that I should take a ride, under the plea that his Majesty would be pleased to know that I was enjoying myself. On one occasion, on our return from a short excursion, the same official, hearing the lash going, told me to proceed at a slow pace, as it was not desirable that we should enter the royal Court while the King was holding an assize in the inclosure. We accordingly took another turn, and reached our own camp just as the King had inflicted about one hundred and fifty lashes with an Abyssinian whip, called a *jeráf*, on a young lady of noble birth, because she had not given due notice that her husband intended to desert and join the rebels in Gójjam. The poor creature swore that she was utterly ignorant of her husband's plans until the day after his desertion, and appealed to the generosity of her inexorable judge not to punish her for the sake of a man whose very desertion proved that he did not care for her. "Throw her down; by my death, scourge her!" was the only reply to her earnest pleadings. Twice, while I was in our camp, he held a Court to try officers charged with high treason, but on neither of these occasions was the sentence of the lash awarded. The victims were ordered to be stripped naked and left day and night in the open air, in the marketplace, for the space of a fortnight, loaded with chains and with a heavy beam, branching out at one end like a yoke, affixed to their necks. On one of these trials he sent to request that I would depute one of my followers to be present, in order that I might be convinced what atrocious subjects he had. The case was one of high treason, and the accuser a notorious tool of the King's, named Bitwáddad Tadla, a Chief of Bagámĕdĕr, the man who was sent to arrest Consul Cameron and his party on their way to the coast from Korâta, and who eventually took us prisoners to Mágdala. His solitary witness was one of his own servants, who could only swear that he once saw the arraigned whisper in his master's ear, but did not know what he said. The charge was, that the accused, who was also a Bagámĕdĕr Chief, had endeavoured to induce Bitwáddad Tadla to desert with him, and to stir up the peasantry of that district against the King, and that he, Bitwáddad Tadla, should be acknowledged as their Chief. The evidence adduced was considered sufficient to condemn the unfortunate man, and when sentence was passed upon him, his Majesty bade my interpreter come and inform me what a treasonable set of people he had to deal with.

One day the King took it into his head to direct that all the great Chiefs, from the Râses downwards, should dismount on meeting me, and stand still to receive my salutation, if they happened to be walking. This despotic order was as disagreeable to me as to the Chiefs; nevertheless we were obliged to submit: they in obedience to the Sovereign, and I, to do honour to his Majesty through them, had also to dismount when they did.

It having been reported, on his own authority, that M. Bardel had been released and taken again into the royal favour, specially in order that he might translate to the King certain letters and books, taken from the captives, which were known to be in his Majesty's possession, and as M. Bardel's friend, I'ngădă Wark, was in constant communication with M. Macraire, Consul Cameron's French servant, we agreed to call M. Bardel "Shrimps," lest any of his intimates should overhear and report that we had been talking about him. The King we nicknamed "Bob," for the same reason. In fact, we were obliged to exercise the greatest caution in our conversation during the whole time of our detention at Zagê. I am bound, however, to mention here that M. Bardel promised not to translate correctly to the King any passages which might prove injurious to the captives. At this same period the King himself was unremitting in his attentions to the Mission. On one occasion he sent us twenty *shámmas* as bedding, and three *márgafs*— the latter an Abyssinian cotton robe, worked with silk instead of twist—because he feared that, as the rainy season had set in, we might feel the cold. The *márgaf* intended for me he had taken from the Queen's person, Itamanyo, the same evening, and the message which accompanied it was as follows:—" I hope that after to-day, when you go out riding, you will wear it, because the ignorant Abyssinians consider that a man is naked unless he wears a *shámma* or a *márgaf*, and I wish you to look well when you go abroad; but if you will not wear it for my sake, I hope you will do so for the sake of the Itêgê, from whom I have taken it to send to you." In my reply, I thanked his Majesty for the honour he had done me, and also for his kind thought for us; at the same time, I begged to be excused wearing a dress to which I was unaccustomed, and one which was unsuited to me as a servant of the British Queen, assuring him, however, that in any other way I should be delighted to please him to the best of my ability; that I should not value the *márgaf* the less because I did not wear it; and that I should carefully treasure it in remembrance of the King and his favourite consort.* This message, I was glad to find, was well received, for he sent back word immediately that I might wear the robe or not, just as I pleased. In reality, there would have been no disgrace in our assuming the robe; on the contrary, the King was justified in saying that we should have been regarded with greater respect by the common people. On the other hand, however, had I consented to wear it, my companions would have been obliged to follow my example, and there are so many formalities attached to the mode of wearing this garment that, situated as we were, the guests of the King and inmates of the royal camp, the least breach of etiquette—such as wearing it round the body instead of over or below the right or left shoulder—might have subjected the innocent culprit to a beating, or to a severe reprimand from the King. His Majesty always held his Court on the outside of an inclosure which had been erected for the purpose within the yard of the royal precincts, so that any one passing to or from our quarter must needs be seen by the King, who was generally squatting on a small platform raised above the hedge surrounding his residence.

My usual ride, during our stay at Zagê, was to the church situated on the summit of the peninsula, about fifteen hundred feet above the Lake, and a mile and a half from our camp. There was always a delicious breeze there, and the scenery of the neighbourhood is magnificent. Zagê was formerly one of the largest and wealthiest towns in Abyssinia, and consisted of as many as two thousand houses, or huts, spread over the peninsula, which is about three miles in length and two in breadth. Every hut was detached,

---

* This robe has been lent to the Managers of the Crystal Palace for public exhibition.

with ground surrounding it for cultivation. The locality was famous for the growth of coffee, and also for the plant called *Gésho*, the leaf of which is used for fermenting *téj* and beer. It is both bitter and pungent. When the King destroyed the flourishing district of Métcha, of which it is the capital, Zagê shared in the common disaster; but when he visited the place in February he determined to consummate its ruin. On the pretext that the priests had supplied the rebels of Gójjam with arms, he imposed a fine upon the inhabitants which he knew full well they were unable to pay, and when the clergy pleaded that they themselves were starving for want of the necessaries of life, he ordered his troops to sack the place, and to level every hut to the ground—the timber of which they were directed to use as fuel—so that the unfortunate residents might be deprived of shelter. In less than two hours not a house was left standing, and hundreds of women and children were driven to beg their bread, with hardly a rag to cover them. The men were allowed the option either of entering the royal service or going wherever they pleased. The latter alternative was a sheer mockery, as it was well known that the guards at the outposts were directed to seize all who left the camp, and that a cruel death awaited them. Even when we were there, although all the dwellings had been destroyed, the whole peninsula was thickly wooded with the coffee plant, the *gésho*, and a variety of other indigenous trees. It is certainly a charming locality, and, blessed with a good government, Zagê might in a few years become the centre of a flourishing and remunerative trade; and the same may be said of many other equally eligible places in Abyssinia proper. The King had declared that he intended to make Zagê his new capital; but, like many other projects of a similar nature, he never attempted to carry it out. He did indeed erect a great number of large rooms, in the ordinary Abyssinian style, and on our first going to Zagé, subsequent to our disgrace, he talked of building us huts for the winter, but finding the place somewhat unhealthy he abandoned the idea of spending the rainy season there. For nearly a month he was engaged in building what he called an imitation of a steamer. Two large boats, sixty feet long and twenty wide, midships, with wooden decks, and a couple of wheels affixed to the sides of each, to be turned by a handle like that attached to a common grindstone, were accordingly constructed; but although nearly a hundred men were taken on board, the wheels were only immersed about four inches. The day they were launched, he invited the members of the Mission to witness the experiment, and the vessel in which he had embarked moved so rapidly after the bulrushes had got well soaked, which made it subside deeper into the water, that he seemed almost frantic with joy, whilst the natives looked on with admiring wonder. He did not take us with him on the trial trip because, as he sent to tell us, he feared the boat might sink so deep that we should get wet. He proceeded to try how the vessel would behave against the wind, and on rounding the peninsula encountered a strong breeze, which soon convinced him of the futility of his attempt. The incongruous materials of which the boat was constructed, one elastic and the other the opposite—no effort having been made to ensure an equal pressure upon them from without—began to give way after a little tossing, and his Majesty deemed it prudent to return as speedily as possible to the smooth water in the bay. From that time he appears to have abandoned all idea of building a royal navy for the Lake of Dámbea.

On another occasion he invited the members of the Mission to witness the national pastime, called "Gûks"—a kind of tournament, in which he himself was to play a part. On our approach he left the field and came forward to welcome us; then, placing us in a convenient spot, he ordered his pages to spread their *shámmas* on the ground for us to sit upon, and left Râs Adilo, of Yadjow, with us as a guard of honour, saying as he returned to the arena that he hoped we should enjoy the spectacle. Theodore himself opened the joust on horseback, but whether or not because they were pitted against the Sovereign, the feigned antagonists soon gave way before him and his party, who always came off victorious. Reeds were used instead of spears, and I noticed that the King made frequent jocular thrusts with this harmless weapon at his favourite warriors. When tired of riding, his Majesty dismounted, and ordered a sham fight on foot. This was certainly a wild and picturesque sight. Hundreds of gaily-dressed soldiers entered the lists with silver shields and glittering spears. The King chooses his party at random, and the officer on whom the high honour is conferred of coping with his Majesty does the same. When the opposing combatants are fully arrayed, about one hundred yards from each other, the side which represents the King's enemies is allowed to attack first. They rush to the onset with a loud yell, the royal party remaining in the mean time on the defensive. When the combatants meet hand to hand, a general outburst of screams and whoops ensues, intermingled with snatches of the native war-song and the ringing of the butt-end of lances on each others' shields—such a clash as baffles description. The King seemed to surpass all the rest in the agility of his movements and his dexterity in the use of the lance, and wherever he appeared in person his adversaries gave way, until at length the royalists remained masters of the field. I could not help deploring on this occasion that Theodore, who had so many qualities calculated to make him the idol of his people, and especially of his army, should possess those qualities in conjunction with other characteristics which neutralized his influence for good, and rendered him the scourge of his subjects. On rejoining us he addressed me as follows:—" I hope, Mr. Rassam, you do not laugh at us for amusing ourselves in this barbarous style. Oh! how I long to see your way of fighting." To this polite speech I replied that it would be altogether unbecoming in me to ridicule the usages of other nations. Every country had its peculiar mode of warfare, and his feelings, I was sure, were reciprocated by many in England, who would have been delighted to witness what we had seen that day. We rode back together, and on entering the royal courtyard the King dismounted and insisted on escorting me to my tent. On reaching it I said, "Now, as your Majesty has done me this honour, I cannot allow you to proceed to your residence without accompanying you thither; and I beg you will grant me that favour." He laughed heartily at this, and remarked that if I went with him he must needs return with me again, and our mutual civility would be endless; "but, never mind," he added, "I shall not vex you by refusing your request to accompany me home."

CHAPTER XVIII.

FROM ZAGÊ TO DEBRA TÂBOR.

Departure from Zagê in rear of the royal troops — Theodore's courtesy and remorse — We cross the Abai — The King's fickleness — Arrival at Korâta — Cholera in the royal camp — Start for Debra Tâbor — The Mission accompanies the King to Gáffat — Theodore and taxation — Abyssinian etiquette in drinking — The European artisans reach Gáffat from Korâta — Theodore handles a broom — Loses his centre of gravity — The Mission and Captives at Gáffat — The King pays the Author a visit and sips Hennessy's brandy — Claims Alexander the Great as well as Solomon as his progenitor — Abyssinian hagiography — Theodore and the Bible — The Author arraigned again on fresh charges — The old charges against Consul Cameron and Messrs. Rosenthal and Stern repeated — Theodore suspects our Government — Dr. Beke's movements — The King detains the Author at Debra Tâbor — Tame lions — Trial of a Chief for high treason.

AT the end of May, Zagê began to be unhealthy, owing to the rain that had fallen during that month. Consul Cameron and Mrs. Rosenthal having suffered from the effects of the climate, I asked the King to allow them to go to Korâta for change of air. I also obtained permission for Mr. Rosenthal to go with his wife, and for Dr. Blanc to accompany them as medical attendant. The King had been thinking of moving his camp to Korâta from the beginning of May; but for some cause or other he had delayed his departure until cholera and typhus fever broke out simultaneously amongst his troops. By the time he began to move, about one hundred persons were dying daily in camp. The King had already sent his female establishment by water to Korâta, retaining only his favourite wife, the Itêgê Itamanyo, to keep him company. At noon on the 6th, the King gave orders for his troops to march towards Korâta, round the southern extremity of the Lake, and appointed Infarâz, about six miles from Zagê, to be the halting-place for the night. He himself, with the Itêgê, went thither by water. Prideaux, the rest of our European party and myself were left to be escorted by Râs I'ngădă and a cavalcade of other Chiefs. The King actually stood on the shore that day to superintend the embarkation of our luggage, and he would not start until he was told that everything had been dispatched. At 1 P.M. Râs I'ngădă was ready for us, and forthwith we accompanied him on our journey. We reached Infarâz after two hours' slow march. The King had also just arrived, and on hearing of our presence he sent a Râs and two Dajazmâtshes with their men to pitch our tents. Being in very good spirits just then, he even ordered Mr. Stern's tent to be put up by an officer of high rank. An hour afterwards he sent us two very large boa-constrictors, each about fifteen feet long, which had been killed by his soldiers in the wood close by, and asked if we had any like them in our country.

In the evening the King sent to tell me that he could not sleep the previous night from thinking about the unfortunate day on which he had arrested me and my companions (he alluded to the 13th April). He said, "I have in my time killed hundreds of people, but I have never had a feeling of remorse for their death, because I knew I was doing the will of my Creator in punishing them as they deserved; but with regard to yourself, I feel that I have done you wrong, and my conscience has suffered ever since."

Early the next morning, 17th June, we heard that the cholera had made great havoc during the night in the camp, and that 500 persons had been attacked, most of whom had died.

When we began to move, soon after sunrise, it was obvious, from the litters which we observed borne by soldiers on all sides, that a great epidemic must have broken out amongst the troops. The King marched in front, and after we had gone on about an hour we came to a standstill, as his Majesty had stopped and was waiting for something. As soon as we reached the royal body-guard, a messenger came to Aito Samuel and said that his Majesty wished to see me. I immediately went to him with Lieutenant Prideaux. We found him sitting on a stone, and when he saw us he looked perplexed and seemed at a loss what to say. He rose and asked Samuel by whose orders he had brought us. It turned out that the messenger had given Samuel a wrong message; nevertheless, his Majesty asked us to sit down. After he had inquired after our health, he told me that in consequence of the number of sick amongst his troops, he was obliged to remain behind and see that all the sufferers were well attended to, and that I had better go on in front with my European party. We then went on, crossed the Abai about 10 o'clock, and arrived at our halting-place, Gádiro, at 11·30. The King did not arrive till four o'clock in the afternoon. He sent me no compliments, as he usually did on arriving from a journey, which seemed to me strange. At six o'clock he summoned Aito Samuel, and, after a short time, sent him back with Wald-Gábir, with an indignant message to the effect that my companion and I had insulted him that day before all his people, by coming on without the horses which he had presented to us. I answered, that we should not think of insulting even a servant of the King, much less his Majesty. With regard to the groundless complaint, I said that his Majesty must be aware that although he had presented me and my companions with horses and mules, yet we had never had them in our possession, and they had always been in charge of the Master of the Horse; that we had only got them when he chose to give them to us to ride; and that I had been informed such was his Majesty's order; how, therefore, could he say that I had insulted him by not taking the horses with us, when the King himself had told us to go on in front?

When a great man travels in Abyssinia, as I have already had occasion to remark, he generally rides a mule for ease, and has his richly-caparisoned horse led behind or in front of him. When the King presented my companions and myself with the horses, he sent to say that as we had no proper stable for them he would keep them for us, but we might send for them whenever we wanted them. On that occasion, when the King told us in the morning to go on in front, he himself sent for our mules, as we had to go before him on foot; and it was he who ought to have ordered the horses to follow us. I have described this affair so minutely, because I wish to show how fickle and unreasonable Theodore was. One day he sends to say, that he could not sleep the night before, because his late ill-treatment of me had troubled his conscience; and the next he asks, in an angry tone, why I had insulted him, when I was all the while doing my best to gratify and to act courteously towards him.

Aito Samuel and Wald-Gâbir carried my reply to the King, and, after a little reflection, his Majesty sent to say that I ought not to take the message he had sent me to heart; that he was quite certain I would never do anything to annoy him; that all the misunderstanding had originated with my Bâldărăbâ, Aito Samuel, and Balambarâs Tasúmma, the Master of the Horse. "Had I known," he concluded, "that you would not be angry with me for it, I would have given them both a severe flogging." He then requested that thenceforward I should order the Master of the Horse, or any other royal groom, to do what I wanted; and that I should reckon them in future as my own servants. He said that the horses must always be led before us, and that I ought never to ride any saddle but the gold one which he had given me, in order that when the Abyssinians saw me they might know at once that I was the servant of the great Queen of England, and the friend and guest of the Emperor of Ethiopia. I then asked the King to forgive the Master of the Horse and Aito Samuel for my sake, and he afterwards sent them to thank me for having interceded for them.

It will be seen from the foregoing that Theodore's outbursts of affection and anger were like those of a spoilt child, or of a madman. The only way I could get on with him at all was by humouring him.

The unfortunate Master of the Horse above referred to was put into chains a few months afterwards for having lost one of the royal mules, and forwarded on to Mágdala, with other Chiefs, when the King was approaching that fortress. On the 8th of April, 1868, he was unfettered, together with six other prisoners; and when the attack was made on our advanced guard, on the afternoon of Good Friday, he was one of those ordered to join in it with spear and shield, accompanied by about one hundred comrades, of whom not a man returned. The poor fellow came to see me on the 9th—the day after his release—and seemed frantic with joy that his chains had been removed. Next day he was numbered among the slain—the victim of the ingratitude and ambitious temerity of a master who did not hesitate to send his most loyal subjects to be slaughtered like sheep by an enemy against whom, he might have known, it was sheer frenzy in him to contend.

On the night of the 7th very few cases of cholera occurred in camp, the King having located his troops in Gádiro, on high ground. We left that place early on the 8th, and reached Korâta after a three hours' slow ride. The King encamped with his troops upon marshy ground, about two miles to the south-west of Korâta; but he was gracious enough to allow me to choose the encampment for myself and our European party. I chose a height between the King's position and the town, and as soon as his Majesty saw our tents pitched, he sent to say that he approved of the spot, and hoped that we might all be preserved from the prevailing epidemic. In returning the compliment, I sent to tell the King that I thought the place he was occupying most dangerous just then; that we always avoided marshy ground at the healthiest of seasons, and regarded such as almost deadly during the prevalence of cholera.

Next morning, the 9th of June, the King sent to say that I was right, and that about one thousand of his soldiers and camp-followers had been attacked during the night by cholera, of whom about three hundred had died already. He asked me if I could recommend a remedy. I replied that the first thing he ought to do was to leave the Lake, and go up to the mountainous country, and, if possible, to disperse the troops in different directions. He immediately followed my advice, and moved with all his camp to high ground on the north-eastern side of Korâta. He gave me the option of going with him, or of encamping in the old place where we had encamped before, on the Lake. I chose the latter, as the ground was rocky, and out of the way of all nuisance. He appointed Kántiba Hailo and Agafári Gólam to superintend the moving of our tents and luggage. The latter was attacked by cholera as soon as he came to our camp, and died three days after. To-day, for the first time since the 13th of April, I was able to go about alone. I had not even Aito Samuel with me, as he had been summoned by the King to receive orders about my burial, in case I should be seized with cholera and die while his Majesty was absent. The King intended to attack some rebels who were reported to be in the neighbourhood, and expected to be away about eight or ten days; and as he was afraid that I might die before he came back, and my remains might not receive proper respect, he deemed it advisable to leave the necessary instructions with Samuel and other Chiefs how I was to be interred.

Early on the 10th the King sent for Aito Samuel and told him that he was afraid to leave me where I was during his absence, as the wicked rebels might carry me off some night, and then, what answer could he give to the English? Consequently, he ordered him to tell me that it would be better that I should go and encamp near his Empress, where we could both be protected by the soldiers. "Besides," he concluded, "I want Mr. Rassam to take care of the Itêgê and my children during my absence." The fact is, the King was afraid that while he was away on the other side of Debra Tábor, whither he was going in pursuit of the rebels, I should take it into my head to decamp with all the Europeans who wished to leave the country. This we might easily have done, if he had left us there where we were, alone.

On the 11th the King returned, having heard on the road that the rebels had been defeated by one of the Chiefs of Bagúmé dér. On his arrival he sent to tell me that, as the cholera was still raging in his camp, he had determined to follow my advice and go up to the heights of Debra Tâbor, requesting me to send at once and tell Dr. Blanc, Consul Cameron and Mr. Rosenthal to join me. Mrs. Rosenthal was to do as she liked: either remain with his European artisans or come with us. As the King was aware that Mrs. Rosenthal was ill, he offered to have her carried in a litter, if she chose to accompany us. She, of course, preferred to be with her husband, and joined us on the 12th June, as she was well enough to travel on a mule. The European artisans, with Mrs. Flad and Messrs. Steiger and Brandeis, were told to follow. On that day Mr. McKelvie and a number of our Abyssinian servants were attacked by cholera, but it only proved fatal to one of Consul Cameron's servants.

On the 13th, we started from Korâta and reached the Gûmâra river in about four hours' ride. The King halted there, and directed two Râses, who commanded the right and left divisions, to disperse with their men. We heard afterwards that no sooner had the troops separated than the epidemic began to decline.

Early on the 14th, we left the Gûmâra river and reached Ondo at 2 P.M., after a four hours' slow ride. Here the King ordered the rear division to disperse as those had done who had been left behind the day before. To-day the King lost a number of his Chiefs from cholera, one of whom had been brought up with him from boyhood. His death made him very sad all the evening.

On the 15th of June his Majesty started very early for Debra Tâbor, and it was reported that he intended to make arrangements for our reception there. On our arrival, however, we were told that the King had determined to let us spend the next three months with his European artisans at Gáffat, about three miles to the north of Debra Tábor. On reaching the foot of the hill on which the royal residence was erected we saw the King descending. He sent us word that as he wished to stay at Gáffat we should accompany him thither. Accordingly, Dr. Blanc, Lieutenant Prideaux and I joined him and rode on with him towards that place. On the road we were overtaken by a severe hailstorm, which obliged us to halt until its fury had abated. His Majesty was accompanied by Râs I'ngădă and twenty other followers. We were conducted to one of the foundries, where the King ordered a fire to be kindled to warm us and to dry our clothes, which were thoroughly drenched. Aito Samuel and Râs I'ngădă were then instructed to go up to the village and select houses for our party. The King himself allotted Mr. Waldmeier's house to me, because it had a large upper room, and on Râs I'ngădă sending to apprise him that the room was unfurnished, his Majesty ordered him to go up to Debra Tábor and bring carpets enough to cover the floor, and to place his own throne in it, to give it the aspect of a royal residence. In the mean time the King conversed with me, through my young interpreter, Dasta, on different topics, sometimes in Arabic and sometimes in Tigrêan. His Majesty dwelt particularly upon the system of taxation in England, and laughed heartily when I informed him how the income-tax was levied and realized. "The people of my country," he said, "would sooner bury their money in the ground than trade with it or pay me a percentage out of it." When I told him of the tax on horses and male servants, he remarked: "Mr. Rassam, you do not know the Abyssinians. Were I to tax their mules, horses and domestics, not one of them would ride, and every man would become his own servant." As the cholera was raging, and the weather was damp, I generally carried a little brandy in a flask, and feeling somewhat chilly at the time I thought a few drops of the stimulant would not be amiss. Sitting, however, as I was, on a plank by the side of the King, I judged that it would be only polite to offer him a little. To my great surprise, he drank off what I poured out for him. I discovered afterwards that I had been guilty of two breaches of Abyssinian etiquette in this matter; for, in the first place, I had partaken of the brandy from the same vessel, which I ought not to have done, because the Sovereign may not drink from the same cup which any one else has used in his presence; and, secondly, instead of passing him the cup with both hands I presented it to him with my right hand only—the sign of a superior giving anything to an inferior. However, as the King doubtless knew that I erred in such matters through ignorance of native customs, he took no notice of these mistakes.

When Messrs. Cameron and Stern arrived from Debra Tâbor they had to come to the inclosure of the foundry, and as they passed the door, I asked the King to allow them to dry their clothes, hoping that he might invite them to join us; but he refused, and ordered a fire to be kindled for them outside. On this occasion he was extremely civil to the members of the Mission: for more than two hours he was quite alone with us, and at last he became so gracious that he told my interpreter to cover himself and sit near the fire, as it was cold. When he heard that Râs I'ngădă had arrived with the carpets, he went up to Mr. Waldmeier's house and assisted personally in carpeting my room and placing the throne at the back of it. This done, he returned to Debra Tâbor to give orders for the remaining front division of the army to disperse. The King was now left with only a few followers. He even dispensed with more than half of his household establishment. From the 13th of April, the King had never intermitted sending rations for my party. Aito Samuel had the charge of everything, and kept open house on my behalf.

17th.—Early this morning his Majesty sent me a large glass bottle containing about three gallons of very old and clear mead, which he requested me to drink for his sake. He was aware, he said, that I was not partial to such beverages, nevertheless as the mead was coeval with his reign he wished me to try it, and to give my opinion of its quality. I drank a little to gratify him, and found it much superior to any liquor I had hitherto tasted in the country. It was as clear as hock, with a flavour of Grave. At 10 to-day the Rev. Mr. Stern celebrated Divine Service in my room, in front of the empty throne, and I could not help contrasting at the time the vanity of the one with the solemnity of the worship in which we were engaged. In the afternoon the European artisans whom we had left at Korâta reached Gâffat, and on their way had visited the King at Debra Tâbor. His Majesty informed them that he had placed me and my party in some of their dwellings, and further expressed his hope that we should enjoy each other's society during the winter; by which he meant that we were to live together. They replied that they would prefer tents to lodging with our party, as they objected to several Europeans who had been consigned over to me by the King; but as they did not wish to make any invidious distinctions, they begged to be allowed to decline living with us. Before I left Korâta, both Mr. Waldmeier and Mr. Moritz Hall had kindly offered me the use of their houses during the winter; and when we reached Gáffat, on hearing that the King had made up his mind to locate us in the residences of his European artisans, I told Samuel of this offer, and suggested that if the King knew of it he would probably allow me to avail myself of one of the two houses. Samuel, however, judged it advisable that I should say nothing on the subject, as the King might be offended with the artisans for taking it upon themselves to allot their dwellings to whom they pleased, seeing that they themselves were merely tenants at the will of his Majesty. Their answer, it appears, vexed the King, as he came early next morning and removed me to the large foundry, not wishing it to be supposed that he wanted to force the British Mission on any one. He left the rest of my party, however, in their different abodes. The King swept the room himself, and he and M. Bardel carried the dust in their hands, and threw it out of the window. He then had the walls covered with cloth to hide the dirt, and, after carpeting the floor, placed his throne in the apartment.

19*th*.—Early this morning his Majesty paid me a visit at the foundry, and told me that he could not sleep last night from thinking that I was uncomfortable. While with me, he sat on the throne, on my invitation, and as it was about four feet high I had to set one of my camp folding-stools to enable him to take his seat there. He went up all right, but on descending he placed his foot on an angle of the stool instead of the centre, and had I not rushed and held it firmly he would certainly have come down head foremost, and there was probably not an Abyssinian in the country, himself included, who would not have attributed the mishap to design on my part. I never saw a man so astonished as the King when I ran and laid hold of the stool. However, on learning the cause, he was much pleased with my attention.

As the King wished to have all my European party to be near me, he said he would select proper houses for us to live in, until new ones could be built for us. He then went to the quarters of the native artisans, below the European village of Gáffat, and, after fixing upon the house that I was to occupy, he ordered that all the houses in its immediate vicinity should be vacated for the use of my companions and their fellow-Europeans. The Kántiba and two other officers were ordered to have my room properly furnished, and the walls covered with cloth. He directed, also, that the throne should be placed as usual in my house; but this I induced him to dispense with, on the plea that the room was too small. In the afternoon we moved to our respective abodes, seven in number, and in addition to these a few extra huts were allowed for our servants. Mr. Stern had to live in a tent, as no good house could be found for him near us. Mr. Flad and Messrs. Steiger, Brandeis, Schiller and Essler were permitted to occupy their old dwellings on an adjacent hill.

20*th.*—The King came early this morning to the second foundry at Gáffat to inquire about some work then in progress. On hearing of his arrival we put on our uniforms, in order to be in readiness to attend him, in case he desired our presence. As he did not, but merely sent his compliments, I dispatched a messenger to ask whether he would allow me and my companions to pay our respects to him. The foundry was not above fifty yards from our huts, and on his Majesty sending a reply to my message in the affirmative, we repaired to his presence. On reaching the inclosure of the foundry, we noticed all the courtiers standing in a very gloomy mood, which augured unfavourably for our reception. We found the King busily engaged in giving angry orders to his European workmen, and looking quite black in the face with suppressed ill-humour. Without asking after our health, as was his wont, he looked straight at me, and said, "Is it not a great shame that I should put you in that dirty and inconvenient house, where you must be very unhappy?" I answered promptly, "Pray don't say so; for I feel that I have one of the best houses in Abyssinia, and, through your kindness, it has been so nicely decorated and carpeted by your servants that it is quite impossible to make it more comfortable." "Are you in jest or earnest?" he rejoined. "If your Majesty will deign to come and see it," I replied, "you will be convinced that I am in earnest, for you yourself will at once admit that it is most comfortable, fit even for the residence of a King." "Very well; I will come with you when I have finished with my people here," was his answer. Thereupon the frown on his countenance began to relax, and when he entered my dwelling, about half an hour afterwards, he was comparatively cheerful. He admired the way I had arranged my three muskets round one of the wooden pillars of the room, with the shield and spear which he had given me above them, and the gold saddle in front. I also took care to spread the Itêgê's *Márgaf* with which he had presented me over the table in the centre of my room. I offered him some Hennessy's brandy, which he drank, without asking any one to taste it first in order to prove that it was not poisoned. This he did, as he stated, to show his people how much he trusted me, and the great respect he entertained for my Queen and her Government, which he did by sitting in their house—for such he considered it—and enjoying himself there. He then spent half an hour talking of the love which he had for the English, asserting more than once that he had conceived that regard from childhood.

21st.—The King came down again to the factory this morning, and on receiving his permission to that effect we paid him another visit. He was in excellent humour, and seemed highly pleased with my attention in having sent an easy chair, covered with red cloth, for his accommodation, which I begged him to occupy while superintending the European workmen. At this time he was busily engaged in making small gun-carriages, to be borne by mules, for his projected expedition against the rebels of Lasta, whom he intended to bring to account during the winter. He related the story of Diogenes and his tub, and asked me whether I thought the cynic was mad or merely eccentric. He then went far beyond my depth into the history of Europe, and told me that he was descended from one of its greatest kings, as well as from Solomon by the Queen of Sheba. On my seeking information from him on that point, he proceeded to narrate how an Abyssinian princess had visited Alexander the Great, just as Balkis did Solomon, and after staying with him some time she gave birth to a child who, when he grew up, governed more than half the world. He then told me that Alexander the Great was held in the highest reverence by the Abyssinians, as being the only person who had visited Paradise during his lifetime. On expressing my wonder how this could possibly be, he directed Kántiba Hailo to go and fetch the book wherein this astounding fact was recorded, in order that I might be assured of that great man having really gone to Paradise and returned again to earth. Kántiba Hailo, who believed in these legends as fully as he believed in the revelations of the Bible, brought the book referred to, and was directed by the King to explain the pictures to me—it contained about thirty. He did so, as he sat by my side, and began describing their import to me one by one, through Samuel. Anything more absurd can hardly be conceived. If I remember aright, the first picture represented the Empress Helena in the act of praying that God would bless her with a male child. Her petition is heard, and Alexander the Great is born into the world. While yet a child, he prays to have a sight of Paradise; whereupon countless angels are employed in making preparations for his trip. He is then transported up to Heaven, where he is permitted to walk about and enjoy its delectable sights. Finally, he is brought back to earth, where dominion is given to him over all the sons of Noah. When the exposition of the picture-gallery came to an end, the King asked me how I liked the history of Alexander the Great. I replied, "To tell the truth, your Majesty, I think Alexander was wise in wishing to obtain admittance into Paradise; but I think he was a fool for returning to earth again. Had I been in his place, once permitted to enter that delightful abode, I should certainly have remained there." When this answer was translated to him, he burst into a fit of laughter, and nearly fell from the easy chair; then turning to me, after his merriment had somewhat subsided, he said, "Do you imagine that I believe in this trash?" I replied, "No, your Majesty; I am sure you have more sense." Poor Kántiba Hailo, who heartily credited the stupid fable, was struck speechless at such incredulity, but looked round upon the grinning spectators with a countenance which seemed to say, "How I pity your infidelity!" After spending two hours with the King, we were permitted to return to our respective abodes; his Majesty also went back to Debra Tâbor.

22nd.—We had another interview with the King under circumstances similar to those of yesterday. He was again in good spirits, and it was certainly very pleasant to meet him when in that mood. After he had finished his work I asked leave to retire, but he insisted on escorting me to my dwelling. On reaching the hut I begged him to sit a few minutes with me, to which he readily assented. He honoured me again by drinking a few drops of brandy from a tumbler; —on the former occasion he had used the metal cup attached to the flask. He was also gracious enough to allow some of the bystanders to taste the liquor, saying that it was useful in time of cholera, and that the weather was cold. On entering the room he sighed, and said how much he wished he could visit the English Queen and her Council, and see all the wonders of England. "However," he concluded, "I fear there is no chance of that, although I feel while in your presence as if I were beholding your masters." Seeing an English book on my table, he took it up and asked if it were the Bible. On my answering in the negative, he remarked, "Handling this book reminds me of the Bible, which England has been good enough to print and circulate amongst us;" then, looking up, he added: "Oh God! how can we Abyssinians forget the English who have given us so many thousand Bibles." Next, turning to me, he said: "I assure you, Mr. Rassam, that before your people printed the Bible for us, we had scarcely four complete copies of the sacred volume in all the churches; and now every village in the country can boast of having one or more. But we Abyssinians are an ungrateful people, and do not deserve such favours." After half an hour spent on these and other topics the King returned to Debra Tabor, but before leaving he directed the men who were engaged in erecting a new fence round the Mission-huts to hasten on the work, in order that our privacy might be respected, and that we should not be annoyed by beggars during the day or by hyænas during the night.

At this time we had no guard at all, and were allowed to do as we pleased; even our horses and mules were sent to us to keep, and I certainly did believe then that we were going to spend the winter in peace; but I was soon disappointed.

On Saturday, the 23rd of June, the King did not come to the foundry, but the following day he sent for his European artisans, and had a private consultation with them; what about, we could never learn. It was reported to me, however, that his Majesty was not in the best of moods and had expressed a wish to have me and my fellow-captives near him, and that he had spoken of having huts built for us at Debra Tâbor.

At dawn on the 25th the King sent one of his domestic servants, named Paul, to inquire after the health of myself and party, and the man would not leave until he had satisfied himself that every European was in his room. As usual, I sent Samuel and one of my interpreters to reciprocate the compliment. They returned instantly, and said that the King had intimated to them that he intended to hold a court that morning, and wished me to attend with my companions, Consul Cameron, the Missionaries, and any other "gentleman" I had with me. The message was, "Be quick." Two days previously, I had heard that a rebel Chief had been brought a prisoner to Debra Tâbor, and I concluded that he was to be tried before us that morning. However, in the course of half an hour, my fellow-officials, Messrs. Stern and Rosenthal and I were ready to start, and as Mr. Kerans came within the category of "gentleman," he also accompanied us on our doubtful visit. On passing the houses of the European artisans, they joined us with Kántiba Hailo, and went on with us to Debra Tâbor. On ascending the hill on which the royal residence was built, I was surprised to find that only the Afâ-Negûs (Mouth of the King) came out of the inclosure, with M. Bardel, to meet us. We were taken to a large black tent made of goats' hair, generally occupied on a journey by the Itêgê, which we found carpeted, but no one was in it. We were told by the Afû-Negûs to take a seat until the pleasure of the King was known. Affairs now looked rather threatening; consequently, while the British officials and the Missionaries sat on the right side of the tent, the artisans took care to sit as far as possible on the other; and as Messrs. Steiger and Brandeis also desired to show that they did not belong to the English party, they went and sat with the artisans.

As soon as our arrival was communicated to the King, he summoned the European artisans. Messrs. Steiger and Brandeis also rose to follow, but Aito Samuel told them that as they belonged to our party they must remain. The dispute was soon settled, however, by the King, who, finding that those two gentlemen preferred the company of his European artisans to ours, directed that thenceforward they should be reckoned with them. In about ten minutes the European artisans returned, with Kántiba Hailo and other Chiefs, with a message from the King to the effect, that a railroad had been laid down between Egypt and Cásala for the passage of English, French and Turkish troops, with a view to the invasion of Abyssinia, and his Majesty wished to know why I had not reported the fact to him on my arrival, as I must have seen the railroad when I passed through Cásala. He said, " Is this the friendship which you profess to have for me?" I replied, that there could be no foundation for the rumour, because when I passed through Cásala, nine months before, no such scheme was thought of. I tried all in my power to dissuade him from believing such reports, which I said were invented by wicked people for mischievous ends.

The second message was, that he had heard from Jerusalem of my having been sent to him by the British Government on false pretences, in order that I might obtain the release of the European captives; and that after we were safe out of the country, England would send troops to avenge the insult offered to her by the imprisonment of her Consul. The King asked, "Is this true or not?" I replied that this report from Jerusalem was false and villanous. Aito Samuel, who acted then as interpreter to the royal delegates, translated my words thus:—"Whoever invented that report is a liar and a villain." M. Bardel, on hearing these words, interposed, and said to his fellow delegates that I had not used the words "liar and villain." As the dispute was referred to me, I replied that I had not actually used the words "liar and villain," still what I had said was tantamount, as false and villanous reports were only invented by liars and villains, and that the delegates might take the words used by Samuel to the King. After this his Majesty sent to say that I ought not to misunderstand him, because he had never changed his friendly feeling towards me, nor failed to place implicit confidence in me; but that my Government was not behaving well towards him, and that he considered it no fault of mine if my Government chose to act insincerely, after sending me to him. I replied that my Government was not in the habit of deceiving any one, and if the King would only trust it, it would be to his advantage. The commissioners came back to repeat the charges against Consul Cameron and Mr. Rosenthal, the former for returning to Abyssinia without an answer to the letter he had sent by him; and the latter for having written that the British Government had laughed at him.

On this occasion I had to make the King understand that the "Clerks" of the Foreign Office were not the Government. M. Bardel bore me out on that point. When this was settled, the King sent to ask me if I was still security for Mr. Stern and others; and whether I would continue to keep to my old engagement. I certainly then began to fear that Mr. Stern had written to his friends in England complaining of our ill-treatment by the King, and that his Majesty had seized the letter. Whereupon I begged to be told at once if any of my party had done anything to displease the King since I became security for them, inasmuch as I conceived it was fully understood that I was responsible for all their acts from that time.

The King sent to say he had always distrusted Mr. Stern, as he knew he hated and abused him; on that account he wanted to be doubly sure that I had not withdrawn my security for him. "Seeing that you still hold yourself responsible for him and the others," his Majesty concluded, "let it be so, and you can all remain together as before; but I cannot let you henceforth live far from me, not knowing what your Government intends to do. You shall always live near me, and I will keep a good look-out upon you until Mr. Flad's return."

I was told afterwards that the King had hoped I would refuse to keep to my old engagement, in order that he might feel at liberty to chain the old Mágdala prisoners, including Consul Cameron.

I had great suspicion on that day that the statement made by the King of his having heard from Jerusalem that I had been sent by her Majesty's Government on false pretences was a trumped-up story, and that the letter which the Greek priest had brought from his Bishop in Jerusalem merely contained a request for a donation to build a refuge for poor strangers visiting the Holy Land. I was at Massowah when the priest arrived there, as has already been stated, and an Armenian merchant who was intimate with him informed me of the object of his visit to Abyssinia, before he left Massowah, in the beginning of 1865. On reaching Adwa, he was detained by Dajjâj Dakla-Guargîs, the then Governor-General of Tigrê, who had orders from the King, after the incarceration of Consul Cameron, to detain every European who might go up to Abyssinia without the royal sanction. When the Wakshum Gabazê took possession of Tigrê, in May, 1866, the priest obtained his liberty, and went up with his letter, which he had had in his possession more than a year. Kántiba Hailo, who was subsequently sent as a prisoner to Mágdala, informed me, in conjunction with others, that there was no foundation for the report alleged by the King to have reached him from Jerusalem.

I am convinced that the King had then heard of Dr. Beke's return to England, after his promise to visit him, *even though the captives were released.* The King had written to him that he was to remain at Massowah until he should inform him what route to take. Although Dr. Beke had then left for Europe, yet the King's reply showed that he did not wish him to leave before he had seen him. Dr. Beke had also written to tell the King that he was imprisoned by the rebels, and asked him to send and have him liberated. The King forthwith wrote to the Tigrê Chiefs, and told them to have

Dr. Beke released and sent down to Massowah. When the royal letter reached them, the supposed prisoner was nowhere to be found. He had returned to his country.

There is another fact which strengthens my belief that, at the time of our second disgrace, the King had heard of Dr. Beke's abrupt departure for England—namely, Messrs. Kerans and McKelvie, two Irishmen, had volunteered to enter the King's employ when Mr. Flad left for England. Their services had been accepted, but their engagement was postponed from day to day until the end of June, two months after Mr. Flad's departure, when Mr. McKelvie was allowed to remain behind, and Mr. Kerans, who was one of those mentioned in the petition sent by Dr. Beke, was ordered to accompany us to Mágdala.

When the trial was over, the King gave me permission to send to Gáffat for whatever I required for myself and party; and as Mrs. Waldmeier was dangerously ill, and Dr. Blanc was attending her, I asked his Majesty to allow him to go and see her for an hour or two; this he acceded to. Towards evening, Mr. Waldmeier returned to Debra Tábor to ask the King to permit Dr. Blanc to remain with his wife two or three days, as she was ill, and required medical attendance hourly. The King replied, "What! is Dr. Blanc my servant? He was sent to me by the Queen of England with Mr. Rassam, and Mr. Rassam is the proper person to ask." His Majesty then sent to say that I was to do as I pleased. Accordingly, it was decided that Dr. Blanc should remain at Gáffat with Mrs. Waldmeier, until she recovered.

When the King told me that I might send to Gáffat for whatever I wanted, he also directed that any of my party might pitch a tent to live in. Mr. Stern accordingly had his brought with that object, and at my request Samuel indicated a spot near our black tent where it might be pitched, advising me, however, at the same time, as Mr. Stern's friend, not to let him be separated from me, as he was only safe in my company. He then went on to say, "You remember, Mr. Rassam, that on your first arrival in Abyssinia I enjoined you not to be too intimate either with Mr. Stern or with any of his fellow-captives, for, as I wished you to succeed and to leave the country, I thought it best at that time that the King should not think that you took part with his enemies. Since his Majesty, however, has chosen to treat you so badly, you will do well to stand by all the late captives, for they will only be safe while in your company. You are all now in the same predicament, and must either stand or fall together." I may here remark that at this same juncture I was being warned by several Europeans to keep aloof from Mr. Stern as much as possible, in order to avoid getting into trouble with Theodore on his account. However, having determined, as I said before, to take my chance with the rest, and to die rather than incur the remorse of having saved my own life at the sacrifice of theirs, I asked Mr. Stern to remain with me in the black tent. I adduce this as another instance of the very false impression which many have entertained respecting Samuel. The man stuck to our cause unflinchingly, when we got into difficulty, and I owe it to him to state, that he never said an unkind word to me against any of my fellow-captives.

On the evening of the 25th I deemed it advisable to send and tell the King, by Aito Samuel, how unwise and unfriendly it was of him to treat me and the Europeans who were with me so rudely, while I was trying my best to befriend and act honestly towards him. I said that our Government would be quite puzzled on hearing of his unjustifiable ill-treatment of us, when perhaps they were making every effort to gratify him. I warned him against the machinations of evil-doers, who were trying all they could to increase his troubles and misfortunes. I told him that he had still time to retrace his steps and show his friendship by trusting us. The only answer I could obtain from him was, "My friend, I believe in you; but there are customs in every country which only the natives of the place understand. You are a foreigner, and know not our rules, nor could you understand why I have acted in this way towards you. You follow your way and I mine, and you will see if I am not right in the end." When Samuel tried to persuade him that I was his true friend, and that he ought to listen to my advice, he said, "Aito Samuel, have you sold yourself like a slave to the English? You are an ass; I want you only to hold your tongue; go and deliver my message to Mr. Rassam."

Next day I obtained permission for Mr. Rosenthal to join his wife. In giving him leave, the King ordered Wald-Gâbir and Aito Samuel to tell me that I need not take the trouble of sending to ask him about everything: I was only to give the order and it would be obeyed. "With regard to your asking me for permission to allow Mr. Rosenthal to go to Gâffat," the King said, "have I not given you all the Europeans to do as you like with? And, besides, are you a prisoner that you should remain in your tent day and night? If you want to please me, go out when you like; and you ought to go down to Gâffat and see your friends; because, if you stay and mope, you will fall ill, and then what shall I, your friend, do? Shall I not be ill too?" He then sent an order to the Master of the Horse to let us have our mules and horses whenever we wanted them.

After the above courteous message we felt somewhat happier for a time, with the privilege also of taking a little exercise; and, in accordance with the King's desire, I visited Gáffat the next day, the 27th of June. I had no guard, but Aito Samuel accompanied me, with the Master of the Horse, as far as the village, and then left me. Thenceforward we were able to go about as we pleased.

The King had business in the foundry at Gáffat, and used to go down almost every day to see his artisans at work. Whenever he went there he sent me his compliments; and on his return he communicated his arrival to me, with a courteous message that through my prayers and good wishes he had reached home safely. Once, he brought four lions which were at Debra Tâbor for me to look at, and directed their keepers to let them loose, in order that I might see how tame they were. They ran about after cattle and mules in the plain below for a long time, and, at a signal from the King, their keepers called them back and conveyed them to their dens. That day he sent me 500 dollars more of the money he had taken from me.

On another occasion he invited me to witness the trial of a rebel Chief and his two associates, who had been seized and brought before him from Wádala, as he wanted to prove to me what bad subjects he had. Three different witnesses gave their evidence in a calm, straightforward manner, unbiassed apparently by any ill-will towards the accused. The latter, on being asked in a quiet tone by the King what they had to urge in self-defence, admitted their guilt, pleading that they had been misled by the devil, and begged his Majesty to forgive them. The King then remarked that Satan was atrociously bad, and must not be encouraged, and that in accordance with the *Fetih-Negûst* they must suffer death, but that he would have them executed in a respectable manner, and then buried. They were taken to the marketplace, and there shot dead, and after the bodies were exposed for an hour or two, as a warning to others, they were interred in ditches made to receive them where they lay. After these rebel Chiefs had been led away, their wives were brought forward, stripped to the waist, in accordance with Abyssinian usage when women fall into disgrace. The King ordered them at once to be covered, and on learning that the only crime they were charged with was that they were the wives of the condemned rebels, he told the soldiers that it was a pity they had been at so much trouble with regard to them, as it was no fault of theirs that they had bad husbands. He then directed the women to be supplied with food and clothing, and told them that they were at liberty to go where they pleased. It was fortunate for these poor females that his Majesty was not in one of his savage humours, otherwise the probability is they would have been adjudged to share the fate of their husbands.

CHAPTER XIX.

FROM DEBRA TÁBOR TO MÁGDALA.

We are to be sent to Mágdala — Theodore changes his plan — Another outburst of royal courtesy — The Author arraigned again — We are confined and guarded in the Treasury — A visit from Theodore — We drink healths all round — The King believes he is mad — The titles "Géta" and "Aito" — Order to set out with the King to Mágdala — Hailstones on Mount Gŭna — We are sent forward to Mágdala under a guard — Arrival at that fortress — We are placed in fetters — The Author's message to Theodore on the occasion — The preliminary location of the Captives — Kindness of the Chiefs — Aito Samuel's services.

The King had been intending for some time to go towards Mágdala, to punish the rebels of Lasta and the adjacent districts. On the 28th he sent me a message by I'ngŭdŭ Wark and Paul (Samuel having been in disgrace since the message I sent by him on the 25th) to say, that he intended to go on a war expedition in the course of three or four days; and that as he did not want to weary us by taking us about with him in the rains, he had resolved upon sending me and my party to Mágdala, there to spend the winter; and he wished to know if I had any objection to the arrangement. I replied, that his Majesty was better able to judge of the salubrity of the different places in Abyssinia than I, and that I was ready to go wherever he wished me to be during the rainy season. The King then asked whether I had mules enough to carry my luggage and that of my party, or whether I required him to transport it for us. I said that we had not mules enough, but that if his Majesty would allow us we could buy more. It was settled, at last, that he was to have it carried for us; and, accordingly, on the 1st of July, he sent all our heavy baggage by some soldiers who were leaving for Mágdala with Ras I'ngădă, and Samuel was sent in charge of it. After the luggage had been carried a day's journey towards Mágdala, the King ordered it to be brought back, as he had changed his mind, and had resolved to let us remain at Gáffat for the winter. It was brought back to Debra Tâbor on the 3rd, by Aito Samuel, and was left in our tents outside the royal inclosure.

About noon on the 3rd, the King, as he was wont, sent me a message to say that, with my permission, he was going down to Gáffat. He asked my interpreter why I remained so much in my tent and so seldom went out. He ordered him to tell me that, if I wished to please him, I must go about oftener, either on foot or on horseback, whichever I preferred, and that I must send to him for anything I wanted. "And you, Dasta," the King added to the interpreter, "mind, I hold you responsible if I should hear that your master has been in want of anything, and you fail to inform me of it. If he requires anything, you must come to me, even at midnight." On the interpreter asking how he could communicate with his Majesty at that hour, the King sent for a page and told him that if Dasta went to him at night with any message from me he was to communicate it. The page replied, that the eunuchs would prevent him from approaching the place where the King was sleeping. On this demur, the eunuchs in attendance were summoned, and orders were given to them that, if a page went to his Majesty with a message from me, he was to deliver it at once; and that if the King was asleep, he was to be awakened; so that if I wanted anything at night, my message would have had to go through the interpreter, the page, and the eunuchs. The King kept poor Mr. Zander and Kántiba Hailo, with a large party of followers, waiting for nearly half-an-hour below the hill of Debra Tâbor to settle that new arrangement of his, which he knew well enough was never to be carried into effect.

The King returned from Gáffat at about 3 p.m., but, instead of the usual civil message, Samuel came running to say that the King wanted to see me, and that I must take the gentlemen who were in my tent with me. I immediately went, accompanied by Lieutenant Prideaux, Consul Cameron and Mr. Stern. I wondered what could have taken place after the polite message which had been sent to me only two hours before. My surprise may be imagined when I found Dr. Blanc standing in front of his Majesty like a criminal, and when, a few minutes afterwards, Mr. Rosenthal was brought in by a number of soldiers. The King looked as if he had gone mad, and the first thing he said to me was, that I hated him. On inquiring what had occurred to make him say so, he said that he had four charges against me: first, that I had read Mr. Stern's book—'Wanderings among the Falashas;' secondly, that he had given Consul Cameron a letter for my Queen, and that he had returned to Abyssinia without an answer; thirdly, that I had tried to send away the Mágdala captives from Abyssinia without taking them to him; and, fourthly, that the Turks had possession of Jerusalem, and that England and France allowed them to keep it. He demanded his patrimony, on the ground that the Holy City had formerly belonged to Kings David and Solomon, his forefathers, and said, "I want Europe to restore to me the Holy Land." The first two complaints I took no notice of, and only answered the third and fourth. With regard to the former, I denied having tried to take the Mágdala prisoners out of Abyssinia without a proper reconciliation, his Majesty having forgiven them on several occasions; that when they left Korâta they did so with his sanction, and that he sent one of his courtiers, Lij Abitu, to escort them. Lij Abitu was called again on this occasion to give evidence; and when the King was satisfied that everything had been done according to rule, he dismissed him. With reference to Jerusalem, I said that the European Powers were not given to interfere in such matters.

He then said to me abruptly, "Are you not aware that India and half the world belong to me?" I replied, that I had not found it so stated in the books which I had read. He next turned and discussed the point with Mr. Stern. (The idea that India and half the world belonged to Theodore originated in the tradition that the Emperors of Abyssinia are the descendants of Alexander the Great, as well as of Solomon. This legend has already been noted in the foregoing pages.)

Aito Samuel looked very downcast during this farce; so the King spoke to him sharply, and said, "Why are you sulky? Is it because I am arguing with your friend? Suppose I put him in chains, what will you say to that?" Samuel answered, "What is that to me? Mr. Rassam is your Majesty's guest, not mine."

The Afâ-Negûs was then called, and the King asked him whether he could watch us better in a tent or in a room. As this functionary knew his master's mind, he said a room would be preferable. Thereupon the King ordered us to be taken into the Treasury and guarded very strictly. The room was so dark that we had to light candles, even in broad daylight, to enable us to see one another. My party, consisting of Dr. Blanc, Lieutenant Prideaux, Consul Cameron,

Messrs. Stern and Rosenthal and myself, were placed in a small circular room not more than twelve feet in diameter; and as a guard of fifteen men was ordered to watch us inside during the night, we should have been in a sad plight had not the King relented in the course of the evening and ordered the guard out of our room. Mr. Kerans was brought in afterwards, but Signor Pietro was allowed to remain in his own tent outside. Mr. Macraire had already entered the King's service and was at Gáffat with the European artisans.

Soon after dark, the King sent to know how we all were, and hoped that I should sleep well. I replied that we were very much obliged to his Majesty for his kind inquiry, and that we were well; but that if our Government or myself had known how the Mission would have been treated, we should certainly not have paid him a visit. "To speak the truth," I continued, "it is our fault for not having believed what we heard before leaving Massowah; but we could not credit what his Majesty's enemies said against him. They will rejoice at what has taken place, and I have no doubt they will spread the report all over the world." The only answer I obtained from the King to this was, "Never mind your Government and my enemies, my friend. Your masters have already decided upon their treatment of me; and my foes would spread evil reports against me, even if I were to carry you on my head. I have only to see that you are happy, and that your heart is not vexed." I replied that I had done my best to maintain friendship between my Government and his Majesty, but that henceforward I should wash my hands of all responsibility, and his Majesty would only have himself to blame for the wrath of my Queen and her Government. To this the King sent the following answer: "God be my witness, my brother and friend, that after to-day I shall not hold you responsible for the future action of your Government. I only want you to be happy, and as I hear from my attendants that you are not so, I must come and cheer you up; I only await your permission to do so." I sent and begged his Majesty not to trouble himself to come and see us. He replied that he could not go to bed without coming to comfort me. "How could I go to sleep," he said, "knowing that you are unhappy, my friend? I will not listen to you, especially after I have refused the entreaty of the Itêgê, who said that I ought to postpone my visit to you until the morning."

Immediately after the last message, the King made his appearance with a horn of arrack (spirits made of mead) slung over his shoulder, and a bundle of wax candles in his right hand to light in our prison, to make it look cheerful. One of his servants also carried a jar of *téj* (mead) behind him. On coming in and seeing a part of the guard with us, he turned them out, and asked how they dared come so near us. As soon as he sat down, he poured some arrack into a tumbler and gave it to me, saying, "I know you do not usually drink, but I feel sure that you will not refuse to drink with me on this occasion, to make me feel happy." After we had drunk to each other's health, he ordered the arrack to be circulated to all my party, and he himself filled the glasses and handed them over to my companions, Dr. Blanc and Lieutenant Prideaux. He then looked towards Mr. Stern, who was standing with Mr. Rosenthal against the wall, and said to the former "How are you, Aito Kokab? Why are you standing in such a disconsolate mood and do not sit down?" After this, his Majesty said to me laughingly, "Comfort Mr. Stern, and tell him not to moan." He then addressed me as follows :—" Do not regard my face, but trust to my heart, because I really love you. I would not say so before my people who are standing by if I did not mean it. It is true that I behaved ill to you this afternoon, but I have an object in what I do. I was obliged to put on a serious face on account of the bystanders, but I never meant to be angry with you. I used to hear that I was called a madman by my people for my acts, but I never believed it; now, however, after my conduct towards you this afternoon, I have come to the conclusion that I really am so; but," he concluded, "as Christians, we ought always to be ready to forgive each other."

After this display of royal affection the King left; but before going he gave orders that none of the guard were to be allowed to enter the Treasury—all must remain outside. While we were both standing at the door with Aito Samuel and my young interpreter, Dasta, the King said to me, "Mr. Rassam, henceforward Dasta shall be my child, and Samuel yours; good-bye." After this I never spoke to him again until he and I met at Mágdala, on the 29th March, 1868—an interval of nearly one year and nine months.

The day Dr. Blanc and Mr. Rosenthal were arrested, it was reported that the King had received a letter from Tigré, on his way to Gaffát; that its contents appeared to make him very angry ; and that this was the reason he had acted so unbecomingly towards us all. My opinion is, that the arrest of Dr. Blanc and Mr. Rosenthal was not premeditated—that the order was given on the spur of the moment. Something had evidently disturbed the King's mind, for when a beggar on the road asked him for alms, and said that formerly the European " Gétotsh " had supported him, the King ordered him to be beaten to death for having applied the word "Gêtotsh" to his European slaves. He had always objected to this title being given to any one but himself, saying that Kings only ought to be called Lords. His Majesty was then at the height of his fury, and seeing Mr. Rosenthal, whom he hated, standing by, he abused him and had him arrested. Dr. Blanc being present came in for his share of the royal displeasure, which vented itself also on a number of the European artisans. Having gone so far, he thought he might go a little further by having them conducted to Debra Tábor, to make another display there.

I interrupt the narrative here to explain the import of the word "Gêta" (plural, Gêtotsh), and also of "Aito," another title which frequently occurs in these pages. *Gêta** means master, or lord; Aito is equivalent to our mister, or sir. Formerly, neither was applied to any but Abyssinian noblemen, but within the last century both have become common, and foreigners as well as respectable natives, such as merchants and others, have adopted them. A servant, ordinarily, may speak of his master as the Gêta, and say that the Gêta had told him to do this or that; but when speaking of his master to a superior, who is then *the* Gêta, he must use the word with the suffix pronoun of the third person, Gêtäu. As the King considered himself *the* Gêta *par excellence*, he could not brook the application of it to any other in his presence. Theodore, however, was very liberal with the title "Aito," bestowing it on all civil officers and respectable merchants, as also on aliens, and did not object

---

* A learned friend of mine suggests whether "Gêta" may not be derived from the Hebrew (or Semitic) root, גאה, to be exalted, majestic. See Ex. xi. 1, 21. "Aito," he thinks, may have the same origin as the Chaldee עֵטָא a counsellor or minister of the king. *Vid.* Ezra vii. 14, 15.

to others being so designated, although, strictly speaking, only princes of the royal blood, and those on whom it is conferred by the Sovereign, have the right of adopting it. It approaches nearer to the Turkish "Effendi" than any other title I know of. When the King was concocting the letter to her Majesty, in April, 1866, which was sent by Mr. Flad, a discussion arose between him and his courtiers as to the title he should give me when mentioning my name. He remarked that the Queen had merely called me "our servant, Hormuzd Rassam," and submitted whether he ought to use a similar phrase. To this one of his courtiers replied, "Your Majesty may not consistently do so, inasmuch as the English Queen is his Mistress, and as such she very properly designates him simply by his name, as her servant." "Very well," rejoined the King, "I will give him the highest civil title in the realm, and call him 'Aito.'" The prefix was accordingly added to my name, and the amanuensis went on with his writing.

On the 4th, the King ordered that we should be allowed to take an airing on the hill, where we had been imprisoned in the black tent a few days before. To do so, we should have been obliged to pass the King's favourite place of resort, both in going and returning, and as his Majesty was as averse from meeting us as we were him, he directed a passage to be made for us through the outer wall of the Treasury. A fence was also to be erected to separate us from his establishment; but our servants were told that they might remain outside it. The fence was finished when we were desired, on the morning of the 5th, to prepare to set out with the King, who was proceeding towards Mágdala. At noon his Majesty started, and at about 1 P.M. we followed him. Dr. Blanc, Lieutenant Prideaux and I were allowed to ride the mules presented to us by the King, but the rest, including Consul Cameron, were told to provide themselves with animals. Mrs. Rosenthal not being well at the time, it was thought advisable to leave her behind with Mrs. Flad, at Debra Tâbor, as we were not certain then where the King intended to take us.

On the 7th July we travelled with his Majesty as far as Ibánkab, a distance of about thirty miles from Debra Tâbor, and nearly fifty from Mágdala. All the time we were with him he treated us with great consideration. One day he sent to tell me that he hoped I did not look upon the guard which slept by our tents as having been placed there to watch us: its duty, he said, was to protect the royal household, and our encampment being near his, the guard was obliged to be close to us.

Samuel's services as Bâldărăbâ were dispensed with, and my young interpreter, Dasta, was ordered by the King to act in his stead, as a temporary measure. For the first time after Samuel's disgrace, the King sent to him, on the 8th of July, to take me to a certain spot, and show me the large quantity of hailstones that had fallen on the mountain of Gŭna, above Ibánkab. When he heard that my companions, Dr. Blanc and Lieutenant Prideaux, and I were pleased with the sight, he sent to tell me that, if we liked, he would send us the next morning up to the high mountain, to see the hail nearer. On our thanking him for his kind offer, he appointed a guard to escort us there and back—to protect us, as he said, against robbers.

Early on the 9th he sent for Samuel, and after telling him he was a "slave of the English" and loved me more than he loved him (the King), he bade him get ready and start at once to keep me company at Mágdala. Bitwáddad Tadla (the Chief who had arrested Consul Cameron and his party on the 13th of April, after they had left Korâta) was then appointed to take me and my party to Mágdala, and to proceed thither forthwith. We were told to take very few things with us, on account of the difficulty of travelling, and that the rest of our luggage would follow us shortly. The King was very anxious that we should reach Mágdala before the rise of the rivers Chetta and Bâshilo, which lay in our way, as he wished us to be in a "safe place" during the winter months. We each took bedding and a few articles of clothing; but after the first stage we found that I was the only one allowed to carry those necessaries. For nearly a week my fellow-captives had nothing to sleep upon except what I could provide them with; as for clothes, we had to put up with what we wore. Our guard consisted of about 100 men, most of whom were either killed or imprisoned by the King before the year was over, and their Chief, Bitwúddad Tadla, was kept in chains at Mágdala until he was released by Sir Robert Napier.

The Europeans who were doomed to keep me company in bondage for nearly two years were seven in number—five of the old prisoners and two new ones. The former were: Consul Cameron, and Messrs. Stern, Rosenthal, Kerans and Pietro; the latter, my companions, Dr. Blanc and Lieutenant Prideaux.

We reached Mágdala in the afternoon of the 12th of July, 1866, and after the ceremony of counting us had been gone through, and our names properly registered, we were ushered into an inclosure near the royal residence, which belonged to the chief minister, Râs I'ngǎdǎ. We were then shown into a room by the Commandant of Mágdala, Dajjâj Kidâna Máryam, where we were told to remain until further orders. This officer had been appointed by the King, through Bitwáddad Tadla, to act as my Bâldărăbă. The Bitwáddad also told me that the orders of his master were, that whatever I required would be attended to by the Commandant. Next to the room, or hut, referred to, there was another, which was also made over to us, for the use of our servants and Aito Samuel.

On our arrival at the fortress I found that Samuel's position with me was quite anomalous: the King had neither said that he was to be treated as a prisoner, nor that he was to act as agent between him and me; but I was told confidentially that he was sent with me as a spy. After considering the matter carefully, I concluded that he would be more useful to us if I availed myself of his services in communicating with the local authorities. This I did a few days after, by sending friendly messages by him to different Chiefs, which gained him and me their confidence.

On the 16th the Chiefs of Mágdala came to us and said that as the King had not sent definite orders about our imprisonment, they were obliged to be on the safe side, and must therefore put fetters on our legs. They accordingly hammered on the chains which they had brought for that purpose. After they had finished with my fellow-captives they began on me, but as one of the rings broke while it was being riveted, I was not chained till next day, the 17th. The Chiefs tried to assure me that the chains were not a sign of ill-will, as they were certain that their master was my friend, and they hoped that before many days had elapsed everything would be right again.

When Bitwáddad Tadla—the Chief who escorted us to Mágdala—was about to return to Debra Tábor, he came to me for a message to the King, as both he and the Mágdala Chiefs judged it expedient that he should not go back without one, and that a pleasant communication from me might induce his

Majesty to relent. When the man came into my room on this errand, I felt very much disposed to give him no answer, as some of my fellow-captives had led me to understand that he was a bad man at heart, and held all Europeans in great aversion. I found out afterwards, however, that he really intended to do me a service. I was in low spirits at the time, and not in the least disposed to concoct a hollow message, for I began to think that our lives hung upon a thread; so I said to him, "Tell the King that my fellow-prisoners and I have reached this jail in safety, and that when this act of his becomes known, it will doubtless serve to increase his fame; especially when people hear that a great Sovereign has imprisoned a man merely because he was his friend." On my repeating these words to Samuel he became ashy pale, and said, "I will certainly not translate what you have uttered, but will send a message suitable to the occasion." He then turned towards Bitwáddad Tadla, and told him that I wished him to convey my best compliments to the King, and to say that, by his Majesty's favour, I had reached Mágdala in safety, and hoped ere long to have the pleasure of seeing him. When the Bitwáddad reached the King, the first question the latter asked was, how he had left me, and what I had said on finding myself confined to Mágdala. His reply was, that I felt highly favoured in having so exalted a locality allotted to me during the rainy season, and one so near his Majesty's *Ilfing*; that my only regret was being so far from the royal presence, but that the thought of soon meeting the King again was a source of great consolation to me. Thereupon his Majesty sighed and merely remarked, "Poor Rassam, he is still friendly towards me, and when I go to Mágdala, which will be in the course of a few days, I will release him and treat him better than ever."

When the messenger, Lih, who accompanied Bitwáddad Tadla from Debra Tábor together with us, returned to the King after seeing us chained, he told his Majesty, on being questioned on the subject, that I had not manifested any vexation, but had simply remarked that whatever came from the King was acceptable to me, from a gauntlet to a fetter round the leg. "Very well," replied his Majesty, "I will soon make him happy, but before then I must send a letter to comfort him; and remember, Lih, when you return to Mágdala you must not forget to take a letter from me to my friend Rassam."

The King had written to the Chiefs to say that Rás I'ngádă's two huts should be occupied by my fellow-captives and their servants, and that another hut next to them, belonging to Fit-awrári Gabriê, should be appropriated to me, and that my own personal servants and Aito Samuel should be provided with two separate rooms near me. For a week, however, my seven fellow-captives and I had to live day and night in one round hut, not more than fifteen feet in diameter; but when we were chained and considered safe, the Chiefs allowed us to be separated as follows: I had the room assigned to me by the King; Dr. Blanc and Lieut. Prideaux the little hut which had been provided for my servant—after the permission of the Chiefs was obtained; and Messrs. Kerans and Pietro occupied a part of the room, or hut, which had been turned into a kitchen.

When the messenger was sent by the Chiefs to Debra Tábor to report to the King that we were safely shackled, they directed him to tell his Majesty what they had said to me about the fetters, in the hope that he would order us to be relieved of them. I was told that when the courier delivered the message, the King said, "Do those asses of

Mágdala Chiefs think that Mr. Rassam is such a fool as to believe that any person could put him in chains without my special order? The thing is now done, and he must wait until I go there myself."

When we left the King at Ibánkab, on the 9th, he had intended to follow in four or five days. He was only waiting for the concentration of his troops, which, since the middle of June, had been dispersed in different parts of Bagámĕdĕr, on account of the cholera. He subsequently changed his mind and went back to Debra Tâbor. I was told that on two later occasions he had moved in our direction, but for some unknown reason he returned to Debra Tâbor, after two or three days' march.

When we were sent to Mágdala the King had ordered— so I was told—that I should be allowed to have all my servants with me, but that my fellow-captives should only have one female servant each, in accordance with the discipline of the fortress. I was also to be allowed rations from his own establishment; but, as for the rest, he did not care what became of them. The Chiefs, who were very exact in obeying every command from their master, were somewhat reluctant to include my companions in the order about the rations and servants. Samuel, however, made their consciences easy at once by assuring them that we three had come to Abyssinia on the same errand, as friends of their King, and that consequently we were all one, and that whenever the King spoke of me he meant the three combined. The rations, which consisted of a few loaves of bread not enough for five persons, I declined; but a small jar of *téj*, generally so sour as to be undrinkable, I accepted for some time, to please the Chiefs. When honey became scarce, and the communication between the royal camp and Mágdala was interrupted, the *téj* was stopped.

During our incarceration at Mágdala the Chiefs never failed to send me, on every great Abyssinian feast, one or two cows, in accordance with orders from their master. On many occasions when they were badly off for cattle they felt bound to present me with the usual offering, though they had none to spare for the royal establishment. The Chiefs became more friendly every day, and never failed to render us a variety of services, whenever they could do so safely. They soon allowed extra servants to our fellow-captives, and before many months had passed they enlarged our inclosure to nearly three times its original extent, and permitted us to build within it as many rooms for our servants as we could. After a while, they permitted Consul Cameron to have a hut of his own, and ultimately they allowed Mr. Stern to occupy a separate apartment day and night. They never interfered with the ingress or egress of our messengers, except on a few occasions, when they thought it advisable, for their safety and ours, to show that they were on the alert.

Aito Samuel never once hesitated to serve me, even at the risk of his life. He was the first who undertook to send our letters to the coast, by one of his own servants, with the report of our incarceration at Mágdala. Being thoroughly acquainted with Arabic and Amharic he was on all occasions of material service to me. As he was still styled the King's Báldárábá, Chiefs, messengers and others could visit him without giving rise either to jealousy or fear. Having always kept open house for me when we were provided with rations from the King, I thought it advisable to allow him to continue the same course of hospitality, notwithstanding our altered circumstances. His frequent entertainment of Abyssinian parties, on my behalf, enabled me to keep up former intimacies and to cultivate new acquaintances among the influential natives, whose friendship proved of essential service to us during our imprisonment at Mágdala.

CHAPTER XX.

OUR GUARDIANS AT MÁGDALA.

The Mágdala Council — Rás Kidána Máryam, the Commandant — Rás Bisáwwir — Bitwáddad Damásh — Bitwáddad Hailo — Bitwáddad Wási — Bitwáddad Bahri — Dajjáj Gojjé — Bitwáddad Bákal — Bitwáddad Hailo, of Chálga — Bitwáddad Dháfar — Our Warders :—Abá-Fálek — Básha Bisáwwir — Yashálaka Ádam — Yashálaka Warké.

BEFORE proceeding with the narrative of our captivity at Mágdala, I must introduce the reader to the different Members of Council who kept watch and ward over us during our incarceration. Formerly, Mágdala had only a Commandant, who was charged with the civil and military administration of the place, but when the King removed the political prisoners from the Sar Amba, in Chálga, to that fortress, he appointed nine Chiefs to various posts there, who were to constitute a Council—the Commandant, however, retaining summary power, subject only to the superior authority of the Sovereign. All the Chiefs were to be consulted on ordinary matters, but more important subjects were to be referred to five only, who were privileged to know the King's secrets. On our arrival at Mágdala, all the Members of Council, including the Commandant, held the honorary title of "Dajazmátsh;" but shortly after they had become our jailors, his Majesty raised the Commandant to the rank of "Rás," and the other nine Chiefs to that of "Bitwáddad."

RÁS KIDÁNA MÁRYAM, the Commandant and President of

the Council, was an hereditary Chief of Bagámĕdĕr, and in the time of Rás 'Ali he, with the other leading men of his family, aided the Chiefs of Gójjam against the Galla ascendancy, which Rás 'Ali represented ; but when Theodore appeared in the field, they forsook their former allies and attached themselves to him. He was very gentlemanly in manners, and had the reputation of being a humane and just man, and would never allow an act of cruelty to be perpetrated, unless ordered by the King. Apathy and indecision were his greatest faults, and he was never known to settle a case, unless backed by the Bitwáddads Bisáwwir or Damâsh, who were far more energetic. Had he wished to rebel against the King, he might have done so easily, as he was beloved by every one in the fortress, and held the command of five hundred Lancers, forming one-third of the garrison. As his Majesty wished to destroy his native province of Bagámĕdĕr, and was afraid to leave Mágdala in his hands the meanwhile, he threw him into chains, on the pretext that he had heard of his having held communication with Menilek, King of Shoa. The poor man ended his days in prison, at Debra Tábor, and when on the point of death he called all his relations, and in their presence appointed me his executor. He wrote me a letter just before he expired, assuring me that God had put it into his heart that I should be saved. He besought me, when I was safe, to look after his wife and children. This poor man behaved very civilly to my fellow-captives and myself while he remained in charge, and never failed to do us an act of kindness whenever it lay in his power.

BITWÁDDAD BISÁWWIR, the next in order, was a nephew to Theodore, and commanded half the Musketeers of the garrison, consisting of 500 men. When Rás Kidâna Máryam was removed, the King made Bisáwwir a "Râs," appointed him Commandant in his room, and placed under his orders the 500 Lancers of his predecessor; hence, as the nominal strength of the garrison was reckoned at 1,000 Lancers and 500 Musketeers, one-half the entire number was subject to his control. Bisáwwir was a native of Infarâz, lying between Bagámĕdĕr and Dámbĕa, and his father, who was the Chief of the place, had married Theodore's aunt—another daughter of the Râs of Amhára-Seint. His family were so wealthy in cattle and land that hundreds of poor people resorted to them for alms. The district where they resided was reputed for rearing the finest vines in Abyssinia, and its wine was sent to Góndar and other places for sale. He was so much given to chanting psalms that he was nicknamed "Dábterâ," or Clerk, and so transported with the services of the Church that he danced at them, in public, like the priests and monks. He was the first Chief sent to Mágdala after its capture from the Gallas, and he retained command of the troops until a few days before the place fell into our hands. He befriended me and my fellow-captives from our first arrival there until we left on the 11th of April, 1868, and never on any occasion refused me a favour, unless he judged it unsafe to grant it. The King had such perfect confidence in him that he made him overseer to his female establishment, which delicate office he discharged faithfully, never failing to keep the inmates in order, yet at the same time acceding to their wishes, provided they were not extravagant. In contrast to poor Kidâna Máryam, Bisáwwir was very easy on the score of responsibility. On one occasion, a doorkeeper of ours—of whom more anon—seized a note which had been sent to our quarters, for Mr. Rosenthal, from one of the native prisoners. As it was contrary to the discipline of the fortress to allow any communication between the prisoners, the meddling doorkeepers—to spite Mr. Rosenthal, I believe—took the note and its bearer before the Râs. Kidâna Máryam, who held that position at the time, was quite bewildered, not knowing how to dispose of the case; for, on the one hand, he was loth to do us any injury, and, on the other, he was afraid to hush it up, or even to reprimand the tell-tale for having brought so trumpery a matter to his notice. In this dilemma he called in the assistance of Bisáwwir, and asked him to dispose of the case, without involving him in trouble. The wary councillor remarked that, in the first place, he must see what the note contained—which, by the way, the Râs had been too timid to read, fearing that it might reveal treason. On perusing the note, Bisáwwir summoned the doorkeepers, and gave them a severe rebuke for having made so much fuss about a trumpery piece of paper which had come from a beggar. "Tell me the truth, you blockheads," he continued, "have you never yourselves tasted the money of the Franks that you should be so punctilious in the matter of alms? Take this paper and eat it, and do not bother us any more about such nonsense. Does not our Master know that Aito Rassam is liberal, and that those who are in want beg of him?" On hearing of this incident, I sent for the mischief-makers and asked what they had to say for themselves. They swore solemnly that they had intended no harm, knowing that what would hurt my fellow-captives would hurt me also; but the note, they said, had been brought in some vegetables, as if it were to be smuggled in, and that as one of our Portuguese servants had snatched the vegetables from the hand of the messengers, the note fell out in the presence of a number of strangers who were standing near the door; consequently, they were obliged to notice it, and to let it be known openly that it was harmless, as it had proved to be. "How can you charge us with being mischief-makers," they added, "when you know, Sir, that we ourselves have brought you a number of letters, and passed your messengers in and out on many occasions? For the sake of our lives, we entreat you to tell your people to be cautious; for if this Indian had not snatched the vegetables from the Abyssinian, the note would not have fallen out; and if the Abyssinian had brought the note to us, and asked us to deliver it to you, we should not have hesitated to do so, since you are a friend of our King, who would not be angry with us for such an act. On the other hand, what would he say if we allowed his enemies, the priests [Missionaries], to correspond with the native prisoners?"

The third Chief in rank and importance, but pre-eminent for his temerity, was BITWÁDDAD DAMASH, one of the King's fathers-in-law, and a native of the same province as Theodore, who had also been brought up with him almost from childhood. He was one of the five Privy Councillors, and commanded the other half of the Musketeers—250 men—of the garrison. It was also his duty to sleep at the Treasury, and see that it was well guarded at night. This man was generally disliked both by Europeans and natives; for my own part, I always found him amicably disposed, and he never failed to support me in the Council, whenever I asked for anything to add to our comfort. I had been given to understand that his relationship to Theodore gave him a high standing in the royal favour, and that his Majesty had commissioned him to report to him all that my fellow-captives and I did. His house adjoined ours, and none of our messengers or servants could come in or go out without passing his door. He had sent his son—a lad about twelve years old—to visit me on our first arrival, and continued the practice almost daily, so that I was enabled, through him, to keep up a regular communication with his father, and by degrees we became very friendly, although, owing to his illness, we did not see each other for nearly six months after I reached Mágdala. Hearing that we were badly off for money, he twice sent us cows and bread, and offered to get me anything from the Treasury, if I needed it. On his recovery, he came to call upon me, and as he knew a little Arabic I could speak to him without the intervention of an interpreter, so that, in course of time, we became fast friends. One morning he took a solemn oath that he would stand by me unto death, and I am bound to testify that he kept his word, and never once betrayed me. He was the only Chief who, for a whole year, had the courage to come and see me alone, without being attended by a subordinate to hear what passed between us; in fact, he considered it beyond the power of any Abyssinian to injure him. He told me, on one occasion, to my great surprise, that he was aware of my communications with the coast, and he actually gave me the names of the messengers and the time they had started. However, he bade me not fear, since he had sworn not to betray my secrets; nevertheless, he advised me to use the greatest caution, lest the letters might be seized at the gate. Thenceforward, I always sent him a private message whenever I intended to dispatch messengers to the coast. When this fact came to Samuel's knowledge, about a year afterwards, the poor man nearly fainted, for he believed that it would be safer to trust Satan himself than Bitwáddad Damâsh; and when I divulged to him another secret—namely, that I had intrusted that Chief with my papers—the hair of Samuel's head nearly stood on end with consternation. None of the Chiefs at Mágdala rendered such good service, through me, to my fellow-captives as Damâsh. He always took our part before the Council, whenever anything connected with us was brought under discussion. Twice while I was playing whist at night with Blanc and Prideaux, he came near our fence and called out to us to be on our guard, as a number of lights had been seen on the heights at Dâwunt, which might belong to the royal camp—the King was then expected at Mágdala—or to a great Râs coming on important business. It happened to be the latter on both occasions, and through this timely notice we were able to dispose of all papers likely to compromise us, in case their seizure had been ordered by his Majesty. Moreover, whenever a messenger arrived from the King, he was the first to report to me that all was "right." On my expressing a wish that Blanc and Prideaux's hut might be enlarged, he it was who told the Council that there could be no harm in allowing my companions, who were the "friends of the King," to increase the size of their abode; and he himself undertook, with the assistance of his Musketeers, to pull down the old building and to erect a larger in its place. When I wished that Consul Cameron and Mr. Stern might have separate huts to live and sleep in, Damâsh and Râs Bisâwwir were the only members of the Council who sanctioned the arrangement. In fact, from the outset, he never shrank from doing us a good turn, sparing us throughout much trouble; and it was probably through his intervention that the life of Consul Cameron's messenger was saved when he was seized in Dalanta, in March, 1868, while the King was on his way to Mágdala. His Majesty had given strict orders prohibiting all communication between his camp and the latter fortress, and any one caught in the act of disobeying was to be executed on the spot. Mr. Flad had also written and warned us against sending any one to the royal camp; but the advice was unheeded: a man was sent, and he was seized at the outpost. Luckily, Bitwáddad Damâsh was in command of the outer guard on the occasion, and, finding that the messenger belonged to our party, he told the sentry that the man was his servant and was not to be meddled with. Damâsh's wife and son, as also his brothers, who were royal couriers, called upon me frequently, in the most open and unreserved manner—with the exception of the lady who, according to Abyssinian etiquette, was debarred from making visits during the daytime. Unfortunately, Damâsh was of a quarrelsome disposition, and during most of our stay at Mágdala he was either in hot water with his wives—he had two—or with Samuel. No sooner had I settled one case of disagreement between them than another broke out; but the task of reconciling the husband with his consorts was easy compared with that of making matters up between Damâsh and Samuel. Sometimes they would not speak to each other for a couple of months, and then, in my presence, would revile one another at the top of their voices. One day the quarrel between the husband and one of his two wives came to a crisis, for the lady left him, and took refuge in the house of a man whom she knew he hated. This step on her part occasioned no little scandal on the mountain, insomuch that even Samuel begged me to interfere, especially as the lady had threatened to expose all her husband's proceedings to the King, and Samuel, being on rather too intimate terms with the family, feared that he also might be compromised. The Commandant and his colleagues also urged me, as a friend of the parties, to reprimand Damâsh for his bad behaviour to his wife, whom he had neglected and almost starved, and, if possible, to induce the runagate to return home. I accordingly appointed a petty Chief, accompanied by one of my interpreters, to wait upon the lady on my behalf, and upon my undertaking to be her guardian and to keep Damâsh in order, she returned to her husband and promised to be obedient to him in future. Before concluding this sketch I must mention one among many of Damâsh's acts of kindly consideration for us. Knowing that my fellow-captives and I only ate wheaten bread, he sowed a field of corn for our special use, and had the produce stored in his granary, in case we might need it during the winter of 1868. Fortunately, we did not require it, but the British force had the benefit of it when they took possession of Mágdala.

The fourth member of the Privy Council was BITWÁDDAD HAILO, a man of good family, who, to use a familiar phrase, had more sense in his little finger than all the other Chiefs combined had in their brains. He was brother to Lij Tasámma, the Chief of the escort appointed by the King to receive the Mission at Chálga, when we reached that place from Matámma, and the eldest son of Wäizero Denké, the lady who entertained us at Wandigè. On our arrival at Mágdala, I was apprised that he was one of the spies selected by the King to watch over my movements and those of the other captives, European and native. I accordingly lost no time in endeavouring to secure his interest. That was an easy task, for I noticed that when we were fettered, he not only tried to select the lightest fetters for me, but manifested much emotion when they were being riveted on. He had heard that I was on the most friendly terms with his family, and his master's treachery towards us had excited his intense disgust. He and Bitwáddad Tadla, the Chief who escorted us to Mágdala, met on the night of the 12th of July—the day we were brought into the fortress—and both spoke despondingly of my fate and that of my fellow-captives. Tadla declared that he felt so utterly degraded by the duty which had been allotted to him, that had his wife and children not been in the King's power, he would have taken us to Wadla, after crossing the Bashilo, and there set us free. He told Bitwáddad Hailo that he ought to use his best efforts to befriend us, inasmuch as I deserved every good man's sympathy. When Hailo heard that we were badly off for money, he sent and requested me to allow him to present me with five hundred dollars, knowing, he said, that as a stranger I should find some difficulty in obtaining funds during the rainy season. Râs Kidâna Máryam also sent me a similar message; but I declined both offers, with my best thanks, stating that I was not in immediate want. In order to put the friendship of the former to the test, I asked him to assist me in procuring money from Matámma, knowing that he might easily do so through his brothers, who were Chiefs of Chálga, unless fear of the King's displeasure stood in his way. He acceded to the request at once, and would not even allow me to write to my agent at Matámma to recompense the messenger, whom he sent with my letter, for his trouble. The man returned in due time, bringing the funds applied for, and it was only after a long debate that he consented to my presenting him with a few dollars. The imprisonment of his bosom friend, Râs Kidâna Máryam, the old Commandant, increased his antipathy to the King, and from that time forward he began to concert measures to get out of Mágdala, and to assist in effecting my escape. For more than a year he was prepared to let me down by a ladder, with one attendant, and send me either to Shoa or Lasta, to be conveyed from thence to the coast. On my representing to him that I could not possibly avail myself of his kind offer, leaving my fellow-captives behind, he consulted with the parties who were to have coöperated in the attempt, and they agreed to include Dr. Blanc and Lieut. Prideaux, but not a man more, otherwise detection would be inevitable, and all would fall in one common massacre. As I gave him to understand that it was utterly out of the question for me to take advantage of his kindness, at the risk of the life even of one of our Indian followers, the subject was dropped. When the King came to Mágdala, in March, 1868, Bitwáddad Hailo was in such dread of encountering him, that he escaped by a ladder, hung over a precipice. The way he managed was this: his mother had come to see him at the time, and was then at Salámgê — the plateau below Mágdala—whither he sent his wife and child to visit her, and by a preconcerted arrangement the three met him during the night, just as he effected his descent from the heights, and then all proceeded together to join the Gallas. On the arrival of the British force, he took refuge with Sir Robert Napier, and according to the latest reports he was administering the government of his native province, Wandigê, and the adjoining districts. Bitwáddad Hailo used his utmost endeavours while we were at Mágdala to induce me to marry, offering, on gaining my consent, to send for his niece, the accomplished belle of Wandigê, and to present her to me as a bride. My excuse was, that a man in fetters could hardly think of offering himself as a bridegroom. It was hinted to me at the time that the suggestion originated with the King, who would have been delighted had I fallen into any such entanglement.

BITWÁDDAD WÁSI, the fifth member of the Privy Council, was a Kamánt, and a native of Chálga. He was a man of unblemished character, and so devoted to the King that he regarded the least reflection on any of the royal acts as akin to blasphemy. He was always forward to do me a kindness, provided that it in no way interfered with his loyalty to Theodore; but as his Majesty always designated me as his "friend" in his letters to the Council, and directed that all its members should visit me and attend to my wants, he was not backward to stretch a point now and then to serve me. So averse was he from receiving presents from any of the prisoners, that before sending him the customary contribution of a cow, bread and mead, towards the wake which he was about to give in memory of his mother, whose death had just been reported from Chálga, I deemed it prudent to ask whether the offering would be agreeable to him. His message in reply was, that he could receive nothing from me while I was a prisoner and he my warden, begging me at the same time not to send him anything; if I did, he would be compelled to return it, however much it might pain him to do so. When the mourning was over, he came to apologize for having declined my proffered gift, praying that I would not consider the refusal as indicative of ill-feeling on his part, inasmuch as he entertained a high regard for me. Conscientious scruples, he said, forbade his receiving any donation from a prisoner; "but," he added, "lest you may still misunderstand me, I will not leave your house until you let me know how I can serve you, in order that I may have an opportunity of proving the sincerity of my friendship to my son's friend." His son, Lij Tasho, one of our Chálga escort, had written to secure his father's good offices for me when we were transferred to Mágdala. I accordingly asked him to procure me a supply of cash from our agent at Matámma, which he undertook to do at once, but before the messenger whom he dispatched could return, the whole country between the Lake and Mágdala had risen in rebellion, and although the man made two efforts to join us, he found it impracticable to do so safely, with a large sum of money in his possession. One day in Easter, Samuel sent him a bottle of arrack and an European shirt; the Bitwáddad returned them immediately, and wished to know why I had acted as I had done, after the explanation which he had given me of his scruples in such matters. The articles were sent into my room with the rude message, "Did I not tell you that you were a prisoner?" As Samuel had taken this step without my knowledge, I reprimanded him for it, and insisted on his going forthwith to explain to Bitwáddad Wâsi how the case stood. Samuel went to the Council, which was then convened to discuss the payments due to the soldiers, and complained of the message which the Kamánt Bitwáddad had sent me. Thereupon the members came to me in a body, begging me to overlook the rudeness of their colleague, who was then sent for and made to apologize, and to declare that I was not a prisoner, but the King's "friend." We were on the best terms ever after, until we parted on the capture of Mágdala.

BITWÁDDAD BÁHRI, the sixth member of Council, was a native of Agówmedĕr. His sole business was to take charge of the Treasury, and to see that nothing was allowed to leave it without an order from the King. He was an upright man, never intermeddled in matters which did not concern him, and was never known to utter an unkind word to any one. He was particularly gracious to me, and although he had presented me with cows on several occasions, he absolutely refused any return until the approach of the King, when he accepted a silk shirt from me for himself, and a suitable dress for his wife. Bitwáddad Güinti Bisáwwir, another member of the Council, was associated with him in the charge over the Treasury; and there was a Deputy-Treasurer besides, named Bajirwand Wald-Taklé, a native of Tigrê.

DAJJÁJ GOJJÉ, the next member, was a native of Wággärä. He was an inoffensive old man, much addicted to mead, and consequently very much attached to those who treated him to the favourite beverage. I was on very friendly terms with his wife, and, although we never met, compliments passed between us every day; but as she resided within the precincts of the *Ilfing*, she was unable to pay me a visit, because those who are privileged to hold intercourse with the royal concubines are not allowed to associate with strangers. The Dajjâj commanded 500 Lancers of the garrison, and although he held an important post at Mágdala, the King, for some reason or other, had omitted him when he raised his colleagues to the rank of "Bitwáddad."

The eighth member was BITWÁDDAD BÁKAL, another harmless old man, whose only fault was excessive devotion to his master. He was one of the guardians of the *Ilfing*, charged with seeing that the eunuchs attended to their duties and did not neglect their royal mistresses. He was very intimate with me, and, from the date of our arrival at Mágdala until our release, his wife, daughter and niece were among my constant visitors. He did all in his power to oblige me in every way, and whenever he heard that we were in want of money, he presented us with a cow. He disliked the Bishop exceedingly, holding that as a subject it did not become him to abuse the "Lord's Anointed." He stuck to Theodore to the last, and when I entered Mágdala with Sir Robert Napier, after the capture of the place, I saw him in the agonies of death, near the gate, where he had been shot. I caused his body to be made over to his family for interment, and deplored the poor old man's fate the more for having sacrificed his life in the cause of one who was unworthy of such unswerving attachment.

The exclusive duty of BITWÁDDAD HAILO, a native of Chálga, the ninth member of Council, was to watch over the native prisoners, in conjunction with Bitwáddads Wâsi and the other Hailo. Though timid and quiet, he succeeded in maintaining order among the hundreds of unfortunate beings who were placed under his charge for political offences. He died in 1867, during an epidemic which raged among the native prisoners for several months. His son, Lij Tasámma, was appointed by the King to succeed him as warder, but without a seat at the Council.

BITWÁDDAD GÁINTI BISÁWWIR was a native of Gäint in Bagáměděr. As already mentioned, he was colleague to Bitwáddad Báhri over the Treasury. He was specially responsible for the cash deposits, and not a dollar could be issued without his sanction.

BITWÁDDAD DHÁFAR, the last member of the Mágdala Council, was a native of Chálga. He was a confirmed toper, and when the mead, or *tėj*, got into his head he was fit for nothing. He had charge of the native prisoners conjointly with Bitwáddads Wâ-i and Hailo. He had a filthy habit of expectorating, which his colleagues endeavoured to restrain, whenever they visited me in his company. If their injunctions were unheeded, they generally sent him home under an escort.

Having described the Chiefs of Mágdala, I must now introduce our official door-keepers, or warders, who held a most important position with regard to ourselves during our imprisonment. For the first week of our captivity they were selected from the guard, which used to be changed every twenty-four hours; the consequence was that we were subject to different treatment every day, some of the men being comparatively lenient, while others went so far as to prohibit our Indian servants from leaving the house, and would not allow others to enter. This interference became so intolerable in a short time that Râs Kidâna Máryam, in conjunction with the other members of the Council, appointed four officers to keep ward over us, two and two in rotation. They were accordingly duly introduced to me, and placed under Samuel, who was to receive his instructions from me as to the persons to be allowed to enter or leave our premises. The names of these men were Abâ-Fâlek, Bâsha Bisâwwir, Yashálaka Âdam, and Yashálaka Warké.

Abâ-Fâlek was cordially hated by every soul on the mountain, and he considered it his bounden duty to reciprocate the general sentiment. He was the most subtle and crafty Abyssinian I ever met with, but at the same time inviolable in his secrecy. He was faithful to me from first to last, and obeyed all my orders with alacrity. My fellow-captives were the objects of his intense dislike, as were also all the Mágdala Chiefs, especially Râs Kidâna Máryam, against whom he used to send stories to the King, and was known to declare openly, on several occasions, that he hoped to live long enough to see the Commandant disgraced. He was between sixty and seventy years old, but as robust and strong as a man of thirty. One day he had a quarrel with the Chiefs in my room, and told them that they had no business there without his permission; and when the Râs bade him hold his tongue he abused him and his colleagues most grossly, saying that he recognized no one's authority but the King's, and, after the

King's, mine, as being his Majesty's friend. I was eventually obliged to interfere and send him out of the room, but he still threatened to divulge all the misdoings of the Chiefs to the King as soon as he arrived. Once it was reported to me that he was about to set out on this errand on the approach of Theodore to Mágdala, and serious mischief would have been the inevitable result. I accordingly sent for him, and expostulated with him on the wickedness of any such talebearing. His reply was, that as everybody hated him, he intended to requite them in a similar manner; but if I judged that he might injure me by so doing, he would rather cut his tongue off than be the cause of any mishap to me. When I was threatened by the King on Good Friday, the 9th of April, 1868, that his friendship for me should be at an end, and that the blood of the messenger whom I employed would lie at my door if I communicated with the British, Abû-Fâlek took charge of a note from me to the investing force, and employed one of his female servants, who disguised herself, to convey it through the royal camp to its destination. She feigned to be going out to gather wood, but was seized at the outpost and kept in custody till the following day, when she was released on the plea of ignorance of the royal order forbidding any one to leave the place. Her delay gave Abû-Fâlek no little anxiety, in which I heartily shared, fearing that she might be discovered, in which case she would certainly have lost her life, especially if the missive with which she had been intrusted were found upon her. But the Abyssinians are unquestionably a remarkable people for keeping a secret. Although this poor woman had many opportunities to destroy the note after her seizure, she nevertheless hesitated to do so, lest it might contain something valuable which could not be replaced.

Abâ-Fâlek's comrade on guard was Bâsha Bisáwwir, who was always stern and morose. His greatest enemies were Samuel and Damâsh, whom he could never allow to pass without some rude speech or gesture of defiance. Whenever these treated him with the slightest disrespect, he retorted by telling the former that he had no right to intrude his presence upon me so frequently; the latter he called a nonentity, who was barely tolerated. On three different occasions he entered Samuel's house and drove out from thence the royal couriers, who were sipping mead with the host after the fatigue of their journey. "How dare you come here," he would say, "to enjoy yourselves in the house of the prisoners, when your master only sent you to deliver his compliments to Mr. Rassam? As for this man, this Samuel, I know nothing about him, since the King has not defined his position here; but as regards myself, I have been appointed watchman under his Majesty's sanction, and I will not allow any one to enter without my permission. So, come; bestir yourselves, and walk out, otherwise I shall be obliged to resort to force." The humiliated couriers never ventured to resist these objurgations, fearing lest the malicious warder might charge them with tippling, and suggest that while in that state Samuel wormed from them some of the secrets of the royal camp. Whenever, therefore, any object was to be gained by detaining the couriers a little longer, I generally sent my compliments to the doorkeeper, and begged him to summon them to me, in order that I might make some inquiries of them. I then placed them in a small by-room—Samuel's official residence—where they and Samuel might chat as long as they pleased. Bâ-ha Bisáwwir was, in fact, Samuel's Gorgon, for he had only to open his mouth and the otherwise fearless Bâldârâbâ was struck dumb. When the warders were appointed to watch over us, I thought it desirable to secure their goodwill by giving them a regular salary; but for three whole months Básha Bisáwwir and his comrade absolutely refused to take a single dollar, on the ground that being a prisoner I might find it difficult some day to procure money. After they once began to receive a monthly stipend, they never asked me for an additional present; and when I occasionally gave them a shirt or a new dress they always accepted the gift with gratitude. Moreover, if they happened to hear that my funds were low, they declined to take their salary when it was due, and begged that I would not think of them until further supplies reached me.

The third doorkeeper, YASHÁLAKA ÂDAM, had attained, according to his own reckoning, the age of fourscore years. He was a harmless kind of man, who never gave himself or others any trouble so long as his stomach was well filled with *brundo* and mead. His worst propensity was begging: if he received five dollars in the morning, he would come again at noon and tell you that his wife's hair required a little butter, or that her shirt was worn out and she wanted a new one. He hated Abâ-Fâlek most cordially, and never lost an opportunity of abusing him—behind his back.

YASHÁLAKA WARKÉ, the comrade on watch with the former, was really a good man, who never annoyed any one —European or native. Warké was liked by all on the mountain as much as Abâ-Fâlek was disliked. When he was on guard, no one knew that such an official was in the house. The only occasion on which I found him strict in the execution of his duty was when the King descended with all his troops to attack our advanced guard. He was himself in great dread of being killed either by the King or by our troops. I am bound to say, however, that the four warders behaved with the greatest fidelity towards me. All communications from the native jail came to me through them, and whenever any of the chief political prisoners sent messengers to me, they always allowed them to pass, and, in fact, were the first to report their arrival to me. After we had been acquainted several months, they even admitted the Bishop's messengers, though if this had come to the King's knowledge they would probably have forfeited their lives. They never interfered with our messengers or servants, although it was their duty to see that the discipline of the fortress was in no way infringed. In fact, had Abâ-Fâlek and Bâsha Bisâwwir wished to annoy us, they might have done so in a thousand ways; and had they not been faithful to their promise never to do me or my party an injury, they might have placed us in serious danger before the King's arrival. After these two men had been with us for some time, the Chiefs wished to substitute others in their stead; but even the brave Damâsh hesitated to remove them, fearing to excite their animosity. Hence, when the matter was discussed before the Council, all the members concurred that the best course would be to leave them under my management, confident that I should be able to keep them from doing mischief.

CHAPTER XXI.

LIFE AT MÁGDALA.

Our domestics -- A complimentary letter from the King — Relaxation of prison discipline — Samuel and a Tigré Chief at loggerheads — Duties of the petty Chiefs — The Guards at the Gates — Meditated escape — Escape impracticable — The Metropolitan, Aṭûna Salàma — His character vindicated — His illness and death — His differences with Theodore — Concessions as to quarters — Abyssinian red-tape — The Author's abode — Abortive sanitary efforts — The Captives' quarters — The Captives' *ménage* — Entertainment of public guests — Society and sympathy — Native lady visitors — Water at Mágdala — Soil and climate — Birds — Religious inquiry among the native soldiery — Reform movement — Conversions to Christianity from Islàm — Christian names — Our own worship.

THE orders which the King had sent when we were taken to Mágdala were, that I should have all my servants with me, but that my fellow-captives should be restricted to one female servant each, in accordance with the rules of the fortress in such cases. The Chiefs added, that a mistress would be allowed to each, if the captives chose to avail themselves of that boon. This statement may seem as incredible as it is shocking to many of my readers; nevertheless, such is the lamentable state of social morality among the Abyssinian Christians generally, that a proposition of this nature comes from them as a matter of course, unaccompanied with the least idea of its degradation. As Samuel and I had succeeded in convincing the Chiefs that Dr. Blanc and Lieutenant Prideaux were associated with me in the same friendly mission to the King—in fact, that they were to be considered as one with myself—they were allowed to have as many servants as they wished; but when I pleaded for the same privilege in behalf of Consul Cameron, they replied that they could not make any difference between him and the other old captives, who were reckoned among the King's enemies, and that it was only by special favour on the part of his Majesty that they were permitted to be located with us, near the royal *Ilfing*, seeing that their proper place was the common jail. Eventually, however, after repeated solicitations, I induced Râs Kidâna Máryam to allow the Consul the services of a lad, who was to be nominally my milk-boy.

On the 9th of August the King sent me a letter containing nothing but compliments; nevertheless, although it consisted of no more than three lines, it created a great sensation on the mountain. "What think you?" one gossip would say to another; "the King has written to Mr. Rassam, who is a prisoner! Surely, therefore, his Majesty does not regard him as an enemy, but must really love him." The Chiefs, who were well-disposed towards me from the outset, communicated the fact to the petty Chiefs of the garrison, and as the former had also received instructions from the King to visit me frequently, and to see to my comfort, inasmuch as I was his "friend" and not his enemy, they caused his Majesty's letter to me to be read in open court, in the Treasury, before the assembled officers of the fortress. Such a thing, in fact, was unparalleled, that the great Theodore should condescend to write to a prisoner, when every soldier of the garrison knew that even his Holiness, the Abûna, had never received a line from him since his imprisonment at Mágdala, and that whenever his Majesty wished to communicate with him he did so through the Chiefs. From that day forward the latter were more disposed than ever to serve me, and, at my solicitation, to extend their favour to my fellow-captives; but all my efforts to convince them that my fellow-captives and I were to be regarded in the same light—having one common feeling towards the King—signally failed. Whenever I expressed these sentiments to Râs Bisâwwir, Theodore's nephew and the foremost in the Council before he was appointed Commandant, he used to smile, wink his eye, and look at me as much as to say, "We know better." However, as his Majesty had given them such positive instructions to attend to all my wants, they thought themselves justified in stretching a point to please me, as regards concessions to my fellow-captives. They accordingly allowed them extra servants, and by making friends with the petty Chiefs who kept the night-watch, I induced them to relax the prison discipline, which requires that all prisoners shall retire to their rooms at sunset, there to be strictly guarded until the morning. Eventually, this watch became a mere sham, for those of my fellow-captives who chose to employ or amuse themselves till very late at night were seldom interfered with. Occasionally, however, some of the petty Chiefs who were at variance with Samuel used to turn restive, and insist on enforcing the prison rules by making all my fellow-captives sleep together in one room. After exhausting every other argument in vain, Samuel would fall back upon "the King's friend," and say to the refractory Chiefs, "Very well; you want all the captives to sleep in one room; so be it. I must first send and tell Mr. Rassam to begin to move, and then I will summon the rest." Thereupon his tormentors declare that they never mentioned my name, and did not intend to include me in the number. Samuel, quickly perceiving the advantage which he has gained, swears "by the death of the King" that all the captives must be watched collectively or not at all. On one occasion, the altercation between Samuel and a Tigrêan Chief, on this same subject, attained such a pitch that they both proceeded to the Council by night to argue the case before them. Samuel, finding that he could not stop the Chief's impetuous garrulity, called out to his confidential servant, and said, "Go and tell Mr. Rassam to prepare to sleep in Mr. Stern's room for the night, in company with the other captives; because a great Chief has come forward to defy the King by ordering him, the King's friend, to betake himself where this grand man may watch him." This sarcastic message put the petty Chief into an awful rage, which he vented on his antagonist by calling him a liar and a villain—a man who had sold himself to the *Franchotsh* for a glass of mead and a fine *shámma*. The *fracas*, which was now at its height, might have resulted in a few broken heads had not Bitwáddad Damâsh, who lived next door, suddenly made his appearance. However, the obstinate Chief would not be silenced; and as he swore "by the death of the King" that he would not be satisfied until he knew whether he or Samuel was responsible for the discipline in the prison-house of the Europeans, the contending parties were obliged to go before the Commandant. Râs Bisáwwir, who was never at a loss in such contingencies, silenced the Chief at once by telling him that as the King had appointed me Bâldărăbâ to all my fellow-captives, and had specially deputed Samuel to assist me, the night-watch was merely nominal; that Samuel and I only were responsible for the rest of the captives; and that the duty of the Chief in charge of the night-guard was simply to see that none of the prisoners left their rooms at night. This decision, as may be imagined, did not tend to soothe the feelings of the exasperated Tigrêan, for whenever his turn came to take the watch, which was once a fortnight, he never lost an opportunity of annoying Samuel, either by prohibiting his servants to leave our inclosure after a certain hour, or preventing others from entering it to join their masters. Ultimately, however, the Mágdala Chiefs brought about a reconciliation between the parties, who afterwards became so intimate that they used to call each other "brother."

The petty Chiefs, who ranked next after the Members of Council, were nominally in command of a hundred men. "Básha" was the proper title of a captain of Musketeers, and "Yasháláka" of Lancers; but when the King raised the members of Council to the dignity of "Bitwáddad," he made all the Báshas and Yashálákas "Dajazmátsh." The duty of the latter was to watch personally over the *Ilfing*, our quarters, the Treasury, and the Bishop; over the native prison and the two gates of Mágdala they might either mount guard themselves, or depute their lieutenants with a certain number of men to each post. At first, the order was that we were to be guarded every night by fifty men, but as some of the captains had not above half that number under their command, it frequently happened that we were left with only three privates and their captain. Two old Chiefs invariably went to sleep as soon as they came, and we might have walked out and disported ourselves on the mountains to any extent, for all they cared. The difficulty with us, as regards effecting our escape, was not how to get beyond the inclosure which surrounded our prison-house, but how to reach Salámgê—the plateau below Mágdala. Indeed, a number of the guard would have willingly joined us, with their families, in any attempt to regain our liberty, but there was no safe way of leaving the fortress. The only exit was by the double gates, at each of which a dozen warders, chosen from different and conflicting tribes, were posted throughout the day and night. They were all introduced to me, and we were on the best terms up to the last. At sunset, the gates were closed and the keys sent to the Commandant, who kept them till the following morning. Fifty men mounted guard over each gate by night, and in case of alarm the Commandant was bound to repair to the Salámgê Gate, double the guard over the native prisoners, and summon all the garrison to assist him. Not a soul, from the highest Chief next in rank to the Rás down to the common soldier, could leave the fortress without a special permit from the Commandant—a stringent rule, first instituted when all the political prisoners were brought to Mágdala, in 1864. Whenever the Commandant granted a pass to any one, he took the precaution of retaining his wife and children as security; but Rás Bisáwwir, an easy-going sort of man, was deceived by a good many who obtained his permission to go beyond the fortress and never returned, having managed somehow or other either to send their wives out beforehand, or to get them to follow.

The King having reiterated his instructions to the Chiefs to attend to all my wants, they appointed one Guangûl, a native of Tigrê, who spoke Arabic well, to act as my purveyor by accompanying our servants to make their daily purchases in the market. As this man was also spirit-broker to the royal cellar, he superintended our distilleries, and produced some very good liquor from *téj*. A female distiller from the royal establishment was also allotted to Samuel. Then, again, when I was at a loss for an efficient native writer, the Chiefs placed the services of Aláká Zánnah, the keeper of the royal archives, at my disposal. This man was an excellent scribe and perfectly trustworthy, so that I never hesitated to confide my secrets to him.

After we were chained at Mágdala, our prospects appeared so gloomy that I judged it a sacred duty to do all in my power to save my fellow-captives and myself from our perilous position. I accordingly wrote to the Bishop — who was then a prisoner himself in the same fortress — through a confidential messenger, asking whether he could assist us in effecting our escape with the co-operation of his friends in the garrison or beyond it, offering at the same time to pay any sum he chose to name for our rescue, provided he could guarantee our safe conveyance to the coast. His answer was that he could not trust the Mágdala people, and that none of his friends outside the Amba, especially among the chief rebels, had sufficient pluck to make the attempt. He submitted that the only way he could assist us was by my aiding him to escape first, and, once free, he would summon all the Abyssinian Christians to arms, and soon make an end of our common tormentor. If I could not manage to get him out of the fortress by any other means, he suggested that our doctor might supply him with a dye to colour his skin, and so disguised he might be able to smuggle himself out of the gates in company with a party of the natives. As there were many serious objections to this scheme, I gave up all hope of succour from that quarter, and tried several others with the same result, until at length the conviction was forced upon me that our deliverance could only be effected by an invading army.

The late Abûna Salâma was strongly attached to the British, and his education at an English school at Cairo had served to imbue him with liberal views, and to divest him of many of those contracted and superstitious notions which are the bane to all progress in the West as well as in the East. He uniformly befriended all British subjects, whether consuls or missionaries, travellers or adventurers. I am persuaded that there is nothing he would not have done, had he possessed the power, to save our lives, without putting Great Britain to the trouble and expense attendant upon a war. To me personally he was extremely kind, and from the time of our imprisonment at Mágdala until the day of his death, in October, 1867, we kept up a regular correspondence. He never grudged giving an English captive a dollar, either before or after my arrival in Abyssinia, and he would readily have shared his last penny with such an one, if he knew him to be in want. His character has been shamefully maligned by individuals who really knew nothing about him, who, nevertheless, have given currency to slanders which are utterly without foundation. He has been reproached with being a merchant, a broker, and a banker; but when the circumstances whereon those charges rest are inquired into, it will be seen that they involved no discredit either to him personally or to his sacred office. The Abûna, in addition to his special duties as Metropolitan, is the guardian or trustee of a large number of monasteries, churches and schools, and as the tithes to these and all similar institutions in the country are paid in kind, the only way in which the grain, wax, ivory and gold can be disposed of is by barter, money being very scarce in Abyssinia. Hence, if the grain collected in Tigré is required towards a contribution in Chálga, it must be exchanged for other articles marketable in that locality, and the Bishop issues instructions to his agents accordingly; or, supposing Massowah to offer a better market, the transaction is ordered to be carried on there. Abûna Salâma generally fed all the poor in the districts through which he travelled on his visitation-tours, and saw to the repair of the churches, as far as the means at his disposal would allow. It is quite true that he lent money to a number of distressed Europeans, but it is equally true that he never charged interest on such loans; moreover, some of those whom he had befriended in that way finally left the country without repaying him, and never sent any remittance afterwards, in liquidation of their pecuniary obligation to him. While we were at Mágdala, the late prelate supplied many a needy prisoner with money, and clothed a number of widows and orphans. Towards the last, however, he became so poor himself—the King having deprived him of all his resources—that he was obliged to apply to me for the cash which he had asked me to remit to Aden on his account. At the outset he was strongly prejudiced against Samuel, regarding him as a "dangerous man," whom it would be sheer madness to trust; but, on further acquaintance with him, he began to suspect that he had done the man an injustice by listening to the slanders of those who were envious of his position and influence. Eventually, the two became bosom friends; during his illness the Bishop always sent for Samuel to keep him company, and when the unfortunate prelate breathed his last, Samuel was sitting by his side.

Before his death, the Abûna begged to see Dr. Blanc, hoping that the skill of an English medical man might benefit him. The Commandant and all the members of the Council accordingly came to me in a body to ask whether I would allow the Doctor to visit the Father of their Church. My belief is that they would have been glad had I refused, and they perhaps thought that I should do so on the score of the distance—the Abûna's house was about four hundred yards from ours—which Blanc would have to traverse, in chains.

However, as my companion expressed his readiness to undertake the task, I told the Chiefs that he would walk over and see the patient. Thereupon they retired beyond our inclosure, and after discussing the grave responsibility of permitting a meeting between the Bishop and any of our party, contrary to the express orders of the King, they returned to say that they must decline acceding to the solicitations of their Metropolitan; they agreed, however, to allow the royal native practitioner to consult Dr. Blanc about his disease, and to act upon his advice. After this, the poor man began to sink gradually, and died on the 25th of October of general debility, brought on by vexation and anxiety. He appointed me his executor before he expired, and I promised to do my best in that capacity, provided the duty involved no reference whatever to the King; but as the latter had already appropriated all the poor man's property, my office as executor was little more than nominal.

While we were at Mágdala together, the Abûna wished very much to see me, and some of our night-guards offered to bring him to me by stealth; but I declined the proposal as often as it was made, judging that it would be indiscreet to imperil our common safety for the sake of a short interview, however gratifying the meeting might have been to both parties. The King, there can be no doubt, would have gone almost mad with rage had it come to his knowledge that we had ever met. With respect to the Bishop's quarrel with Theodore, all that can be fairly urged against the former is, that he stood up in defence of what he conceived to be the rights of the Church; and that, as the spiritual head over all the Abyssinians, the Sovereign included, he deemed it his bounden duty to remonstrate with his Majesty, whenever he knew him to be guilty of treachery or cruelty. On the King's approach to Mágdala, I sent and begged him to say nothing which might irritate his Majesty's peevish temper, and to do all in his power to conciliate him. His reply was, "My son, I am ready to do all that you may require of me in this matter; I will even carry a stone on my neck, and, bearing that token of humiliation, will kneel and kiss the ground before the King. But it will be of no use: the man is going from bad to worse, and is beyond recovery."

My friendship with the Mágdala authorities increased from day to day, until there was nothing that they would not have done for my comfort and that of my fellow-captives, provided they could do it with immunity. Râs Kidâna Máryam spontaneously undertook to make an alteration in my chains, by substituting a ring in the centre of its length, instead of one of the links, thinking that thereby I should be able to walk more easily. I objected to the proposal, on the ground that if carried out it might displease the King. The Râs, who was then in my room with all the other members of Council, immediately replied: "Mr. Rassam, if we thought that the change suggested would offend his Majesty, you may rest assured we should not have dared to make it; therefore, you must let us follow our own bent in this matter." When the new rings were made, I found that they were twice as heavy as the old links, which I consequently begged to be allowed to retain. They were afterwards made lighter however, and weighed just half a pound less than the original links, and as they also increased the length of the chain four inches, I was able to take a longer stride in walking. I then begged that a similar change might be effected in Dr. Blanc and Lieutenant Prideaux's fetters, hoping that eventually the remainder of our fellow-captives might share in the boon. At first, the Chiefs promised to do all they could to accede to the request, but after meeting in council three times to discuss the matter, they came to the conclusion that by granting the same concession to my companions they might incur the King's displeasure, with the additional risk that his Majesty might order their chains to be made more unbearable than they were before. It was discovered afterwards that the Chiefs had not acted wholly on their own responsibility in this instance, the King having sent them express instructions to render my imprisonment as light as possible in every respect. It was owing to a similar order that I was allowed to have a separate room, and was not to be guarded at night, like my fellow-captives, who were all condemned to sleep in one apartment, and to be strictly watched. Fortunately, the Chiefs were well-disposed from the outset, and did what they could to alleviate the restrictions imposed upon my fellow-captives. They felt that they might stretch a point in favour of Dr. Blanc and Lieutenant Prideaux, who were my associates in the Mission, while I was regarded as the King's "friend;" but with respect to the other captives, who had formerly been lodged in the common jail, and were generally called the "enemies of Theodore," they felt bound to keep up a certain show of enforcing the prison discipline of the fortress. With the exception of a few months, therefore, before the end of our captivity, when the Chiefs became somewhat more venturesome, and allowed me to build a separate apartment for Consul Cameron and another for Mr. Stern, which they were permitted to occupy without a watch being set over them, those two gentlemen, together with Mr. Rosenthal, were obliged to live in one room day and night, under a guard. Prior to that, the Chiefs had given their consent to my erecting a couple of huts for Mr. Kerans and Signor Pietro;

but these they were only allowed to inhabit during the day, and were compelled to sleep in the kitchen, where they were watched by a guard. To my repeated solicitations that this restriction might be removed, I received one and the same answer—that it was impossible. Eventually, Mr. Rosenthal also was allowed to live with his wife in a separate hut, without being watched during the night; but when the King came to Mágdala, he ordered us all, without any exception, to be guarded in our rooms at night-time. The order was soon rescinded as regards myself and the members of the Mission; but thereafter Messrs. Stern, Rosenthal and Pietro had to sleep in one room, with a guard. Consul Cameron and Mr. Kerans would also have been obliged to share it with them had not the Chiefs, on my representation that the Consul was unwell and required some one to be near him, allowed them to occupy their own huts, which were to be watched on the outside only during the night.

No officials in the world can surpass the Abyssinians in red-tapism and punctilious adherence to routine. Shortly after our incarceration I instructed Samuel to assist my fellow-captives generally in all their requirements, and authorized him to use my name whenever he had to refer to the Chiefs on their behalf. Nevertheless, on every such occasion, they insisted on his stating positively whether he was sent by me, alleging that on no other ground could they justify their compliance with his requests, in the event of question by the King. One day Samuel fell into dire disgrace for asking their sanction to build an extra hut, without having previously received express directions from me to that effect. My apology in his defence—that I had empowered him to ask for what was necessary—was of no avail; thenceforward, the Chiefs refused to listen to his applications, unless he was attended by one of my interpreters.

Having already related how our respective quarters were allotted, I shall proceed to describe what mine was when first made over to me. It was a round hut—more like a barn than a dwelling—twelve feet in diameter, constructed of branches of trees, with a straw roofing, and was still being used as a kitchen by two native families on our arrival at Mágdala. As the fire-places were in the centre of the room, and there was no other vent for the smoke but through the crevices of the walls, the whole interior was begrimed with soot. The floor had never been levelled, and was furrowed here and there to make stands for water-jars. In fact, every part of the place was wretched and filthy in the extreme. One of my first cares was to make my prison-house tidy. Then, in order to get rid of the dust and soot which fell from the thatch whenever there was a strong breeze, I caused the old roof to be replaced by a new one, in which work the Abyssinian soldiers, who were always ready to assist the humblest prisoners, lent me a helping hand. Eventually, I had the whole structure pulled down, and a better room erected on the site, which I continued to occupy until the arrival of the British force. There was one great inconvenience, however, beyond effectual remedy. The ground where our general quarters were located was so low and soft, that when the rains began the water oozed through the floor in all directions, despite all my efforts to divert it by having trenches dug round all the huts, and the inclosure well drained. The floor of my room, in particular, was always as yielding as mud, although I took the precaution of having it laid with rubble; and the water which collected in the trenches made to convey it to the main drain occasionally flowed day and night, as if issuing from a spring.

I was not successful, however, in my efforts to keep the general inclosure clean, which was invariably so filthy that the Chiefs frequently complained to me of the state in which it was allowed to remain. At first, I undertook the office of sanitary inspector myself, but was obliged to relinquish it on Samuel's representation that it would lower me in the estimation of the natives. I then appointed the interpreters to see that the public walks were swept, and kept clear of all nuisances. But the opposition which they encountered neutralized all their efforts. Next, I tried the doorkeepers, who were charged to insist that all rubbish should be carried to the edge of the plateau and thrown over the precipice; but the arrangement gave rise to so many squabbles that I finally commissioned Aito Samuel to try his hand at the duty. He was eminently successful at the outset, by dint of an indiscriminate use of the whip, but on my strictly forbidding any such treatment of a female he resigned the task, saying, " How can I effect what you wish, when you will not allow me, after our own custom, to flog the women, who are as obstinate as mules, to make them do their work properly?" I never allowed a domestic of mine to have a hut within the inclosure of my house, or any Abyssinian male or female servants to stay there. Whenever the latter were employed on any special work during the day, I insisted on their quitting the premises at night. My Indian servants slept in the kitchen, as it was unadvisable that they should sleep beyond the inclosure, where they might have got into some affray with the natives.

The annexed plan, in conjunction with the subjoined refer-

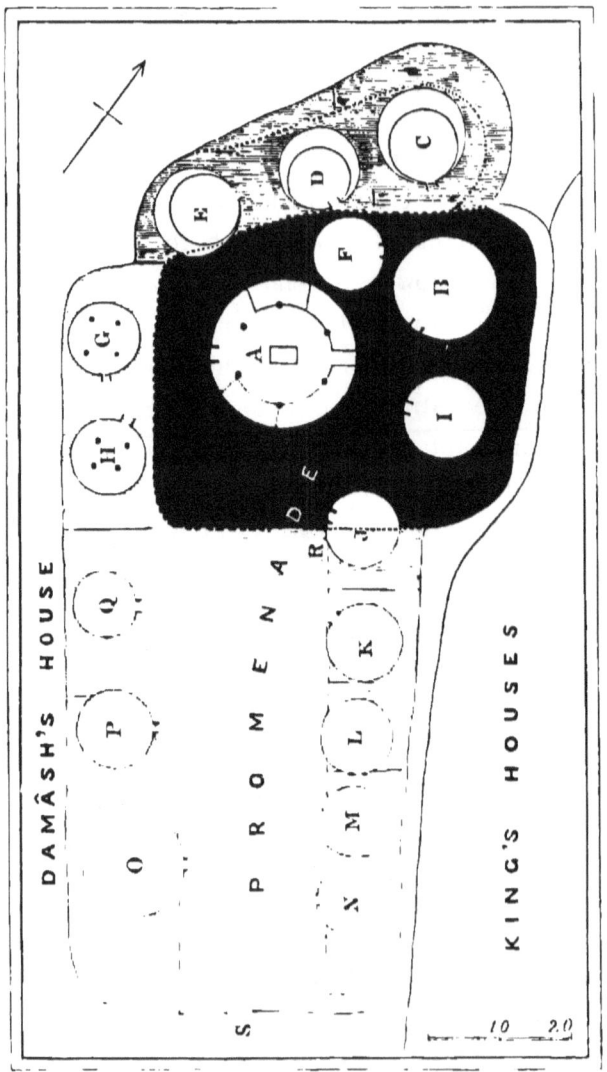

DESCRIPTION OF PLAN.

Darkest Ground. Formerly Râs I ngâdâ's residence. This was the first locality allotted to the captives. It then comprised huts A and B only. The surrounding fence was removed when the *lighter ground* was attached; as was also the fence round C, D, E.

Lighter Ground. Belonged to Fit-awrâri Gabriē. Allotted by Theodore to Mr. Rassam and his servants, and Alto Samuel. The double outline of the three huts, C, D, E, shows the original size and subsequent enlargement.

Lightest Ground. Additional space eventually granted by the Mágdala Chiefs for the accommodation of the captives.

ences, shows the location of the captives, and the different changes which were made in their respective quarters from time to time, from our first arrival at Mágdala until our liberation.

As regards furniture, the members of the Mission had, luckily, lost nothing necessary to comfort. We had our own bedsteads, bedding, chairs and tables, and the King had provided us with carpets; but the old captives, who had been bereft of everything, were in a far less enviable plight in that respect. Even they, however, had it in their power to make themselves comfortable. As to food, all fared alike: all were well supplied with what the country afforded, and enjoyed a privilege above the natives of the place generally, for on several occasions, when certain articles were scarce in the market, the Chiefs directed that we should share what was procurable with the purveyors for the royal household. We made our own bread, always used table-cloths, and sometimes napkins, and never sat down to dinner, barring the first few days after our arrival, without beginning with soup,

DISTRIBUTION OF HUTS.

A. Kitchen.
B. Occupied by all the captives for a week; then by Messrs. Cameron, Stern and Rosenthal; then by the latter alone. Finally by Messrs. Staiger, Brandeis, Schiller, Esseller and Macnairc, when Mr. Rosenthal removed to D.
C. Mr. Rassam.
D. Occupied first by Samuel; then by the Interpreters; lastly by Mr. and Mrs. Rosenthal.
E. Dr. Blanc and Lieut. Prideaux.
F. Samuel's official room.
G. Samuel's *Ijing*, or Female Establishment.
H. Samuel's reception-room.
I. Mr. Stern.
J. Consul Cameron.
K. Mr. Kerans.
L. Signor Pietro. Here Theodore's remains were deposited until interred on 14th April, 1868.
M. Consul Cameron's servants.
N. Messrs. Stern and Rosenthal's servants.
O.⎫ Dr. Blanc and Lieut. Prideaux's
P.⎭ servants.
Q. Guard-room.
R. Entrance of the first locality.
S. Entrance of the enlarged inclosure.

The black dots in A, G, H, represent the wooden pillars supporting the roofs of the huts.

which was occasionally followed by fish; then two or four *entrées*, then a joint, then a pudding or tart, winding up with anchovy-toast, or cream-cheese — the latter made by our Indian servants. In fact, a millionnaire could not have lived better than we did, under similar circumstances. My two associates in the Mission, Consul Cameron, Mr. Stern and I boarded together till the beginning of 1867, when Mr. Cameron and Dr. Blanc preferred messing each in his own hut. Lieut. Prideaux, Mr. Stern and I shared the same table until we were liberated. As to pecuniary and other means of living, we were much on a par, with the exception of those whom I had to support on the public account, as distressed Europeans. Whenever funds reached me from the coast, or by any other route, the amount was divided according to the requirements of each.

Not one of the captives can justly complain that his imprisonment, during my time, was aggravated by privations. It is true that we were fettered, to our no small discomfort; but our worst trials consisted in mental anxiety, protracted for nearly two years; in the ever-present consciousness that our lives hung upon a thread; that a mere caprice on the part of the ruthless despot who held us in his grasp might lead him to order us to be mutilated, or to be hurled headlong from that fatal precipice, where hundreds as innocent as we were had met an untimely end. These fears were shared alike by all, and mine, I need hardly say, were intensified by a weight of responsibility which at times quite overpowered me.

The task of entertaining public guests, whose interest it was desirable to secure for the common benefit of all the captives, was undertaken by Samuel, to whom I had intrusted it since our first arrival at the Court of Theodore. Being a native of the country, and holding a recognised position with the King, Samuel was the fittest person available to discharge the important functions which such hospitality involved in our case. My personal assistance in that respect was chiefly limited to receiving visitors, in which occupation I was often engaged for six hours at a stretch, and few can conceive how irksome the duty was. As a rule, I offered every guest a cup of coffee, and one or two small glasses of arrack—when I had a supply of the latter on hand; but *téj* I never allowed to be brought into my room until towards the end of 1867, when I was advised to give it to my Abyssinian visitors, in order to cultivate a closer intimacy with them. The first time I permitted it to be introduced was when an attack on Mágdala was threatened by several rebel Chiefs, at which juncture the local authorities used to assemble in my house to discuss the matter among themselves, and to settle certain disputes which had arisen between some of the inferior Chiefs. It was a time when policy demanded that I should humour them as much as possible; for our prospects then, for good or for evil, depended in a great measure on the part they might take for or against us. This course was fully appreciated by my associates in the Mission, for on one occasion when our funds were very low, I consulted them about stopping the allowance to Samuel to provide *téj* for public guests, and we unanimously agreed that it would be most unwise to make the retrenchment. Painful as was my captivity in Mágdala, it would have been intolerable but for the society of genial companions. Dr. Blanc and Mr. Prideaux were always at hand and ready to coöperate towards the common welfare of our little community, especially in times of difficulty and danger. The Rev. Messrs. Stern and Rosenthal, as well as other of my fellow-captives, were never backward to contribute to the same end. Mr. Waldmeier, also, one of the most favoured of the King's European artisans, did us many a good turn. On our departure from Debra Tâbor for Mágdala, Theodore sent to inform me that if we wished to leave anything behind, Mr. Waldmeier would take charge of it, and that he had further directed that gentleman to act as my agent, after we reached the fortress. I accordingly availed myself of the King's offer, and Mr. Waldmeier frequently obtained money for us from his friends at Gáffat, against bills drawn on Europe, procured for us other necessary supplies, aided our messengers, and did all in his power to serve us until he and his fellow-artisans fell under the royal displeasure, in the beginning of 1867. On one occasion when the King heard that Mr. Waldmeier was sending me five hundred dollars—it was at a time when the roads to the fortress were unsafe—his Majesty took the money and sent me an order for the amount on the Mágdala Treasury. I have much pleasure in bearing my grateful testimony also to Mr. Flad's unwearied exertions in our behalf, and especially for having kept me informed, even at the risk of his life, of the King's movements—intelligence which often pointed the clue what measures should be taken for the common safety. Isolated as we were from all other sources of aid from without, such cordial sympathy was like a silver lining to the dark cloud which perpetually hung over our prison-house at Mágdala.

My evening visitors were for the most part ladies, the wives either of the local magnates, or of the attainted political Chiefs, who came to me from the native prison with news of their husbands. They were not over clean, so that it was no great pleasure to sit near them; but their sweet voices—Abyssinian ladies of rank are remarkable for softness of speech—and kindly sympathy alleviated my otherwise wearisome existence. They never entered the room without glancing at my fetters, and breathing a sigh of condolence; whilst the wives of the political prisoners encouraged me to bear my lot with fortitude, and not to forget the mercy of God, who had implanted an extraordinary affection for me in the breast of their Sovereign—a man bereft of every other trace of humanity. "Except that you are fettered," they would say, "your imprisonment, and that of your brother captives, is bliss compared with what our husbands have to endure; for if, in addition to your fetters, you were encumbered as they are with hand-chains fastened to your feet, life would be intolerable to you. Ask your brothers who were incarcerated in the native prison before you came, and they will tell you the difference between their circumstances now and what they were then." A photographic album which I had with me was a source of great interest to these lady-visitors. They often sent for it on their return home, in order to show it to their friends, and it was sometimes retained for a fortnight together. I always lent it on condition that the portraits were not to be touched, and that those who undertook to exhibit them should previously wash their hands. These injunctions must have been obeyed most scrupulously; for although the book was externally the worse for wear, not one of the portraits was soiled. While at Mágdala I received the *carte* of a lady-friend of mine in England, and as soon as the fact became known the new "picture" was in great request on all sides. Concluding that it was a portrait either of my wife or my betrothed, these simple, good-hearted souls shed many a tear over it, and kissing it would say, "Oh, did you not weep when you heard that Mr. Rassam was in chains? May the Lord comfort you!" Even the Chiefs were so fond of looking at this portrait that, to be rid of their importunity, I eventually fixed it to a pillar in my room.

A plentiful downpour in the monsoon suffices to provide the garrison of Mágdala with water the whole year round; but as very little rain fell during the last two years of our captivity, the inhabitants generally suffered from drought. A hollow near the common jail, which used to be well replenished at the rainy season, and which served to supply the royal household throughout the summer with sufficient water for culinary purposes, as well as for making mead and beer, was nearly dry towards the end of 1867. Water is more abundant in the adjoining plateau of Salámgê, where there are two perennial streamlets, whenever the monsoon rains fall copiously. These also ceased to flow about the same time, and the wells had to be deepened before a supply could be obtained from them. The wells connected with the Mission stabling, which was situated below a cliff about twenty feet high, were considered the best in Salámgê. The stables were eventually appropriated by the King, and converted into a jail, and this locality was the scene of that general slaughter of the native prisoners which took place on the 9th of April, 1868, by order of the inhuman monarch. Most of the victims, on being thrown over the ledge of rock, fell first into our wells, from whence they were barbarously dragged by the soldiers, and then hurled down a much steeper precipice.

The soil and climate of Mágdala are favourable to vegetation; but the great drawback is scarcity of water for irrigation during the hot season. Soon after our arrival there, I obtained a few tomato shoots from an Egyptian in the King's service, and planted them in front of my hut. In the course of a month they grew up like a vine; in a few weeks more they formed an arbour large enough to shelter half-a-dozen persons, and, eventually, the luxuriant tendrils covered the entire frontage of the room. The most extraordinary feature was, that they bore fruit all the year round, which enabled us to indulge in the luxury of tomato soup and cutlets. Subsequently, I sowed a quantity of the seed, and distributed the plants among the natives of the place. These thrived so well that just before the invading British force reached Mágdala, tomatoes were so abundant that we did not know how to dispose of them. One of the plants measured eighteen feet and a half in length.

Green peas sprung up in front of my house eight feet five inches high. Potatoes also throve well; the beet and long radish were rather hard; the turnip-radish grew too fast, and became spongy a fortnight after the seed was sown. Almost all herbs flourished, as also several kinds of lettuce; French beans succeeded better than any other vegetable. As I fully expected, when we were sent to Mágdala, that we should remain there some time, I wrote to Colonel Merewether at Aden for a supply of seeds, smiling to myself as I did so at the idea which the request might convey—that I intended to make the place my abode for an indefinite period. However, I was not deterred by any such reflection, knowing that if we did not use the seeds ourselves, we might leave them behind us for the benefit of the country. The seeds came to hand in due course, and were sown; and not only did we eat of the produce, but obtained fresh seeds from them, which we should have sown in turn, and again have partaken of the fruit, had not the scarcity of water discouraged the attempt.

One of my greatest sources of amusement, and one which afforded me real pleasure during our captivity, was to keep open house for the beautiful little birds to be found at Mágdala. A few casual visitors at the outset, venturing up to the door in quest of crumbs, were induced by a scattering of *téf* grain to repeat the call, bringing companions with them of several other species. The entertainment provided for them was so much appreciated, that in less than a month there were from fifty to sixty of these pretty creatures, of various hues and colours, warbling in my arbour all day long. They generally came to feed in batches, and as one party left it was succeeded by another, beginning at sunrise and ending at sunset, when all sped away to their respective roosts. How I envied their freedom! The ungrateful little things deserted me at harvest time, when they found abundant provision elsewhere; but, as water at Mágdala became scarce, they recommenced their calls, evidently in search of it. I accordingly had a trough made for them, and in less than a week the drinking far outnumbered my eating guests, and among the former were several new species that fed on flies and insects, none of which had visited me before. They seemed to enjoy bathing even more than drinking, for on a hot day there was quite a scuffle among them which should have the first dip. The Abyssinians, who have a strong prejudice against washing themselves, used to be highly amused at the scene, and I generally took the opportunity of suggesting that the example was one which they might imitate with advantage. Among the birds were two handsome species which changed their plumage at different seasons of the year, the feathers assuming a variety of the most lovely hues during the transition—I counted as many as eight just as the change began. Another of my visitors, not larger than a goldfinch, was arrayed in red. These used to come in dozens, and after narrowly watching their habits for some time, I noticed a peculiar instinct in them which greatly amused me. When a male loses his mate and is on the look-out for another, he seizes a wisp of straw, or a twig, and hops about with it in his beak among the fraternity, as an indication that he is a widower in want of a consort. On one occasion, there was evidently a widow present who was similarly situated. The fact was soon apprehended by the widower, who proceeded forthwith to woo her, which he did by simply dropping the twig at her side. Her consent was unmistakeable, for she immediately joined him and both sped away on their honeymoon. As my occupations generally were duly reported to the King, my amusements also did not fail to reach his ears, and he seemed highly interested in my feathered visitors; for, whenever the couriers were charged to convey my respects to him, the first question he asked, if he chanced to be in a good humour, was, "How are Rassam's children?"—meaning my pet birds.

When I became tolerably well acquainted with the different classes of people at Mágdala, I was surprised to find that a great number of the more intelligent soldiers of the garrison were well versed in the Sacred Scriptures, knowing many passages by heart, and understanding their true import. They had accordingly abandoned the superstitious doctrines and ceremonies of their own church, and adhered simply to what they called the "Creed of the Bible," or, in other words, Protestantism. These results were due to the missionary efforts of the Rev. Mr. Stern, in 1865, when he was first sent as a prisoner to Mágdala. It appears that during his incarceration he never lost an opportunity of imparting Scripture truth to such of the guard as were willing to listen to him. The subjects of his discourses, and the texts of Holy Writ which he adduced by way of confirmation, were afterwards discussed by his hearers at their own homes, and eventually they arranged to meet together once a week, in a private house, to peruse the Scriptures, referring to Mr. Stern to explain any difficulty which arose in their minds in the course of these readings. Their champion in the fortress was Bâsha Negûsê, a devout Christian, and, by all accounts, a man who led a most exemplary life. He was shot accidentally at the storming of Mágdala on the 13th of April, 1868, as has been already stated.

The private meetings above described had been discontinued before my arrival at the Amba, but the movement was kept up by Bâsha Negûsê and several of his zealous colleagues, who used to go publicly from house to house preaching the Gospel to those who were disposed to receive it. The priests did all in their power, by threats of excommunication and other ecclesiastical penalties, to arrest the good work, but as none heeded their menaces, they eventually appealed to Râs Bisáwwir, the Commandant, to prohibit the promulgation of the doctrines of the *Franchotsh* in the fortress. The only reply they received from the bluff Chief was, that as soon as it came to his knowledge that the parties complained of taught anything contrary to the Word of God, he would certainly put a stop to their proceedings; in the mean time, however, he advised the priests to try and imitate the piety of Bâsha Negûsê, for whom he had a great regard. Of course, a considerable number of the petty Chiefs and soldiers who attended the lectures of their devout countrymen did not wholly abjure the false tenets in which they had been brought up; nevertheless, many of them so far profited by the truths inculcated that they endeavoured to lead a more moral life, and, as a first step in that direction, married their wives according to the solemn rites of the Church. In consequence of this reform, the Mágdala garrison, made up of men from all parts of the country, comprised twice the number of duly wedded couples that were to be found in any of the most populous towns of Abyssinia. I give this statement on the best native authority.

During our stay at Mágdala, no less than eight of the Mussulman servants of the Mission embraced Christianity. Of these, the only conscientious convert was 'Omar 'Ali; a love affair, or a desire to be reckoned among the members of the dominant community, were the chief motives which induced the others to abjure Islâm. Their consequent duties and privileges as proselytes to the Abyssinian Church may be summed up as follows :—The hair of their heads was shaved, and a priest besprinkled them with a few drops of water; besides which, they were allowed to wear the "Mâteb"—a cord made of blue silk, worn round the neck by Abyssinian Christians, to distinguish them from their non-Christian countrymen. They were never to address prayers to God in Arabic, or to praise Him in that language; and they were expressly forbidden to partake of meat slaughtered by Mohammedans. Of course, their conversion necessitated a change of name: 'Omar was turned into Guargis—George; Mohammed into Gabra-Yasûs—the Man of Jesus; 'Ali into Wald-Salassé—the Child of the Trinity; 'Amir into Wald-Máryam—the Child of Mary; and so forth. As the Abyssinians, however, never call a man simply George, or Peter, or John, without the prefix "Wald" or "Gabra," Samuel's insistance that 'Omar-'Ali should be baptized "Guargis," and not "Wald-Guargis," gave rise to considerable discussion. The Chiefs accordingly met together in my house to consult the Bible, in order to discover whether it was not a sin to call an ordinary man by the same name as a saint, which, in their opinion, was equivalent to placing saint and sinner on a par. Samuel, however, carried his point by contending that the inference would be justified if it were proposed to give 'Omar 'Ali the name of " Saint George "—although it was quite possible, he argued, that the convert might hereafter attain to that dignity. Most of the proselytes having expressed a wish to receive Christian instruction, the Rev. Mr. Stern appointed certain days in the week to catechize them.

Divine Service, according to the ritual of the English Church, was celebrated in my room every Sunday during our captivity at Mágdala, by the Rev. Mr. Stern, one or two Sundays only excepted, when that gentleman was too ill to officiate. The Abyssinians always behaved with decorum, and never interrupted us while we were at prayers. On more than one occasion, royal couriers arrived with messages from the King, while we were so engaged, but they waited at Samuel's house until the conclusion of the service before seeking to communicate with me.

Those who do not wish to break the continuity of the narrative may reserve perusing the succeeding chapter until they reach the conclusion of this volume.

CHAPTER XXII.

MARRIAGE AND ETIQUETTE.

Abyssinian marriages — Marriage according to the rites of the National Church — How dissolved — Infidelity of the husbands — Continence of wives married sacramentally — Theodore's canonical marriage with the daughter of Rás 'Ali — Obliges Mr. Bell to follow his example — His marriage with the daughter of Dajjáj Oobé — He gets tired of her — Marries Itamanyo, the wife of a Mussulman Galla — Itamanyo's conversion and devotion — Secondary marriages — Third-degree marriages — Native etiquette — "Girding" — The *Shámma* described — Various styles of wearing the same — Modes of Address — Etiquette in presentation — In drinking — Covering the head, an insult — Privilege of priests, monks, and nuns.

IN the foregoing narrative, occasional mention has been made of first, second, and third degree marriages—a phraseology which I have no doubt many of my readers have been at a loss fully to comprehend. The Abyssinians are a peculiar people in many respects, and, with regard to marriage, I believe their customs to be unique, and withal so closely interwoven with their social and domestic life as not to be readily understood by a foreigner. The same remark applies to the conventional formalities which prevail among them, and to which the highest importance is attached by every class of the community. As much of the subjoined information on these two subjects was acquired during my prolonged captivity, I insert it here as a sequel to our 'Life at Mágdala.'

The most binding marriage with the Abyssinians consists of an interchange of vows between the bridegroom and bride, confirmed by their jointly partaking of the holy Eucharist; in fact, the union in this case is solemnized much in the same way as in other Christian Churches. Here, however, as elsewhere, certain breaches of their mutual vows by either party dissolves the tie and renders the transgressor legally obnoxious to punishment; but as Abyssinian law in such matters has been disregarded for centuries, and Might has taken the place of Right, it follows that an offending husband generally escapes with impunity; so also does the guilty wife, if she happens to belong to the family of a powerful Chief. Hence, an unprincipled husband, when tired of his wife, finds no difficulty whatever in getting rid of her; and such repudiation is undoubtedly very common. Many cases of the kind fell under my own cognizance, and, in nearly all, the husbands were leading incontinent lives; on the other hand, I never heard of a single instance of a wife who had been sacramentally married proving unfaithful to her husband, even after his repudiation of her. Most women so situated remain single, and many become nuns. In consequence of this deplorable state of things, Abyssinian females generally entertain a great distrust of the opposite sex, and not one in twenty would willingly contract the more binding marriage. A case in point happened while I was at Mágdala. The husband was in such dread of losing his partner, knowing that as he had been united to her by the secondary marriage only—to be described anon—she might leave him any day, that her refusal to accompany him to the altar, there to partake of the Lord's Supper with him, in token of their more indissoluble union, nearly drove him mad. The matter was eventually referred to the Abúna, my intervention being also sought, and after considerable trouble we overcame the obstinacy of the lady, and induced her to consent to be sacramentally joined to her love-sick lord, in the holy estate of matrimony.

The late King Theodore—who was devout, moral and humane, by fits and starts from boyhood to the end of his career—took it into his head, after he was crowned, to lead a virtuous life, and to imitate the Christians in the East and West by uniting himself to one wife. He accordingly espoused Tôbet, the daughter of Râs 'Ali, and ratified the marriage by partaking with her of the holy Eucharist. On that occasion, moreover, he announced to the royal troops that they could not better manifest their regard for him than by following his example in this respect; but as the Abyssinians are rather stubborn in such matters, he found very few proselytes among his own subjects. It is a curious fact, that the only person he actually compelled to do as he had done was the late Mr. Bell; and, what is more extraordinary still, he obliged that gentleman to marry, not the wife who had already borne him four children, but another woman.

On the death of Tôbet, Theodore judged it politic to ally himself to the family of Dajjâj Oobê — the second greatest Chief in Abyssinia whom he had overthrown—by marrying his daughter Têru-Wark, according to the solemn rites of the Church. The Dajjâj, then a prisoner in the camp of his successful rival, was almost frantic with joy on hearing that the great Theodore had espoused the young Princess— she was only twelve years old at the time—very naturally inferring that such a union would restore him to his native province of Semên, and lead to his being re-invested with the regency over Tigrê and the northern districts. He was set at large for a short period, but when Theodore had gained his object, he made the poor old man a closer prisoner than before, and although he repeatedly promised to liberate his sons—now the King's brothers-in-law—he detained them in captivity at Magdala, where they were almost starved, nor were they released until that fortress fell into the hands of the British.

After a year, during which he was constant to his new Queen, Theodore became dissatisfied with her charms and temper, and reverted to his former practice of making any woman his wife to whom he took a fancy. He allowed no religious scruples or any other considerations whatever to interfere with the gratification of his passions in that particular. It signified little to him whether the bride elect was married or single. If the husband objected, he could easily be intimidated into compliance; if not, there were summary modes of chastising those who dared to stand in the way of the "Lord's Anointed." Still, I never heard of the late King having taken a Christian woman to wife during the lifetime of her husband; but he observed no such moderation towards Mussulmans. Itamanyo, who was his favourite Itêgê, or Empress, while I was in Abyssinia, was the wife of a Mohammedan of the Yadjow Gallas. From the accounts which reached him of her beauty, he ordered her to be brought to his Court, and prevailed on her to embrace Christianity, while the hapless husband was glad to effect his escape in order to avoid the alternative of losing his life or abjuring his creed. Itamanyo eventually became very assiduous in the performance of her religious duties, and spent much time in reciting prayers. The Abyssinians, like the Roman Catholics, use rosaries in their devotions, and, as a matter of course, the Queen adopted the same practice. This was scarcely a novelty to her, since Mohammedans generally use a similar though much longer chaplet, but without any symbol attached, called a *Músbahah*, each bead serving the devotee as a tally in his enumeration of the names and attributes of God. Being unable to find a suitable rosary, Itamanyo applied to me, through Samuel, to assist her in procuring one. I accordingly directed a native craftsman to make a string of silver beads, with a large cross of the same metal appended, and had it presented to her. According to Abyssinian canon law, no man can contract a second sacramental marriage during the lifetime of a former wife, whether she be divorced from him or not. But for this prohibition— his wife Téru-Wark being still alive—there can be no doubt that Theodore would have ratified his union with Itamanyo by wedding her according to the ritual of the Church.

In what, for want of a more appropriate designation, I call the "Secondary" or "Second-rate Marriage" among the Abyssinians, the contracting parties simply swear, in the presence of two witnesses, that they will live together as husband and wife. This bond may be dissolved at any time by mutual consent; in that case, the wife is entitled to retain whatever property she possessed before wedlock, as also any presents which she may have received from her husband during coverture, unless a stipulation to the contrary was agreed to by both sides, on their union. Most Abyssinian marriages are of this sort, and the generality of the respectable classes so wedded live together as husband and wife until separated by death, few only among them reverting to the subordinate or third-degree marriage.

This last is little better than concubinage. The contracting parties merely engage to cohabit during pleasure, and while so living are regarded as husband and wife. The children of such unions, however, have an equal right of inheritance with the offspring of first- and second-rate marriages. The national Church, indeed, recognizes only the first as valid; but the laity as a rule set all ecclesiastical law in such matters at defiance. Hence, a wealthy Abyssinian Christian, who is debarred by the two higher degrees of wedlock from having more than one wife, may nevertheless have as many third-rate wives as he pleases, and cohabit with them simultaneously. In the course of my inquiries into these matrimonial customs, and the laws affecting inheritances among this peculiar people, I applied to the Abûna to aid me in the research. His reply was, "My son, you have asked me questions which I am unable to answer. This only I can tell you; Abyssinian marriages, with few exceptions, are so abominably revolting that the issue are all bastards."

With respect to etiquette—the remaining subject to be treated of in this short chapter—the Abyssinians are most punctilious. In fact, their adherence to conventional formalities is extreme, and may be regarded as the offspring of that admixture of barbarism and civilization which characterizes their social, religious, and political economy. It is confined to no class, and pervades all the relations of private and public life. The style in which a superior should address an inferior, and *vice versâ*, is with them a point of the highest importance; so much so, that the meanest peasant will stand upon his dignity in that particular. In rank, the King of course occupies the highest place; next in order is the Abûna, or Metropolitan; but both claim to be addressed in the third person plural, which is the highest formula. When speaking to each other, however, the Sovereign assumes the subordinate position of "son" towards the Prelate "father." The latter also addresses the former in the second person singular; whereas the King is bound to address the head of the Church as "they." Further, according to the letter of the ceremonial law, the Sovereign should *gird* himself in the presence of the Abûna—a token of deference which the latter is not expected to imitate. Whether this arises from the fact that the Metropolitans, being always Copts from Egypt, never adopt the Abyssinian costume and consequently do not wear the loose native outer robe, I am unable to say with certainty. When the King and the Abûna enter the same room, the former may not be seated before the latter. Nevertheless, in all such observances, Theodore followed his own inclinations, and treated the Bishop accordingly. If in a good humour, he even condescended to kneel and kiss the Prelate's feet, in recognition of his "sonship" to the spiritual "father" of his people; but if his temper happened to be ruffled at the time, he would exclaim, "Who is his father? If he is a Bishop, he is a Turk notwithstanding; whereas I am the offspring of David and Solomon, and, withal, his Sovereign."

Before proceeding further with this subject, I must explain what is meant by "girding." It refers to the different modes in which the native outer robe is worn, and involves niceties of etiquette far surpassing any connected with the ordinary salutations in vogue, either in the East or West. The robe, which is called a "Shámma," is common to all classes—the texture of course differing according to the means of the wearer. It is a long sheet of cotton cloth, doubled, of native manufacture, with a broad red stripe crossing the width at one end a short distance from the extremity. The size varies: one in my possession measures 30 × 2 yards. Thrown over the back, keeping the red stripe on the right side while the other end is first brought over the left, then thrown over the right shoulder, under the striped end, which is next cast over the left shoulder, so as to exhibit the coloured stripe falling perpendicularly down that side, from the shoulder to the foot—such is the highest style of wearing this vestment, and one so clad, who is not obliged to re-arrange it in deference to another person, is regarded as the superior of all present on the occasion. If, in addition to these lappings and over-lappings, the wearer can manage to muffle his chin, mouth and nose in the folds, he thereby adds to his consequence. Wearing the *Shámma* as above, but with the red stripes downwards, like the hem of a skirt, is also reckoned as dignified as the style just described. When two persons of equal rank meet, they move the corner of the robe from off the left shoulder with the concealed hand, and then replace it as it was before. This, however, is not called "girding," but "dressing." When one so clad meets a superior, to whom he is bound to pay homage — whether in passing him, giving him a message, or taking leave of him—he must move the red stripe from off his left shoulder and arrange the folds so as to exhibit it stretching in a horizontal line from shoulder to shoulder. This is reckoned the highest degree of "girding."

The next in order, which is styled "girding at ease," because it simply indicates respect without obsequiousness or humiliation, consists in withdrawing the right arm and shoulder from under the robe. Theodore conferred upon all his European employés and artisans the privilege of appearing before him so girt; and on three different occasions, when his Majesty wished to make himself particularly gracious, he received me with his right arm uncovered—a condescension which he had never before manifested to any foreign official. Servants waiting on their masters, while on a journey or at a grand feast, when strict ceremony is dispensed with, or petty Chiefs in attendance upon their leader —other than the Sovereign—may also adopt this style.

Winding half the robe round the waist, tying it in front, and then throwing the other end over the right and left shoulders, so as to cover the body, and yet show the girding, is the third mode of wearing the *shámma*, and denotes inferiority.

The lowest style is accomplished by taking the robe from the shoulders, winding it round the waist, tying it in a knot in front, and then tucking the ends within the girding. Every subject in the country, from the heir-apparent to the throne down to the lowest peasant, is bound to appear before the Sovereign "girded" in this manner. Moreover, throughout the length and breadth of the land, whenever a royal letter is read, or a royal message publicly proclaimed, all present must listen to the announcement standing, with the *shámma* worn as just described. Before I was consigned to Mágdala, no Abyssinian from a Rás downwards could appear before me otherwise than in the same guise. My repeated attempts to induce visitors and others to dispense with the ceremony were always met with the objection, that it might cost the defaulter his life to disregard the Sovereign's order in that respect. On our way to Mágdala, as prisoners, whenever I addressed Bitwáddad Tadla, the Chief of the guard, he threw the robe off the left shoulder and exposed his right arm; but, on reaching the fortress, all the members of the Council, with the exception of Damásh, used to appear before me muffled up to the nose, regarding themselves as my warders. After a while, however, they took to moving the end of the *shámma*, bowing at the same time; all the inferior Chiefs adopted the lowest style, and Damásh, who vied with his master in his civility towards me, always bared his right arm. When Theodore reached A'rogê, on the 20th of March, 1868, he asked the Mágdala Chiefs whether it was true that they had muffled themselves in my presence. Fearing to tell the truth, Damâsh replied for his colleagues that they had all used the third style in their intercourse with me; whereupon his Majesty abused them roundly for not having paid me greater respect than he did, since even he had always received me with his right arm bared. Poor Damâsh, being in bad odour at the time, came in for the largest share of the royal vituperation, whereas he was the only member of the Council who had treated me with the higher tokens of deference. On dismissing them, Theodore bade them go forthwith and inquire, as from him, how his "friend, Mr. Rassam," fared; adding, "I shall find out how you visit him in future."

Next in importance to girding the *shámma* comes the mode of address between equals, and between superiors and inferiors. In the former case, it is optional with the parties to address one another in the second or third person singular; but the latter is considered more polite, even amongst domestic servants and peasants. In such cases, however, a man venerable from age will address his juniors in the second person; whereas they, out of respect for his years, address him in the third. It is discretionary with a superior to address a subordinate in either way, but the latter must always subjoin the third to the second personal pronoun, singular or plural, in addressing superiors. Theodore employed the honorary style towards four persons only, namely, the Metropolitan, the puppet-Emperor, Dajjâj Birro, and Aito Odisso—the latter the old Chief of Dâwunt, whow as burnt alive by the rebels in the month of July, 1867. The Metropolitan, as head of the Church, addresses all indiscriminately, not excepting the Sovereign, in the singular number. The corresponding etiquette among ladies is not so clearly defined, and, exclusive of those belonging to the highest class such as the wives of Râses and independent Chiefs, seems to be regulated by the age as well as the rank of the parties. Of course, a domestic servant always addresses his mistress in the third person, even if she happen to be a negress; whereas she uses the second person towards him, although he may chance to be descended from a good family. The hoary head among females, however, enjoys the same privileges as it does among the other sex, in this respect. I was told that holding the position which I did in the country, the Itégé was the only personage whom I ought to address in the honorary style. The first time I was made aware of this was on hearing Samuel ask Râs Kidâna Máryam, on my behalf, how his wife was. The members of the Council, Damâsh excepted, always addressed me as an equal—in the third person singular, and, had I been able to speak Amharic, I should have been expected to reciprocate the courtesy.

An inferior, in presenting anything to a superior, should always convey it with both hands, standing the while, or rising a little from his seat; a superior, however, is bound by no rules in this respect. At my first meeting with the King, after my imprisonment, he had a cup filled with mead, of which, agreeably with the prevailing custom, he first drank a little himself, then rose slightly from his sitting posture and presented it to me with both hands—a condescension on his part which I never expected from the haughty Monarch.

An inferior may not drink out of the same cup which his superior has used, or of the vessel from which he is about to drink; but as the superior always expects that any beverage brought to him should be first tasted by the domestic presenting it, on receiving the cup he pours a little into the hands of the latter, and after he has quaffed it the master of the house disposes of the remainder. According to the etiquette which obtains among the higher classes, a fly or any other insect falling into the mead or beer renders the liquor undrinkable, and the cup has to be replenished.

Enveloping the head in one's robe, even by a superior in the presence of an inferior, is considered a gross insult. This was the charge brought by the King against M. Bardel at the trial on the 15th of March, 1866. Ladies who are obliged to go abroad during the day, either walking or riding—when, in accordance with conventional usage, they generally cover their heads—are expected, out of courtesy, to uncover on meeting a superior whom they recognize; this, however, is not obligatory. A person who has shaved his head may cover it with a kerchief or cap, which he may wear in the presence even of royalty, without a breach of etiquette. All priests are privileged to wear turbans, and monks and nuns skull-caps. In travelling, the late King Theodore allowed considerable latitude in all these conventionalities, and he went so far as to announce that he did not wish ladies, on passing him, to uncover their heads.

CHAPTER XXIII.

REBELLION AROUND MÁGDALA.

Theodore's continued courtesy — He sacks Góndar — He receives her Majesty's letter sent by Mr. Flad — Sends it to the Author requesting him to write for the English artisans to be forwarded on from Massowah — His letter to that effect — The Author's reply — Theodore repeats his request — The peasantry between Debra Tábor and Mágdala become disaffected — The Commandant of Mágdala sent in chains to Debra Tábor — The district of Bagámédér rebels — Intercourse between Mágdala and the royal camp cut off — Rumours of Theodore's having fled to Kwára — His bloodthirstiness at this time — Horrible atrocity perpetrated by a band of rebels — The outrage avenged — Theodore learns a new lesson in cruelty — Honesty and fidelity of Abyssinian servants illustrated — Native agents beyond the fortress protect the messengers of the Mission — How regular intercourse was kept up between the Mission and the coast — Scheme organised for rapid intercommunication between Mágdala and Massowah — Kindness makes friends — The devotion of Mr. Stern's native servants — Where is Theodore? — Rival candidates for the possession of Mágdala — Overtures from Ahmed, the Imam of the Wello-Gallas — Menilek the king of Shoa's futile display — The Wakshum Gebazé and his army retire on the approach of Theodore — The Wakshum's friendliness towards the British Expeditionary force.

In reply to the King's letter which reached me on the 9th of August, after our imprisonment at Mágdala, I sent him a few lines containing my personal compliments, but I also commissioned the couriers to convey similar salutations to his Majesty from my fellow-captives. This I did as a feeler; besides, I wished him to understand that we all entertained the same sentiments towards him — in fact, that our interests were identical. On the 15th of the month following, I received the subjoined polite note from him, wherein I was glad to find that, for the first time since my arrival in the country, he deigned to notice the old captives:—

(After compliments.)

"Lih's party left in a hurry, and I could not answer you by them. How have you and your brothers [Dr. Blanc and Mr. Prideaux] spent the rainy season? By the power of God, be of good cheer; I am coming to you shortly, and we will meet.

"Since we separated, a large gun has been cast for me; when it is finished I shall let you know.

"By the power of God, I shall not forsake you; so, be of good cheer. Ask Mr. Cameron, Mr. Stern, and their parties, how they have passed the rainy season."

(Without date.)

To the foregoing I replied as follows, the day after its receipt:—

"*Mágdala*, 16th *September*, 1866.
"Most Gracious Sovereign,

"I have had the honour of receiving your courteous letter by your servants, Dasta and Kasa, and I was glad to learn therefrom that your Majesty was in perfect health.

"Thank God, both my companions and I have spent the rainy season in good health, and I trust that your Majesty has passed it auspiciously. I am not a little rejoiced to find from your letter that you will soon join us here. I pray our Heavenly Father to show us the light of your countenance ere long in health and prosperity.

"I have also been greatly pleased to hear of your success in casting a large gun, and I trust that your next attempt may prove even more satisfactory to you.

"Dr. Blanc, Mr. Prideaux, Mr. Cameron and his party, and Mr. Stern and his party, beg to send your Majesty their respectful compliments."

3rd Oct.—Received the stores to-day which had been sent on for us from Matámma, and which the King forwarded in charge of Rás I'ngŭdă; in fact, it was through his Majesty's intervention that the supplies had been transmitted from the above-named place. The circumstances of the case were these:—Hearing a few days before we left Zagê that I was sending to Matámma for European stores, the King immediately sent to ask me why I had not applied to him for assistance in the matter. He accordingly directed a petty Chálga Chief to accompany my messenger to Matámma, who was also instructed to apply to Sheikh Jumä'ah to provide the requisite number of camels to convey the effects as far as Wahné, to be transported from thence to the royal camp by the subject peasantry. Before they reached the King, we had been sent to Mágdala, and the rains having in the mean time fairly set in, and the rivers become unfordable, his Majesty had caused the loads to be deposited in the Treasury until the opening of the fair season. The accompanying messenger had also a packet of letters and some newspapers. These he managed to keep concealed for two months, and delivered them to us safely, together with a sum of money which he had obtained for our use.

During the months of October and November friendly letters and bland messages passed between the King and myself. He had so often announced his advent, that we now began to regard such intimations in the same light as the hollow compliments with which he occasionally honoured us.

Hearing, towards the end of November, that certain stores had been forwarded for us from Massowah to Matámma, and knowing that it would be impossible to smuggle them through the intervening districts, I thought it best to seek the King's permission to send for them. Being also anxious to learn the fate of one of my messengers, whom I had despatched to Massowah from Zagê in May, and who was reported to have been plundered and imprisoned by the rebels near Góndar, I referred that subject also to his Majesty in the following letter, which I sent to him, together with the men who were deputed to the several duties to be carried out:—

"*Mágdala, November* 29, 1866.

"MOST GRACIOUS SOVEREIGN,

"I have the honour to inform your Majesty that I am necessitated to write to Matámma for stores, as those provisions you kindly sent me some time ago are nearly finished.

"I am sending for this purpose Garankail, with a few mules, and I beg that your Majesty will give him permission to go, and will extend to him your protection thither and back.

"I have heard with regret that Dábtcrâ Dasta, whom I had sent to Massowah a few months back, for the purpose of bringing for your Majesty some books for showing the mode of casting guns and shot, and for teaching artillery-practice, and other things, has been seized and imprisoned by the rebels while passing through Wággärä.

"As I am anxious to know the facts of the case, I am sending one of my servants to the house of Dasta, at Góndar, to inquire about him, and the things he brought with him; and I trust that your Majesty will grant him leave to proceed on his duty.

"I hope your Majesty will pardon me for the liberty I am taking in sending Hailo to convey to you this letter, and in troubling you with the above matters, as I have no one in this country, except your Majesty, on whom I can rely for assistance.

"My companions, Dr. Blanc and Mr. Prideaux, also Mr. Cameron and his party, and Mr. Stern and his party, beg to send their respectful compliments to your Majesty.

"Hoping that this letter will find you in perfect health and prosperity, I remain," &c.

When my messengers reached Debra Tábor, the King had already left for Góndar, whither he had gone to chastise a rebel who had usurped the Government there for some time. He made a sudden attack on the place, hoping to surprise the insurgents, but they had received intimation of his approach, and evacuated the place a few minutes only before the royal troops surrounded it. Their escape so exasperated the foiled Monarch that he ordered the capital to be utterly destroyed, not excepting the churches. No resistance was offered: even the priests, who allowed themselves to be made prisoners, professed to be satisfied with the King's flimsy promise that he would build better churches for them. Under ordinary circumstances, the native clergy would have preached a crusade against a Sovereign who had been guilty of such an outrage upon their religion, and have had him killed or deposed; but the mighty Theodore had effectually broken the haughtiest spirits in the country, and none dared to utter a word or move a finger even in deprecation of his violence.

On his return to Debra Tábor, he received my messengers well, and told them that he had laid Góndar in ruins because its inhabitants had betrayed my courier to the rebels. As to the stores, it was his duty, he said, to see that all my wants were provided for; consequently, only one of my people was to proceed to Matámma with the instructions to my agent; the remainder were to return to me, and the mules also, and he would undertake to have the stores forwarded from Matámma to Mágdala by his own subjects.

Before my messengers left Debra Tábor the King received a communication from Mr. Flad, who had reached Massowah from England, transmitting to him the following copy of her Majesty's letter, of which he was the bearer:—

"VICTORIA, by the grace of God, &c., to Theodore, King of Abyssinia, sendeth greeting.

"Relying on the assurances contained in your Majesty's letter of the 29th of January, which duly reached us, we were in daily expectation of the arrival in England of our servant Hassam, together with our servant Cameron, and the other Europeans, so long detained in your country, but whom your Majesty had announced that you had sent with our servant Rassam. When Flad arrived bringing your Majesty's further letter of the 17th of April, in which, while repeating that you had released and made over to our servant Rassam, our servant Cameron, and the other Europeans, in order that they might leave the country, you stated that you had kept our servant Rassam for the sake of consulting together upon the extension of the friendship between us. We will not disguise from your Majesty that we found it difficult to reconcile your assurances with the obstacles which were still opposed to the departure of our servants and the other Europeans from your country; but we were willing to accept the desire expressed by you for the extension of friendship between us, and we accordingly admitted Flad to our presence, and having heard from him your Majesty's wishes, we gave directions for the transmission to your Majesty by the hands of Flad of such articles as we understood from Flad your Majesty desired to obtain, and we also gave our sanction to the engagement in your Majesty's service of skilled workmen, such as you desired to employ in Abyssinia. These arrangements were made, and Flad was on the point of leaving England to rejoin your Majesty, when intelligence reached us that you had withdrawn from our servant Rassam the favour which you had hitherto shown him, and had consigned him, together with our servant Cameron and the other Europeans, to prison. We have received no explanations from your Majesty of the grounds of a proceeding so inconsistent with the assurances and professions formerly made by your Majesty, and we have, therefore, lost no time in allowing Flad to depart, and have given to him this letter for your Majesty, not allowing ourselves to doubt that immediately on its receipt you will redeem your promises, and give effect to your professions, by dismissing our servant Rassam, with our servant Cameron and the other Europeans, in conformity with the statement made in your letter of the 29th of January.

"Your Majesty must be aware that it is the sacred duty of Sovereigns scrupulously to fulfil engagements into which they may have entered; and that the persons of Ambassadors, such as our servant Rassam, and those by whom they are accompanied, are, among all nations assuming to be civilized, invariably held sacred. We have, therefore, the more difficulty in accounting for your Majesty's hesitation, and we invite your Majesty to prove to the world that you rightly understand your position among Sovereigns, and do not desire to neglect the international duties which it is incumbent on all Sovereigns to fulfil. Your Majesty may be assured that we shall be disposed to attribute to misapprehension on your part, rather than ill-will towards us, the delay that has occurred in the return of Rassam, and those whom you had engaged to send with him; but in the uncertainty which we cannot but feel as to your Majesty's intentions, we cannot allow Flad to be the bearer of those tokens of goodwill which we purposed that he should convey to your Majesty. But, in full confidence that the cloud which has darkened the friendship of our relations will pass away on the return of Flad, and desiring that you should as soon as possible thereafter receive the articles which we had proposed to send to your Majesty in token of our friendship, we have given orders that those articles should be forthwith sent to Massowah, to be delivered, for conveyance to your Majesty's Court, to the officers whom you may depute to conduct our servant Rassam, and our servant Cameron, and the other Europeans, so far on their way to our presence. And so we bid you heartily farewell.

"Given at our Court at Balmoral, the 4th day of October, in the year of our Lord, 1866, and in the thirtieth year of our reign.

"Your good Friend,

(The large Signet.)   (Signed)   "VICTORIA R."

(Not countersigned.)

Superscribed—
"To Our Good Friend Theodore,
 King of Abyssinia."

It was reported that the King was not displeased with this communication; but he appears to have tried, at the same time, to put a more favourable construction upon it than its tenor really warranted. However, he forwarded the copy to me by my own messenger, inclosed in the following letter from himself:—

"In the name of the Father, Son, and Holy Ghost—one God.

"From the King of kings, Theodorus. May this reach Mr. Hormuzd Rassam. How have you passed the time? I, by the power of God, am well. Ask Dr. Blanc, Mr. Prideaux, Mr. Cameron and his party, and Mr. Stern and his party, from me, how they have passed their time.

"Your servant, whom you wished me to forward to Matámma, I have sent for you. I have ordered your things to be brought to Wahné, by camels, and from thence I have ordered my people to bring them hither, by the power of God.

"Mr. Flad has returned to Massowah, and transmitted to me the inclosed letter. Peruse it, and wait till I arrive, as I am coming to you, by the power of God. I will consult with you as to the answer I shall send."

(Without date.)—Received December 28, 1866.

The receipt of her Majesty's firm yet conciliatory letter by the King, and the announcement of his intention to consult me personally on the subject, led me to hope that I might be able to persuade him to convey us to Tigré, there to negotiate for our release. The pleasing delusion was of short duration, for, a few days after, I received the following letter from his Majesty, through Râs I'ngădă, wherein he notifies his determination to retain me and my fellow-captives at Mágdala until he had secured his object, requiring me at the same time to write and request her Majesty's Government to send up the artisans:—

(After compliments.)

"Mr. Flad has written to me again, and I send you herewith the letter which he has enclosed.

"Now, in order to prove the good relationship between me and yourself, let it be shown by your writing and getting the skilful artisans and Mr. Flad to come, viâ Matámma. This will be the sign of our friendship. When you hate my enemies and love my friends, and I shall prove wanting in my friendship towards you, leave me to God [as my judge]. Even Solomon, the son of David, the great King, God's created being and slave, when he wished to build the Temple in Jerusalem, was perplexed [about finding skilful artisans]. Falling at the feet of King Hiram of Tyre, he begged him for carpenters and skilful artisans, who assisted in building the Temple. And now, when I used to fall girded at the feet of the great Queen, her nobles, peoples, and hosts, I found Mr. Stern and his party abused me and lowered me. Also, when I sent a friendly letter to the great Queen of the English, the Defender of the Faith, the succour of the needy, the friend of God, the favourite of God—Victoria, Mr. Cameron refused me an answer. Also you, Mr. Rassam, said that you were coming from the Queen, and came to me. Consenting to this, I received you in a friendly manner, and treated you to the best of my ability. When I read the letter which you brought me, which asked me to release and pardon all the Europeans whom I had hated and imprisoned, I consented, and sent and had them released at once, by the power of our Creator, before I passed the night. Before they came to me I gave them over to you, in order that the Queen and her Government might be pleased. But you, before you asked them as to the crime which they had committed, and which caused their imprisonment, and without finding whether I was wrong, in order that I might compensate them, or, if they were guilty, in order that I might obtain a favour from the Queen—before you brought them to me, you sent them away.

"I had also heard that the English and the Turks had entered into an alliance. I kept my vexation to myself and said nothing.

"Now Mr. Flad has sent me a most friendly and pleasing letter. As Solomon fell at the feet of Hiram, so I, under God, fall at the feet of the Queen, and her Government, and her friends. I wish you to get them [the skilful artisans] *viâ* Matámma, in order that they may teach me wisdom, and show me clever arts. When this is done, I shall make you glad, and send you away, by the power of God.

"Written in the year of St. Luke, on Saturday the 28th day of the month Tahsáss" [answering to January 5, 1867].

Received January 8, 1867.

To have refused the King's request in this case would have placed all our lives in jeopardy; even Mr. Waldmeier wrote to me on behalf of his Majesty's European artisans, begging me to accede to the demand for their sakes as well as our own. Moreover, I knew full well that I should be able to communicate twice or thrice with the coast before the letter which was to be sent through the King could reach its destination.

My reply was as follows:—

"Mágdala, January 7, 1867.

"MOST GRACIOUS SOVEREIGN,

"I have had the honour of receiving your Majesty's two letters: the first by my servant, Hailo, and the second by Râs Ingáda, together with a copy of my Queen's letter to you, which was forwarded to your Majesty from Massowah by Mr. Flad.

"Agreeably to your Majesty's desire, I have written to my Government about what you have communicated, and I hope that your request will be complied with. I send Mohammed Sa'id, one of my servants, with the letter, which I have given to him, open, in order that your Majesty may have it read, if you please. Allow me to return you my best thanks for your Majesty's kindness in having sent to Matámma for the stores I required, and I trust that our Heavenly Father will reward you for your acts of friendship. Dr. Blanc, Mr. Prideaux, Mr. Cameron and his party, Mr. Stern and his party, desire to present their respectful compliments to your Majesty."

I had just dispatched the foregoing, when another special courier arrived, bringing the subjoined extraordinary epistle from his Majesty, enclosing a note to my address from Colonel Merewether:—

(After compliments.)

"Mr. Flad has sent [written] to me as follows:—' I had formerly sent to you Mr. Rassam in the affairs of Cameron and his party, and we heard that you had received him with favour and with friendship. We had also consented to all the things you required, and had given them over to Mr. Flad, but after that we heard that your friendship towards him had changed; but we hope that the friendship existing between us and yourself will not be changed.'

"That is what was sent to me, and I am going to reply as follows:—'Formerly England and Ethiopia were on terms of friendship, and I also, having knowledge of this, used to love you exceedingly. But [since then] having heard that they [the English] have calumniated me to the Turks, who hate me, I said to myself, Can this be true? and I felt some misgiving in my heart. However, I trust there is no enmity between Ethiopia and the English, but that there is friendship. We do not esteem those who calumniate and hate the English; so you, for our sake, should not esteem those who calumniate and hate the people of Ethiopia. Mr. Rassam and his party, whom you sent to me, I have placed in my house, in my capital at Mágdala, and I will treat them well, until I obtain a token of your friendship.'

"I shall write the above to Mr. Flad, and I wish you also, for the sake of obtaining for me their [the English] friendship and love, to write at the same time to the proper authorities, and send the letter to me, by the power of God. It is necessary that you should send a man immediately to me, in order that he may bring Mr. Flad to me quickly."

(Without date.) - Received January 7, 1867.

Here was a batch of complaints, reproaches and solicitations, all put together, in order to induce me to write for the transmission of the artisans from Massowah. As I had anticipated, the letter which I addressed to Lord Stanley on the subject, and which had been forwarded, open, through the King, did not reach London till four months afterwards, by which time the artisans had left Massowah, on their way back to England; and, in the mean time, her Majesty's Government had been apprised by me of all that had taken place. However, I replied to the foregoing letter, on the same day, as follows:—

"*Mágdala, January* 8, 1867.

"Most Gracious Sovereign,

" I have the honour to acknowledge the receipt of your Majesty's letter of the 28th Tahsáss, which reached me this morning.

"I return you my best thanks for the letter you kindly inclosed me from Massowah. It is from Colonel Merewether, the Resident at Aden, who it appears has been intrusted with the management of what my Queen wrote to you about.

"He writes to say that he is anxiously awaiting your Majesty's reply to Mr. Flad's communication.

"I have already written regarding Mr. Flad and the articles which my Queen had ordered for your Majesty, as a token of her friendship, and that they are to be sent at once to Matámma.

"I must take this opportunity of reiterating to your Majesty my assurances that up to this time I have always deemed it my sacred duty, though in chains, to do everything towards cementing the friendship between Ethiopia and England.

"It is no little consolation to me to find, from my Queen's letter to your Majesty, how anxious she is to continue her friendship with you.

"I pray our Heavenly Father to grant that the friendship which I have been anxious to cultivate between my Queen and your Majesty will be fully established to the satisfaction of all.

"Dr. Blanc, Mr. Prideaux, Mr. Cameron and his party, also Mr. Stern and his party, beg to send their respectful compliments to your Majesty."

From the date of the above until the middle of March I received only complimentary messages from the King, but on the 19th of that month he sent me the subjoined note, together with the stores which had been brought for us from Matámma, by his orders:—

(After compliments to all.)

"Your servants have brought your things from Matámma. As I found them too bulky, I divided them into light packages in the presence of Mr. Waldmeier and his party. I now send them to you in small parcels, because I want you to receive them speedily.

"Dated 6th of the month Magábit, A.D. 1859."—(2nd March, 1867.)

Râs I'ngárlá came in charge, and the packages were brought on the shoulders of the royal troops, as most of the peasantry between Debra Tâbor and Mágdala had become disaffected since the King had commenced imprisoning the Chiefs of Bagámĕdĕr. Râs Kidâna Máryam, the Commandant of Mágdala, had been put in irons on the ostensible charge of having been in correspondence with Menilek, King of Shoa; the real fact was, that Theodore feared he might rebel on hearing that his district, Bagámĕdĕr, was being devastated by his ungrateful master. He was conveyed to Debra Tâbor to-day by Râs I'ngădă, together with Wakshum Tafâré, cousin to the Wakshum Gobazé, and two other great Chiefs of the King's creation. It was apprehended that his Majesty intended to put these men out of the way; such, however, was not the case. He had merely subjected them to the torture for a few days, in order to extort money from them, and they were sent back to Mágdala when Theodore himself approached that fortress in the beginning of the following year.

I sent the subjoined letter to his Majesty by Râs I'ngădă, thanking him for the trouble he had taken about our stores, and requesting his permission to send him some of the wearing apparel which I had received:—

"*Mágdala, 20th March,* 1867.

"Most Gracious Sovereign,

"I have had the honour of receiving your Majesty's welcome letter by Râs I'ngădă, dated the 6th of Magâbit, and I was glad to learn therefrom that you were in perfect health.

"I beg to inform your Majesty that the things you so kindly forwarded to me have reached safely. Allow me to return you my grateful thanks for your kindness in having had them brought from Matámma, and for the trouble you have taken in transmitting them hither.

"I take this opportunity of informing your Majesty that when, on a former occasion, I asked your permission to obtain a supply of eatables and drinkables from Matámma, I was not aware that anything had arrived there for me, from Massowah; but it appears that a few days before my letter reached that place, some wearing apparel had arrived for me and my companions, which was accordingly forwarded to me, together with what I had written for. Part of the former consists of a supply of calico and shirts, and as we have already more than we require of those articles, I trust your Majesty will allow me to send you ten pieces of calico and thirty shirts, for the use of your servants. I hesitate to send them by Hailo, the bearer of this letter, before obtaining your sanction, which I hope you will be pleased to accord.

"Dr. Blanc, Mr. Prideaux, Mr. Cameron and his party, and Mr. Stern and his party, beg to send your Majesty their respectful compliments. Thank God, we are all well, and I trust this letter will find you in the enjoyment of perfect health."

When I wrote for the above-named articles in May, 1866, I had intended some of the shirts and calico for the King, and as they had reached me through him, and he himself had actually seen them when they were re-packed, I could hardly do otherwise than make him the offer which I did. Being a prisoner, however, I deemed it expedient to ask his consent before sending the present. His reply, which came to hand on the 15th of April, was characteristic:—

(After compliments to all.)

"I have received your communication, and thank you for it. It is not convenient for the present that I should receive anything from you; but, by the power of God, whatever you require I will give you. I am much obliged to you [for the proffered gift]; let your servants wear the articles for me. Oh! my beloved, send to me for whatever you need, and I will supply it. Don't fear.

"What I require from my friend, the Queen, and from you, my brother, is your friendship. Not that I can say that I am rich, and am in no want of worldly goods; but, by the power of God, I am anxious that you should open my eyes, for I am a blind donkey."

Only once after this, subsequent to Mr. Flad's return from

England, was I able to correspond directly with the King through my own messengers, as the whole of Bagámĕdĕr had risen in rebellion and effectually cut off all communication with Mágdala. Dalanta and Dáwunt, in the vicinity of the fortress, remained faithful to the royal cause till July, when they were driven, under compulsion, to join the Gallas for a time. For seven weeks, Theodore was unable to hold any intercourse with Mágdala, except through secret messengers obtained from among the native prisoners and peasants. For three months, even these emissaries failed to accomplish their errands, and matters had come to such a deadlock that all kinds of conjectures were afloat as to what the upshot would be. The rumour that the King had been driven to such straits that he was obliged to take refuge in his native district, Kwára, filled all the captives with joy, and at one time there was not one amongst us who would not have wagered a hundred to one that we should never see his face again; nevertheless, we were once more doomed to disappointment. Were I to record a tithe of the exaggerated and unfounded reports which obtained temporary currency at that period, this narrative would cover many additional pages. There can be little doubt, however, that the proceedings of Theodore, during the greater part of 1867, were characterized by a savage brutality quite diabolical. His thirst for blood had attained such a pitch, that he is said to have ordered one hundred thousand head of cattle to be shot dead, between sunrise and sunset, on hearing that his soldiers, who had already plundered more cows than they knew what to do with, were selling them to the rebels for one dollar each. It appears, also, that he had learnt from the rebels a more summary way of disposing of his captured enemies, namely, by committing them to the flames. A petty insurgent of Dâwunt, near Mágdala, is stated to have been the first to perpetrate this horrible outrage, before that district revolted. The district was presided over by a Chief, named Aito Odisso, who was reputed to be upwards of a hundred years of age, and yet walked and rode with the energy of a man of fifty. I saw this venerable patriarch as we passed through Dâwunt, on our way to Mágdala, in July, 1866. He certainly did not look more than seventy years old, and yet the people assured me that he was a Chief of Dâwunt in the time of Râs Guksa, the grandfather of Râs 'Ali, that is, about eighty years ago. This man was so devoted to Theodore, that he maintained the loyalty of the district to the royal cause when the whole country around was convulsed with anarchy, and on two occasions he repulsed the rebels who appeared in the immediate neighbourhood, and utterly routed them. One rebel, however, with a party of about eighty followers, determined to get rid of the old Chief and his family. They accordingly concerted together to set his house on fire by night, and to massacre any of the inmates who attempted to run from the flames. The devilish scheme was carried out to the letter. Aito Odisso, who was the first to awake, rushed out of the burning house, and was speedily dispatched by the ruffians, who were on the look-out for him. Eight or ten members of his family were either burnt alive or speared; the remainder, including his son and heir, managed to effect their escape under cover of the darkness. The marauders then collected all the booty they could from the village, including horses, mules and cattle, and by sunrise the following morning reached that part of the Bâshilo river which divides Dalanta from Dâwunt, where, fancying themselves safe from surprise, they halted to have a feast on *brundo*.

Meanwhile, the son of the slaughtered Chief was busy at work, and swore that he would not bury his father before he had avenged him. The conflagration of the houses, and the resoundings of the war-cry during the night, brought all the Dâwunt warriors to the spot, who, on seeing the mangled corpse of their Chief, took an oath that they would not return home until they had wreaked their vengeance on his murderers. About five hundred mustered to go in pursuit, and the scouts sent in advance to reconnoitre returning with the intelligence that the band had halted near the Bâshilo, the young Chief divided his followers into two parties, one of which was placed so as to cut off the retreat of the enemy, while the other attacked them. The rebel Chief fought bravely, and, refusing to surrender himself alive, was almost hacked to pieces by the assailants; whereupon his adherents, finding themselves surrounded on all sides, laid down their arms. The corpse of their leader was then transported to the old Chief's village in Dâwunt, where it was left to rot in the fields, and about eighty of the captured prisoners were sent to the King at Debra Tâbor. So severely did Theodore feel the loss of Aito Odisso, that he is reported to have wept when he heard of his death, and kept himself secluded for a whole day. Even during the old man's lifetime, the King never exacted any taxes from the people of Dâwunt; the only burden imposed upon them was the duty of supplying the garrison at Mágdala with a tenth of the grain raised in the district. Moreover, he always addressed the hoary-headed Chief in the third person, as if speaking to a superior. The rebel prisoners underwent a fair trial, and all pleaded guilty; whereupon the King adjudged them to a death similar to that which they had devised for his dear and faithful friend. They were accordingly placed in a large hut, on the outside of which heaps of grass were piled by the executioners, who then set the whole on fire. Such was Theodore's first essay in this species of cruelty, and, finding that it was an expeditious way of dispatching those whom he styled "rebels," he thenceforward frequently adopted it. By all accounts, some hundreds of men, women and children were subsequently burnt alive by his orders.

An incident occurred on the murder of the old Chief of Dâwunt which is worthy of being recorded, as illustrative of the honesty and fidelity of Abyssinian servants. When I was sent a prisoner to Mágdala, the King instructed that Chief to act as my agent, and to assist me generally in my requirements. He also directed, that in case I wished to send mules belonging to the Mission to graze in Dâwunt, he was to supply them with forage, and also to provide quarters for the muleteers and for any servants or messengers of mine who passed through his district. On the afternoon preceding the night of the outrage, one of my trusty messengers, named Golja, reached the Chieftain's house from Gáffat, with two companions, carrying no less a sum than 1,700 dollars—nearly 400*l*.—for my fellow-captives and myself, which had been obtained from the King's European artisans against orders drawn on Europe. They were located, during the night of the attack, in a small hut just beyond the Chief's inclosure. Luckily, Golja happened to be awake when the first onset was made on the premises. Suspecting foul play, he roused his companions and hurried them out of the hut, bearing the money, and the three concealed themselves in a clump of bushes, away from the village, until the morning. When everything was quiet, they pursued their journey, and arrived at the fortress without the loss of a dollar.

During the interval that the roads between Debra Tábor and Mágdala were closed by the rebels, I occasionally employed the King's private messengers to bring letters and money from our friends at Gáffat. Though twice attacked by marauding parties, they never lost any of the parcels confided to them; in fact, the readiness of these royal couriers to serve me, and their fidelity to the trusts they undertook, are beyond all praise. Aito Samuel also had two servants, named respectively Obíshet and Dábaj, whose devotion to their master induced them to risk their lives on our behalf. Any communication from a party who feared to make it through a third person generally reached me through Obíshet, with unerring punctuality and truthfulness. As I never allowed the letters which we dispatched to the coast, or those sent up to us from Massowah, to be taken from Mágdala or to be brought there by the messengers charged with their conveyance, it was the joint duty of Obíshet and my interpreter, Dasta, to carry them about their persons until they found a safe opportunity of delivering them to the parties selected to transmit them. Dábaj, on the other hand, was the principal medium of carrying on our communications with the royal camp during these critical times, and although well known to the King's courtiers, and even to Theodore, he never hesitated to undertake my errands to Debra Tábor or elsewhere. If seized, he was instructed to say that he had been sent by me to procure funds—the only plea which was likely to save his life. Once, when not another soul would venture between Mágdala and Debra Tábor, owing to a stringent order that no stranger was to be allowed either to enter or leave the camp, he volunteered to visit Mr. Flad there, in order to obtain a supply of money for us, of which we were in the greatest need. He travelled with one of the King's private messengers, and after getting the money—about two hundred dollars—he consigned half of it to his companion, and both set out on the return journey together. On reaching the district of Gaïnt, in Bagámēdĕr, they were attacked by a party of rebels, who seized Dábaj, while the royal courier managed to escape. The latter brought us the sum which he carried, just as we had expended our last few dollars; the former was first bound by the marauders, and then lightened of his burden, with the exception of a sum of forty dollars, which he had carefully secreted in his trousers. Two of the forty dollars he gave to one of the servants in the house where he had been confined, to connive at his escape, and he eventually reached us in safety with the balance by travelling only during the night.

On finding that we were close prisoners at Mágdala, I appointed agents at different places between the coast and the fortress, and also between the Amba and the King's camp at Debra Tâbor, to protect my messengers and render them every assistance in their power. I found, also, that guides were necessary to insure the safety of the letters when they arrived near Mágdala, and I accordingly employed a number of men on that service. These guides carried the letters when I did not think it safe to trust the messengers directly, lest they should be detected. The latter acquitted themselves from beginning to end most honourably, and only on a few rare occasions did they lose any of the money confided to them.

Of all the assistance, however, which I received from the Abyssinians, none proved so valuable as the co-operation of the Chiefs of Dalanta. I'rkina, one of their number, never failed me in a single instance from the time I first employed him until we finally left Mágdala. During that interval, Dalanta changed its governor no less than six times, having been ruled alternately by the King, the Wakshum Gobazé, and the Gallas. I'rkina and his two brothers harboured my messengers and afforded them protection, whenever it was needed. Without them I could not have sent our mails regularly to the coast, nor could we have received, as we did, supplies of money from without, when the whole country was in a state of anarchy. Many a time did I'rkina retire to sleep in the most lonely spots, fearing lest the letters which he carried might be seized, in the event of his betrayal either to Theodore or to the Imâm of the Gallas. On one occasion, when five batches of messengers arrived together on the borders of Dalanta from the coast, with several sums, amounting in all to 2,000 dollars, a large party of rebels concerted to attack and plunder them. On hearing this, I'rkina mustered all the fighting-men from among his relations— seventy in number—and proceeded with them to the rendezvous, took charge of the money, and brought it intact to Mágdala.

Before the King reached the fortress I managed to maintain a regular bi-monthly communication with Massowah. So trustworthy had I found the Abyssinians, that when news reached us of the landing of the British troops, I commenced organizing intermediate stations between Mágdala and Sakôta, to serve as a more expeditious line of conveying intelligence between ourselves and the invading force. According to my calculations at the time, a letter might have been transmitted from Mágdala to the coast, and *vice versâ*, in twelve days. I had even appointed the respective station-masters—men who could read and write—and commissioned a silversmith at Mágdala to make different seals for each, with which the letters passing through their hands were to be stamped. Four men were allotted to each station, who were to travel in couples, forty miles, once a fortnight. I had nominated the couriers, and the seals were being prepared, when the King's approach was announced, and the people of Wádala—the district where the two first stations were to have been established—suddenly left their homes and fled towards Lasta. This unforeseen occurrence of course upset my scheme, but I mention these incidents to show the trustworthiness of the Abyssinians generally, and their fidelity towards their employers and those who treat them with proper consideration. Nothing, indeed, that either my fellow-captives or myself experienced at their hands would warrant us in speaking otherwise of them. If a few isolated cases to the contrary are enough to brand a whole people with dishonesty, faithlessness and ingratitude, then, forsooth, no nation is free from the stigma. It is perfectly true that I did fall in with disreputable individuals in Abyssinia, especially among the common soldiers, who regarded me as an inferior being, because I neither wore a *shámma* nor buttered my hair; but such characters were comparatively few, and many of them were afterwards won over by kindness to serve me with almost abject devotion. It should be remembered, moreover, that ours was a most anomalous position at Mágdala; we were, to all intents and purposes, "prisoners," and the soldiery regarded us as such. It is not to be wondered at, therefore, that we did not receive from them those outward tokens of deference which, under other circumstances, might have been expected. An European guard is not bound, and I believe not allowed, to salute its prisoners, whatever their rank may be; corresponding discipline prevails in the Abyssinian army, and it would be as unreasonable to inveigh against it in the one case as in the other.

I offer no apology for adducing another eminent example of the fidelity of the Abyssinians towards their employers. When the Rev. Mr. Stern was brutally beaten, and two of his native attendants were flogged to death by the King's orders, simply because they were in that gentleman's service, not one of his remaining followers deserted him; on the contrary, they stood by him to the last, though they were imprisoned, tortured, and had a yoke hung round their necks by the cruel tyrant who had shed the blood of their innocent comrades. Moreover, even when some among his own countrymen shunned the disgraced Missionary, his Abyssinian friends still clung to him, despite the risk which they incurred by their sympathy. My most ardent wish is that the poor Abyssinians could be provided with better rulers and a more stable and equitable government, for I am persuaded that in the course of a few years, under an enlightened administration, they would make rapid advances, as well in morals as in civilization generally. They are without any caste prejudices, they are observant and shrewd, fond of learning, and by no means deficient in intellectual ability; indeed, I am disposed to rank their natural powers in the latter respect as equal to those of most European races. A large portion of the educated and enlightened members of the community were sadly disappointed on finding that England's sole object in invading the country was the liberation of the captives, and that the British force would retire without taking any steps to introduce law and order among them. "We were born in bondage and must die slaves," was their desponding remark. The day after Mágdala was captured, I was asked whether it was true that we were going to abandon the wretched people, without leaving a competent governor behind to rule over them, and to lead them in the steps of other Christian nations. On my replying in the affirmative, telling them at the same time that they must learn to govern themselves, they rejoined, "You mean that we must cut each other's throats."

For a long time we were absolutely ignorant of the whereabouts of the King, or when he intended visiting Mágdala. (The march from Debra Tábor thither eventually occupied him six entire months.) During this interval, both the Wakshum Gobazé and Menilek, King of Shoa, were most anxious to obtain possession of the fortress, and with that view tried to ingratiate themselves with the Abûna, promising him immunity and honour when the power of Theodore fell into their hands. I was repeatedly asked to use my influence with the Chiefs to surrender the place to one or other of the contending parties, when the royal cause was thought to be desperate. Ahmed, the son of Mastyât, the youthful Imâm of the Wello-Gallas, also sent me a singular letter, while I was still in chains, asking me to make over Mágdala to him, promising faithfully to send me down, with all my fellow-captives, to the coast in safety. It did not seem to have occurred to Mastyât, the Imâm's mother—it was she who dictated the letter—that if I had possessed the power of giving up Mágdala to them, I should have got out of it myself. He wrote an equally absurd letter to the Bishop, telling him that if he assisted him in securing Mágdala, he, the Imâm, would protect his "idols," that is to say, the pictures and crosses used in the Abyssinian churches. Mastyât, who was acting as Regent for her son during his minority, often threatened to starve the Mágdala garrison by stopping its supplies, which she could easily have done, if the Gallas had

only supported her in the design; but they preferred their
own detestable way of revenge—lying in ambush behind trees
and rocks, whence they issued forth to kill helpless boys,
women and inoffensive priests. I believe that on the defensive the Gallas fight well, but they are contemptible as
assailants, except in harassing a hostile army by hanging
on its outskirts and cutting off stragglers.

Menilek and the Wakshum Gobazé did approach at last,
but they took care to keep at a good distance, thereby making
themselves the objects of ridicule to the Mágdala garrison,
who despised their cowardice. Menilek came first on the
30th of November, and pitched his camp on the plateau
opposite Mágdala, not less than five miles off. It was said
that he had at least 30,000 fighting men with him. One
afternoon he approached about 500 feet nearer, with about
2,000 Musketeers and some artillery; but after making a
little display of his fire-arms, he returned to his tent, and
nothing more was seen of him. He remained there three
days, and we hourly expected that he would approach and
invest the place; but he seemed to have feared an encounter
with the fierce defenders of the fortress, and instead of
coming towards us, when he moved on the 2nd of December,
1867, he returned to Shoa, on the plea that the provisions
for his troops were exhausted. The fact was, he had then
heard of the approach of Theodore, and thought it better
to decamp in time. Menilek was much liked, and would
have found many friends among the garrison, if he had been
bold enough to commence operations.

After Menilek's departure, the Wakshum Gobazé appeared
in the field, but did not come as near to Mágdala as the
King of Shoa. The movement was made just as we heard
that Theodore was approaching, and he halted about thirty

miles off, with an army computed at 30,000 fighting men.

Although the Wakshum Gobazé did not behave bravely on that occasion, he was one of our first and best friends in Abyssinia, and never failed to serve us to the best of his ability. Soon after we were sent to Mágdala he gave orders, at the Bishop's recommendation, that his officers on the road between Mágdala and the coast should assist our messengers, and protect them in case of danger. This co-operation continued until the arrival of the British army at the fortress. On one occasion, I sent to tell him that I had a large packet of documents which I was anxious to send safely to Massowah, and asked if he could help me in the matter. He immediately sent a priest to me, who took charge of the packet and conveyed it to its destination. When I heard of the landing of our troops, I sent to inform him of the fact, and asked him to assist in providing them with carriage and provisions. He accordingly caused to be proclaimed through his districts, by beat of drum, that all his subjects were to supply the British army with whatever they required, and that they were not to fear, as the troops were Christians, and would pay the full price for everything. He said he was sorry that he could not wait to receive the army himself, as he had engaged to go and settle the governments of Bagámědĕr and the other districts round the Lake of Dámtča, and could not delay any longer, on account of the rainy season, which was then fast approaching.

Since our seizure at Zagé, on the 13th of April, 1866, when we judged it prudent to destroy all our papers, I abstained from keeping a regular journal, lest by some mishap it might fall into Theodore's hands. Hence, many portions of the foregoing pages are compiled from official dispatches, from private letters which had been sent to friends in England, casual notes, and from memory—a faculty which comparative seclusion from the work-a-day world, pending a two years' captivity, has a marvellous power in refreshing and rendering more retentive. However, when at the end of 1867 nothing was heard of the King, and nobody believed that he would ever be able to reach our prison-house, I re-commenced a diary from November of that year, and dispatched the memoranda by the messengers who were sent from time to time to the coast. But as it would tire the patience of the reader to peruse a mere record of repeated visits from different Chiefs, and of the local occurrences at Mágdala, I shall skip over such trifling matters—important as they were to us on the spot—and take up the narrative of events connected with the Mission from the time that the communication between Mágdala and the royal camp was reopened, and the King resumed corresponding with me.

CHAPTER XXIV.

THEODORE REACHES MÁGDALA.

Theodore hears of the landing of the British troops — Sir Robert Napier's Proclamation — Death of Hailo, a messenger — Submission of the Dalanta people — The road open to Mágdala — Death and burial of Theodore's sister — Transport of artillery — The Author sends dispatches to the British camp — Abyssinian mourning for the dead — Native and five European prisoners forwarded to Mágdala — Theodore's polite messages and speeches — Sir Robert Napier's ultimatum — Theodore in prospect of the impending invasion — He reaches the Dalanta plateau — Breaks faith with the Dalanta people — The Amháras — Messengers arrive from the British camp — The Author released from his chains — Letter and present from Theodore — Communications to and from the British Camp — Theodore reaches the plateau of Salámgê.

ON the 2nd of December, 1867, the King heard of the landing of the British troops, and about the 20th of the same month an Amharic copy of Sir Robert Napier's Proclamation reached him from Tigrê. It was reported at the time that the announced invasion made him furious, and that his European artisans narrowly escaped being put into chains in consequence. Such, however, was not the case, for I was assured on the best authority that the Proclamation only elicited a smile from the inscrutable Monarch. Nevertheless, he would not allow the document to be seen by any of his own people; not even by Aläkä I'ngădă, his chief scribe. It was placed with other papers in the tin box which I had given him. His Majesty was then in Wádala, near the Chetta river. The following is a copy of the Proclamation:—

"To the Governors, the Chiefs, the Religious Orders, and the People of Abyssinia.

"26th October, 1867.

"It is known to you that Theodorus King of Abyssinia detains in captivity the British Consul Cameron, the British Envoy Rassam, and many others, in violation of the laws of all civilized nations.

"All friendly persuasion having failed to obtain their release, my Sovereign has commanded me to lead an army to liberate them.

"All who befriend the prisoners or assist in their liberation shall be well rewarded, but those who may injure them shall be severely punished.

"When the time shall arrive for the march of a British army through your country, bear in mind, people of Abyssinia, that the Queen of England has no unfriendly feeling towards you, and no design against your country or your liberty.

"Your religious establishments, your persons, and property shall be carefully protected.

"All supplies required for my soldiers shall be paid for; no peaceable inhabitants shall be molested.

"The sole object for which the British force has been sent to Abyssinia is the liberation of Her Majesty's servants and others unjustly detained as captives, and as soon as that object is effected it will be withdrawn.

"There is no intention to occupy permanently any portion of the Abyssinian territory, or to interfere with the Government of the country.

"R. Napier, *Lieutenant-General*,
"*Commander-in-Chief, Bombay Army.*"

1st *January*, 1868.—News reached Mágdala that the Wakshum Gobazé had announced his intention of attacking Theodore as soon as the latter descended into the valley of the Chetta. He had nominated two Dajazmâtshes, with about ten thousand men, to proceed to Dalanta in order to prevent his Majesty's progress to Mágdala. In the afternoon, the

Commandant and other Chiefs came to condole with me on the loss of Hailo, the faithful messenger whom I had employed to carry my messages to the King, his Majesty having sent to inform me that the poor man had died in Zabît, after a lingering illness. I had dispatched him with a complimentary letter to Theodore as far back as May, but as the roads had been closed since then, he was obliged to remain in the royal camp, and eventually came on with his Majesty. In the evening the Râs's wife and other ladies visited me on the same errand. It is worthy of remark that the Abyssinians generally are very kind to servants, treating them as members of the family, especially on their marriage or death. When native ladies go to condole with any one, they usually wear their dirtiest clothes; hence, my fair visitors on this occasion were, externally, far from prepossessing.

2nd.—Private couriers arrived this evening, bringing me a polite message from the King. They reported that his Majesty had reached Beitahôr, on the top of the northern side of the Chetta valley.

3rd.—News reached us that the people of Dalanta had submitted to the King. The Wakshum Gobazê having failed to protect them, they judged it prudent to take advantage of the royal amnesty which Theodore had held out to them. I received another polite message from his Majesty this afternoon.

4th.—The road being now open between the royal camp and Mágdala, the King was able, for the first time after a long interval, to re-commence employing his regular couriers. His Majesty had been so long without proper food that he sent to request his favourite wife, Itamanyo, to prepare some good dishes and dispatch them to the camp, in order that he might enjoy himself at the Abyssinian Christmas. The couriers came to me shortly after with the following message from their master:—"How are you? How are you, my friend? Thank God, I am well. I have now reached Beitahôr, and hope to be with you soon. The nearer I approach towards you the happier I feel, knowing that the pleasure of meeting you is at hand. I sent you to Mágdala to be in my house, with the Queen Consort and my son, and I hope they have been kind to you and attended to your wants. Your servant, Mohammed Sa'id, has reached Chálga, with stores for you, and he is now with my people there. I have also received everything that was sent for from the coast. I have had a large mortar cast, which has detained me on the road; but when I reach Mágdala, and you see and admire it, I shall forget all the trouble which it has given me. Ask your brothers [fellow-captives] how they are, from me. I am obliged to dispatch the messengers in haste, otherwise I would have written to you." On the strength of this very courteous message the Mágdala Chiefs advised me to write a congratulatory letter to his Majesty. I accordingly addressed him as follows:—

(After compliments.)

"I have had the honour of receiving your Majesty's kind message by Yashálaka Lih, and I was delighted to hear of your safe arrival at Beitahôr.

"I was also not a little pleased to learn that your Majesty was in perfect health.

"May the Lord give your Majesty health and prosperity, and show us the light of your countenance soon; and may you enjoy a happy Christmas.

"Dr. Blanc and Mr. Prideaux, Mr. Cameron and his party, and Mr. Stern and his party, send your Majesty their respectful compliments."

The articles referred to by the King were some books and fusees which I had ordered for him from Aden, as far back as May, 1866. Mohammed Sa'id was the messenger whom he had asked me to dispatch with the letter he had requested me to write, in January of the following year, to get the artisans sent up from the coast. He was fully aware that the man had returned without an answer, and yet he forbore manifesting any displeasure towards me, or finding fault with the Government on that account.

In the afternoon the remains of the King's sister, to whom he had been very much attached, were brought from the royal camp to be interred in the church. She had died on the road to Mágdala, and had been placed in a coffin. To prevent the effluvia arising from decomposition—whenever it is desired to transport a body to a distance—the Abyssinians wrap the corpse in several folds of cerement, much in the same way as seems to have been practised by the ancient Egyptians, and after exposing it to the sun for some time remove it into the shade. By this process the waxed cloths adhere closely together and form an impervious shroud. The Mágdala priests received the remains of the Princess in full canonicals, with chants and the beating of drums, and outdid themselves on the occasion, knowing the proximity of the King, and being anxious to make a great show of their loyalty, in order to win his approbation.

6th.—Received another polite message from Theodore. Orders came to-day directing that half the Mágdala garrison should be sent to assist in transporting the heavy baggage, and in moving the guns and mortars through the Chetta valley. Damásh was to go in command of the detachment. This being the Abyssinian Christmas I gave an entertainment to the royal couriers, a number of the Mágdala Chiefs, and several courtiers who had come from the King's camp on different errands, and treated them with *brundo* and *téj* to their hearts' content.

7th.—Bitwá:ldad Damâsh and all the other officers who were going to the royal camp came to take leave of me, offering to convey anything from me to the European artisans, or to bring anything back for me on their return. As the near approach of the King and the submission of Dalanta rendered it dangerous to dispatch letters to the coast, I sent messengers to accompany the detachment as far as Dalanta, from whence they might proceed onward to the British camp without risk of being seized.

11th.—My agents in Dalanta—who, in common with the generality of the people of that district, had accepted the royal amnesty—called to assure me of their constant readiness to serve me faithfully as long as I remained in the country.

12th.—Another message from the King this morning. As we were at prayers when the couriers arrived, they waited until our service was over. His Majesty apologized for having detained 'Omar 'Ali, my interpreter, but said that he did not wish to send him back without an answer. The following day 'Omar 'Ali returned with the subjoined note :—

(After compliments.)

"By the power of God, I am coming to you. Oh, my friend, do not think that I bear any hatred towards you. Be of good cheer. I have placed you in your present position in order that I may have intercourse with the people of your country. The friendship which I have always entertained for you has not diminished. When God vouchsafes us a meeting, we will talk together from the heart. God knows that I really have no hatred towards you."

'Omar 'Ali reported that the King had received him very

well, and both he and the Europeans who were with the royal camp stated that his Majesty had publicly spoken of me in flattering terms. Theodore at this time was engaged from sunrise to sunset in widening and levelling the roads down the valley for the passage of his huge waggons.

17th.—Heard that his Majesty had reached the bottom of the Chetta valley, with all his heavy baggage, guns, &c.; that upwards of two hundred prisoners had been made over to Damâsh, to be conveyed to Mágdala; also Mrs. Rosenthal, who had received the King's permission to join her husband. Dispatched a post to-day to the British camp with the latest intelligence.

19th.—This being the Feast of the Epiphany with the Abyssinians, the priests and warriors of Mágdala made no little uproar in conveying the sacred *Tábot* from the springs near which it had been deposited the previous night, and where it was newly affused with water prior to its re-committal to the Holy of Holies within the church. A description of this ceremony has already been given in Vol. I. pp. 225-7.

22nd.—The King sent me word regretting his long detention. He found road-making a harder task than he had anticipated.

23rd.—Samuel's wife having heard of the death of her father and mother in the royal camp, through fatigue and anxiety, there was great wailing in his house this morning. As usual, a feast followed the lamentation for the departed, all the friends of the family, and those who wished to manifest their sympathy on the occasion, contributing the customary viands.

On the death of a near relative, the Abyssinians either shave their heads or crop their hair short; many of them also try to disfigure themselves by scratching their cheeks and temples till the blood runs. Samuel, however, who disliked all such barbarous customs, would not allow his wife to cut off her hair, and was obliged to place women over her to see that his injunctions were obeyed. Feeling aggrieved at this prohibition to observe the usages of her country, the lady refused to allow her hair to be buttered. All other resources to induce her to comply with her husband's wishes in that respect having failed, my intervention was sought, and after considerable effort I induced the mourner to submit to the usual buttering. Theodore hated all these obsequies, which he regarded as pagan, and on his accession to the throne he forbade them, and decreed that any one, male or female, who disfigured his or her face, in token of sorrow for the departed, should be amenable to punishment. He also prohibited all loud wailing for the dead in the royal camp.

Menilek, King of Shoa, sent me some money to-day and a note, informing me that the English Queen had written him a letter recognizing him as King of Abyssinia. It was fortunate that this communication did not fall into Theodore's hands.

26th.—The Mágdala detachment returned this afternoon with 180 native and five European prisoners. The latter were those who had tried to effect their escape from Debra Tábor when M. Bardel betrayed their design to the King, namely, Messrs. Staiger, Brandeis, Schiller, Essller and Macraire. Mrs. Rosenthal and her infant came also with the escort. Among the native prisoners were Wakshum Tafâré and the other Chiefs who were taken with him by Râs I'ngādā when Râs Kidâna Máryam was removed to Debra Tábor; Kántiba Hailo, the ex-Mayor of Góndar; Râs Wald-Máryam, and Râs Gabriê, the Chiefs who had guarded the members of the Mission on our disgrace at Zagê; the Master of the Horse;

Balambarâs Tasámma; Bitwáddad Tadla, who had brought us as prisoners to Mágdala; T'issoo Hailo, the merchant who was afraid to accompany me on board the steamer at Massowah at the end of 1864 (see Vol. I. p. 36), and a large number of courtiers who had incurred the royal displeasure for trivial offences.

After the native prisoners were safely lodged in the common jail, together with about four hundred inmates who had been confined there previously, Dajjáj Dasta, one of the petty Chiefs of Mágdala, who was then in great favour with the King, accompanied by several other Chiefs, brought the European captives, each chained to an Abyssinian soldier, and made them over to me, in accordance with the King's orders. His Majesty, he said, had directed him to repeat the following message to me :—" How are you? How have you passed the time? I send five of your countrymen whom I wish you to receive and keep with the other Europeans who are with you. Be of good cheer, my son; I shall soon be with you." It appears that when the native prisoners were consigned to the Mágdala Chiefs at the royal camp, the latter inquired where the five Europeans were to be lodged. After considering a little, his Majesty asked the Chiefs whether they thought I should feel hurt if they were located with the native prisoners in the common jail. On their replying in the affirmative, he directed them to be made over to me, with the foregoing message. With regard to Mrs. Rosenthal, he said, " Take her and deliver her over to her brother, and say from me, ' I send your sister, as you desired.' " The poor lady was detained at the gate of the fortress nearly two hours, and was not admitted until the Chief had terminated his task of delivering over, categorically, all the native prisoners to the local authorities, agreeably with a list which had been drawn up at the royal camp. The exigencies of Abyssinian red-tape demanded not only that the prisoners should be made over numerically, but the Jail Wardens must have each individual identified, lest a common convict should be substituted for an attainted political offender of rank. So apprehensive was Theodore of losing Wakshum Tafâré, that he sent him to Mágdala with his hands shackled to his feet, and twenty trusty men, selected by the King himself, were appointed to keep watch over him day and night until he reached his destination. All the formalities over, seven guns were fired to announce that the prisoners were safely lodged within the impregnable fortress. The King, knowing the time when they might be expected to arrive, sat on a hill awaiting the expected signal. On seeing the smoke of the guns he breathed freely, and exclaimed "Thank God!" As there were some thousands Amhâra as well as Galla rebels in arms in the neighbourhood, and as he could only spare an escort of five hundred men to guard the captive Chiefs, he was in dread lest their rescue should be attempted. In this apprehension he seems to have overlooked the fact, that the smoke of his camp-fires was enough to scare the cowardly rabble from his path.

News reached us to-day that the British force was being concentrated at Senâfé.

27th.—Received a budget of letters from the coast; also some newspapers. A short paragraph in one of the journals stated that "Calcraft had been engaged by her Majesty's Government to accompany the Abyssinian Expedition"—a pleasant announcement to Theodore had the paper fallen into his hands and been rendered into Amharic for him by a malevolent translator. The day following, all the officers of the returning detachment came to take leave of me.

30*th.*—Dispatched other messengers to the British camp. I have now three guides and several agents between Mágdala and the Täkkäzê river, to insure the safe transmission of letters out of the reach of the King.

1*st February.*—Theodore has been publicly talking about me and some of the other captives. Mr. Flad's version of the royal speech was as follows:—" Mr. Rassam was my best friend before I sent him to Mágdala, and although I put him in chains he is still my friend, and for that reason I esteem and love him, and shall do him good as long as I live, though those who are above him in England laugh at me, and deride my poverty; but Messrs. Stern, Cameron and Rosenthal I cannot esteem more than my own Abyssinians." His remark about our Government having ridiculed him referred to a passage in one of Mr. Rosenthal's letters which has been explained in Vol. I. p. 301.

3*rd.*—After I had retired for the night, I was aroused by Aito Samuel, who came to inform me that couriers had arrived from the King with a message which they were ordered to deliver to me without delay. The message ran thus:— "How are you? I must apologize for not having written when I sent you the five Europeans. I have been hard at work of late making a good road for the gun-carriages. I hope it will not be long before I ascend Dalanta, when I trust to have the pleasure of meeting you—a joy which has been long deferred. Ask your brothers how they are," &c. We were induced to infer from the tenor of this communication, that as soon as the King reached the Dalanta plateau he would send for us and keep us there. It was no small satisfaction to us that he never carried out that project, if he had ever intended it.

8*th.*—Almost every alternate day since the 3rd, complimentary messages have come to me from his Majesty. On the 13th there was a tremendous hailstorm, which partly destroyed the beautiful arbour in front of my hut. The day following a quaint message reached me from Theodore, which I must give in full :—" How are you? How are you, my friend? Thank God, I am well; but the people of your country have made fools both of you and me. In a few days I shall be up with my guns in Dalanta, when I shall communicate to you what I know." This was quite a riddle to us, and the messengers were equally at a loss to know what the King meant.

The Wakshum Gobazê forwarded me a copy of his Excellency Sir Robert Napier's ultimatum, addressed to the King. He had opened and read it, and on ascertaining its purport had exclaimed, "Alas! for the poor *Franchotsh*. Should this fall into the hands of Kâsa [the name which the rebels always gave to Theodore], he will certainly kill them all." He accordingly directed the messenger to bring the paper to me, in order that I might decide whether it was to be forwarded to its destination or destroyed. To insure its reaching me first, he instructed his agents to see that the bearer came to me before going elsewhere. When it reached me, I submitted it to several of the intelligent natives who were in my confidence, and they unanimously agreed that the worst consequences might be apprehended if the document found its way to the King. I also referred the matter to those of my fellow-captives whose opinion I felt bound to consult in such a case, and as their views concurred with my own I decided to arrest the dangerous missive.

The following is a copy of the ultimatum :—

"I am commanded by her Majesty the Queen of England to demand that the prisoners whom your Majesty has wrongfully detained in captivity shall be immediately released and sent in safety to the British Camp. Should your Majesty fail to comply with this demand, I am further commanded to enter your Majesty's country at the head of an army to enforce it, and nothing will arrest my progress until the object shall have been accomplished.

"My Sovereign has no desire to deprive you of any part of your dominions, nor to subvert your authority, although it is obvious that such would in all probability be the result of hostilities.

"Your Majesty might avoid this danger by the immediate surrender of the prisoners.

"But should they not be delivered safely into my hands, should they suffer a continuance of ill treatment, or should any injury befall them, your Majesty will be held personally responsible, and no hope of future condonation need be entertained."

15*th*.—Received a letter from Mr. Flad to-day, wherein he informed me that the King had broached the subject of the impending invasion to his European artisans. The feeling which pervaded Theodore's mind, in anticipation of that event, is so clearly indicated by his utterances on the occasion, that I shall give them in Mr. Flad's own words:—

"*Royal Camp, Dalanta,* 11*th February,* 1868.

"You will be glad to hear that his Majesty informed Mr. Waldmeier, on Friday last, that he had received news from the coast that the English had disembarked at Zoolah; and on Saturday morning he called me aside and told me, 'The people of whom you brought me a letter, and of whom you said that they will come, have arrived, and disembarked at Zoolah, and they are coming up by the salt plain. Why did they not choose a better road? The road by the salt plain is very unhealthy.' I said, that as they bring their troops from India, they could not take a better road than this. From the sea-coast they would, in three or four days, reach the alps of Agamay; and that with little difficulties, as already, at the time of King Fasil, the Portuguese had made a way up, and the salt plain they would leave to their left. He then said, 'We are making roads, and what will it be to them but playing to make roads everywhere? Well,' he said, 'it seems to me to be the *will of God* that they come. If He who is above does not kill me, none will kill me; and if He says, you must die, no one can save me. Remember the history of Hezekiah and Sennacherib.' His Majesty did not say more, but this he said most solemnly. To-day he said to Messrs. Waldmeier, Saalmüller and Bender, 'I long for the day on which I shall have the pleasure to see a disciplined European army. I am like Simeon who would rejoice, having the Saviour in his arms; but he was old and died, and I am old too, but I hope God will spare me to see them. I am no more proud of my soldiers. We are nothing in comparison to a disciplined army, where thousands of men act on the command of one man.'

"On Friday he said to Mr. Waldmeier, 'We have a prophecy that the time will come when an European King will meet with an Abyssinian King in this country; and the Europeans will then take their mouthful and speak the truth before the people of this country; and after this time a *great* King will reign in Abyssinia, as great as none will have been before him. This time has come.' He said, 'but I don't know whether I shall be that great King, or some one else.' From all he now and then says, the Europeans here make their conclusions, that he is glad that they are coming, and that he thinks only of a reconciliation, and that nothing is to be feared for any Europeans in his hands."

In the afternoon, messengers arrived from the royal camp to announce the King's arrival on the Dalanta plateau, with all his guns and mortars. They brought me a most polite message from his Majesty, and I was delighted to find that he had not sent for us. A salute was fired from the fortress on the receipt of the foregoing intelligence. If Theodore's circumstances and prospects hardly warranted such a *feu-de-joie*, the feat of having transported huge pieces of artillery through the deep and difficult valley of the Chetta, with thousands of rebels hovering around him, certainly did.

16*th*.—Unlike all other Churches, the Abyssinians begin

their Lent on Monday; consequently, those who up to yesterday (Sunday) feasted on raw beef and mead, or beer, look rather downcast this morning. Messengers, escorted by my Dalanta agents as far as the fortress, reached me from the coast to-day, with money.

17*th*.—Dispatched letters to the British camp this morning, under the protection of the same escort. Three hours after they had started, the astounding news reached Mágdala that the King had broken faith with the Dalanta people, who, since accepting his amnesty, had done all in their power to assist him. Not only had they helped in transporting the guns and heavy baggage through the Chetta valley, but they had fed the royal army from the beginning of January. I deplored this fresh outrage, especially on account of my agents, I'rkina and his cousins, who had left their families to the tender mercies of the ungrateful King, to accompany the messengers bringing the money. The intelligence reached them just as they were entering Dalanta; nevertheless, they sent to tell me, by a special courier, that the letters were safe, and that I was to be in no anxiety about them. "Although our property has been plundered, and our families probably slain"—so said they to the messengers who were going down to the coast—"we may not neglect Mr. Rassam's business by sending you back to Mágdala with the letters. God's will be done! but we shall be faithful to our benefactor."

18*th*.—The road between Mágdala and the royal camp is entirely closed by the peasants of Dalanta and Dâwunt, who have taken up a position in the Bâshilo, and sworn to kill any one attempting to convey communications between the King and the Mágdala garrison. On the morning of the 20th, the messengers whom I had dispatched to collect what information they could respecting the proceedings at the royal camp, and the fate of my agents' families, returned to report that the Dalanta people had fought bravely, and killed a number of the royal troops, when attacked by the latter; but that his Majesty had seized a number of helpless women and children, among whom were several of I'rkina's relatives. I was glad to learn, three days after, that these captives had been released by Theodore.

The circumstances connected with this contest were as follows:—the Wakshum Gobazê having failed to render the Dalanta people any assistance, the only alternative they had was to submit. All the Chiefs accordingly went to Theodore in a body and asked forgiveness. They were received most courteously, and the King called them his beloved children, and said, "How can I blame you for submitting to the rebels, when I rendered you no protection? Can I forget the assistance you have always rendered to my Mágdala garrison? Would they not have starved, if you had not provided them with food? Come nearer to me, all of you, my children and friends, as I cannot see too much of you. I shall treat you all well for your good conduct to-day, that the world may know how well you have deserved my gratitude." The Dáwunt people subsequently followed their example.

After these people had submitted, the King was able to communicate freely with Mágdala. He made them transport all his heavy baggage, and by their assistance managed to send all his prisoners to the fortress, and to go on with his road-making and moving the guns. At the same time they had to feed his almost famished army; to grind and bake as well as to provide the grain! On reaching the plateau of Dalanta, he asked the Chiefs why they had not submitted earlier, and on their answering that they were prevented by the Gallas and the Wakshum Gobazé, he told them they were as bad as the others, and ordered them to be plundered. They offered no resistance to this outrage; but, knowing that Theodore was not to be trusted, they had taken the precaution of keeping most of their cattle out of his reach, and had always remained on their guard. Consequently, when the King further ordered them to be attacked, they all fought bravely, and, in conjunction with the inhabitants of Dâwunt, killed a great number of his soldiers and seized their mules and arms. As the two clans mustered about 10,000 men, they might have put an end to Theodore's reign at this time; but they had not the courage to assume the offensive, and were without a commander to lead them on. Had his Majesty kept faith with these people, the districts of Wádala and Yadjow would have submitted before many days were over. Indeed, it was reported that a deputation from the latter was coming to him with proposals to that effect; but on hearing of the King's treachery, they returned to their country more quickly than they had left it.

For some time after, nothing was heard of the King, as all the roads were closed around him by the Gallas, as well as by the Amhâras. Had not his tents been visible from Mágdala, we should have inferred that he had either gone back to Debra Tâbor, or had been utterly routed, as a messenger might easily have come from his camp in less than five hours; yet a fortnight elapsed and no news from him reached us. The Mágdala Chiefs, however, were watching his movements, and reported to me daily that he was approaching nearer and nearer.

I take this opportunity of remarking that the term "Amhâra," as now used by the Abyssinians, in an ethnological sense, designates the inhabitants of the country lying west of the Tăkkăzê, and also south of that river, as far as the province of Gójjam. Socially the word indicates a native Christian, in contra-distinction to Jews, Mussulmans and Kamánts. It is also frequently applied to Christians generally; for on several occasions I overheard Abyssinians, in speaking of us amongst themselves, describe us as "Amháras," when they wished to distinguish us from "Turks."

2nd March.—Messengers arrived from the coast with money, escorted to within three miles of the fortress by the Dalanta agents, from whence they were brought on by Galla guides. The day following, I dispatched a post to the British camp, through the same medium. The roads are so unsafe now that I have to employ no less than six agents and guides to transmit the letters, from one place to another, as far as the Tăkkăzê. The letters are not consigned to the messengers until they are beyond danger. When travelling through a district where there is a chance of their being seized by the King's adherents, they carry a note from me addressed either to Colonel Merewether or M. Munzinger, containing a request for money, and are instructed, in case of arrest, to say that they are my servants, proceeding to the coast for supplies. Very frequently, I forbear giving the messengers any letters, lest they should be seized. In such cases, I give the men an impression of my signet-ring in sealing-wax, as a token both to the King's people and to the rebels that they are employed in my service.

4th.—Couriers arrived to-day from the royal camp for the first time since the 17th of February. They brought me a message from his Majesty, bidding me keep up my spirits, as we should soon meet; they also reported that the King had effected the descent of the Báshilo. The couriers were four hours on the road.

5th.—Messengers arrived this afternoon from the British camp. The Commandant and other Chiefs of the garrison read Sir Robert Napier's ultimatum again, and approved of my having detained it. All that I could say in reply to their repeated questions as to the probable upshot of the existing complications was, that I hoped they would be adjusted amicably.

Courier after courier arrived with polite messages from the King on the 7th and 8th. One of these was:—"I am so near you now, that I must not ask you, how have you passed the time? but must bid you 'Good morning.'" (This remark illustrates the prevailing usage among the Abyssinians, who have an appropriate salutation for a number of sections into which they divide the day.) Mrs. Flad received the King's permission to leave the camp and reside at Mágdala. His Majesty's instructions were, that she should have a house near our inclosure, and be allowed to visit me. Mrs. Rosenthal also might communicate with her.

On the 9th I dispatched messengers to the British camp, but they returned the following morning, not having found the Dalanta agents at the rendezvous; the latter had been driven away by the Gallas, owing to the recent breach between them and the Dalanta people. However, on the 15th I'rkina managed to let me know that he had sent guides to take the messengers through the disturbed districts to their destination. The British force was now reported as having approached the Tăkkăzé.

In addition to a complimentary note from the King, I received a few lines to-day from Mr. Flad, telling me that his Majesty had given out that, in the event of our people treating him well, everything would be satisfactorily arranged; otherwise, a "blood-bath" would be the consequence.

On the 16th I sent Theodore a complimentary letter, through Dasta, congratulating him on the feat which he had achieved in bringing his heavy guns through the difficult valleys. On the 18th I received a note from M. Munzinger, who was then at Koso-Amba—about two days' journey for a good messenger when the roads are safe—informing me that he had been dispatched in front by the Commander-in-Chief to reconnoitre the route, and also to communicate with me. In the afternoon, Dasta returned from the royal camp, and informed me that his Majesty had sent Mr. Flad, Alâkâ I'ngădă and Yashálaka Lih, with an order directing that I should be released from my chains. Accordingly, shortly after, these officers appeared, accompanied by the members of the Council and the officers commanding the troops, all dressed in their fine silk shirts and looking much pleased. They evidently thought that matters were about to be brought to a favourable termination.

The first thing the royal Commissioners did was to place in my hands a letter from the King. This, agreeably with native usage in like cases, I opened, and then caused it to be read in public. It was as follows:—

(After compliments.)

"Oh, my friend, I have no quarrel with you, nor have I any rancour towards you. Formerly, when I sent you to Mágdala, I told my people to watch you only, but they sent me an answer that, out of precaution, they had put you in chains; but now when I, your friend, am brought by God near you, your chains shall be opened; but until I see the object of your masters [Government] we will watch you, but without chains.

"Mr. Flad brought you stores and money from your country, which he made over to me. My country was then in rebellion, and I had no bearers to convey them to you; they have therefore been wasted. You will receive from Mr. Flad, Alâkâ I'ngădă and Yashálaka Lih the sum of 2,000 dollars in lieu of the things you have lost; also 100 sheep and 50 cows, which I hope you will accept.

"If, by the power of God, I reach you safely, and see you face to face, I will consult with you. Be of good cheer."

Some of the Chiefs assisted in striking off my fetters, whilst others placed their fingers between the flesh and iron to prevent my ankles from being hurt. I was greatly disappointed to find that my fellow-captives, especially the members of the Mission, were not included in the dispensation, and on first hearing the contents of the letter I had resolved to decline the royal favour. Luckily, I was better advised, and accepted the boon with simulated pleasure; otherwise, as I was assured on all hands, matters would have been brought to a dangerous crisis, either by our being all consigned to the common jail, or sent for by the King, who would not have failed to make us feel his displeasure.

19th.—I wrote the following reply to the King, asking him at the same time to relieve my companions of their chains:—

"I have had the honour of receiving your Majesty's kind letter by Mr. Flad, Aläkä I'ngädä and Yashálaka Lih, and was glad to learn therefrom that your Majesty was in the enjoyment of perfect health.

"I am much obliged for your Majesty's kind consideration in having released me from my chains. May the Lord reward you for all your acts of kindness.

"Your Majesty has always tried to befriend me since my arrival in your country; and I trust it will not be long before you perfect my joy by granting a similar boon to my companions.

"I return you my best thanks for having sent me by Mr. Flad, Aläkä I'ngädä and Yashálaka Lih, two thousand dollars; also one hundred sheep and fifty cows, which I have received with pleasure."

The cows were miserably lean; the flesh of those which we had slaughtered was uneatable, and finding that they were not valued even as a gift by those to whom I thought of offering them, I sent the remainder to pasture near the Bâshilo river, under the charge of one of my Galla agents who resided in that locality. They were carried off a few days after by the royal troops, together with other herds of cows, when the King, as will be noticed in the sequel, ordered the plunder of all the peasants between the Bâshilo and Mágdala. Of the sheep, twenty had died on the road; the rest, which were in a most wretched condition, having been without food for three days, I disposed of as presents to different parties, who, I believe, only killed them for the sake of the skins, which, when tanned, the Abyssinians use to sit upon.

In the afternoon the royal couriers brought a message from the King, congratulating me on my being relieved of my fetters. If not fatalists, men in authority among the Abyssinians practically reject the doctrine of free-will in their official capacity. It is a common custom with them, on committing an individual to prison, to conclude the judicial sentence with the prayer, "And may God set you free!" On releasing the culprit, the same magistrate will piously say to him, "The Lord hath delivered you."

In the course of the day I forwarded the latest intelligence to the British camp, through M. Munzinger; and the day following I received a communication from Colonel Merewether, reporting his arrival at Antâlo and the progress of the invading force. I also received an answer from the King, inquiring how I had passed the night, and expressing a hope that God would "bring us together propitiously," but without any allusion whatever to the request which I had made that my companions should be freed from their fetters.

21st.—Dispatched Dasta, my interpreter, with an answer to the King, and received intimation from Mr. Flad that his Majesty had promised to unshackle my companions when he met me. Dasta returned, accompanied by two royal couriers, with the following message from Theodore, who was too busily engaged in blasting rocks to write :—" A good day to you, my friend. I am now so near that I can see the top of your house plainly; and if you come out and look down you will see my tent. Our meeting is at hand."

Received two communications from M. Munzinger to-day. He is now in Dalanta, only a few hours' journey from Mágdala.

22nd.—Bitwáddad Hailo, one of the members of the Mágdala Council, made his escape last night by means of a ladder. He dreaded meeting the King, as his cousin Balambarás Gabra-Mádhané 'Âlam, Governor of Waudígé mentioned at pp. 74 and 90, had rebelled, and it was extremely probable that as the principal was beyond his reach, Theodore would visit his defection on the Bitwáddad. Dispatched messengers to the British camp.

The King forwarded all his valuables to-day, including a bar of gold fourteen inches long and four inches square, to be deposited in the Treasury; he also sent me his compliments, which I reciprocated.

23rd.—The advanced guard of the royal army, commanded by Fit-awrári Gabrié, encamped on the Salámgé plateau this afternoon. The remainder of the King's effects were lodged in the Treasury to-day. An interchange of courteous messages between his Majesty and myself.

24th.—Received an intimation from Theodore that he had

reached the foot of Salássê, with all his guns and mortars. He was engaged in repairing the road leading from the base of Fála to the saddle which joins that mountain to Salássê. (*Vide* Plan of the Amba Mágdala.)

25*th*.—This morning his Majesty unshackled three Râses—I'ngŭdă, the Prime Minister; Tágga, the Commander-in-Chief; and Barráko, a courtier; also Moritz Hall, the Pole. The poor fellows had been dragged in chains from Debra Tábor—the two former hand to hand; the latter with the right hand attached by a chain to their fetters. In the evening Mr. Flad came to me with a complimentary message from the King, accompanied by Bitwáddad Damâsh and three Dajazmátshes. They were all wet through to the skin with the heavy rain. His Majesty announced to me, through them, that he should sleep at Salámgê that night. All the members of the Mágdala Council, including Râs Bisáwwir, were summoned to the royal presence this evening, and were graciously received by the King. The *de jure* Queen Tĕru-Wark, and her son Dajjáj 'Alamâyo, as well as the favourite queen, Itamanyo, were also ordered down to Salámgê this evening, but before they started the King sent to say that he would not see Tĕru-Wark, who was consequently obliged to remain behind.

26*th*.—Received a message from the King this morning, apprising me that as there was now only a "span" between us, our meeting would soon take place. A silk tent and carpets were ordered down to Salámgê, and it was generally supposed that his Majesty intended to send for me during the day; however, if such had been his intention, he subsequently changed his mind. Poor Samuel is sadly dejected, owing to the King having taken no notice of him. Every one else in

Mágdala, whether chiefs, courtiers, priests, or servants, has been allowed to pay his respects to the Sovereign, while the disgraced Báldárábá has received a hint to stay away. A note with some money reached me this afternoon from M. Munzinger.

During the day Theodore dismantled Mágdala of all its artillery, ammunition, and other warlike stores, and had them conveyed to Salámgé. This proceeding was evidently designed to indicate that, if called upon to fight, he intended to meet the enemy in the open field.

CHAPTER XXV.

THEODORE AT MÁGDALA.

Theodore enters Mágdala — Tries two Priests for defamation and three Chiefs for treason — He returns to Salámgé — His message to the Author about the advance of the British troops — Changes the Mágdala garrison — The European Captives placed under strict watch — Bitwáddad Hásani, as a soldier and a man — Old acquaintances among our new guard — Mágdala garrison reinforced — We burn our papers — Theodore's second visit to the fortress — Receives the Author in state — His altered appearance — His condescension on the occasion — Is undecided whether he will fight the British or not — Requests the Author to see him buried, in the event of his death — His miscellaneous conversation — Unshackles Dr. Blanc and Lieutenant Prideaux, and receives them graciously — The King "in labour" — Introduces Prince 'Alamáyo to the Author — Abuses his Chiefs at Salámgé — Asks them if they are prepared to fight the British — Damásh's reply — A sally from Mágdala against the Gallas, an episode — Origin of the expedition — Theodore's charmed rifle — A night attack — The Amháras are successful — Are pursued by the Gallas on their return march — Rout of the Amháras — Letters from the British force at Ashangi — The Mission invited to inspect the great mortar, "Sevastopol " — Theodore's queries on European warfare — Recounts his troubles — Complains again of Consul Cameron and Mr. Stern — Contrasts his soldiers with the British troops — All the European Captives are unshackled — The Author's proposal to report his Majesty's recent civility to Sir Robert Napier declined — Theodore is anxious for news from the British camp — Espies some of our troops descending into the Báshilo valley.

27th.—Theodore entered the fortress this morning, and on passing through the gate sent me a message, that he hoped to see me soon. After performing his devotions in the church, he proceeded to the open space in front of our prison-house, where a temporary throne had been erected for him, and the ground around covered with carpets. There was quite a panic among the inhabitants, as no one knew what these preparations portended, and the King's most cherished friend felt that his life trembled in the balance. On taking his seat, Theodore first sent for Samuel, a summons which created no little alarm among our small community. This was dispelled, however, a few minutes after by the announcement that the disgraced official had been well received by his royal master, and that my interpreters, who were standing outside our inclosure to do obeisance to the King as he passed, had been graciously noticed by his Majesty and asked how I fared. The next case brought forward was that of two priests, who had publicly called the King a "Frank" to his face for having failed—so they had heard—to keep the Lenten fast, and for having granted a similar dispensation to those of his soldiers who preferred meat and butter to dry bread. When arraigned before him, his Majesty denounced the culprits as "fools" and "asses" for their meddling, and then ordered them to be unfettered and forthwith banished from Mágdala. "If I find you in my camp again," was the judge's valedictory, "I will have you flogged." The wretched priests received the sentence with downcast looks and without uttering a word; inwardly in ecstasy, however, at having got off so easily, as every one in the place had expected that they would have been condemned to be hurled over the fatal precipice. How we all envied their summary banishment, and wished that a similar fate awaited ourselves, even with the superadded disgrace of being kicked out of the loathsome place!

The case of the priests disposed of, the whole garrison was then summoned to attend the trial of three of its Chiefs for high treason, namely, Rás Bisáwwir, the Commandant, who was cousin to the King, and Bitwáddad Damâsh—both members of the Council—and one of the petty military Chiefs, who were severally accused of having invited Menilek of Shoa, "the Usurper," to come and invest Mágdala with his army. A great number of witnesses were called to give evidence, but as the King himself acted as judge and jury as well as prosecutor in the case, a conviction was inevitable. Damâsh seemed utterly cowed in the presence of his royal master; but the Râs and the military Chief indignantly repelled the false allegations, and undertook to prove, if his Majesty would grant them time, that some of the witnesses had themselves been guilty of holding treasonable communications with Menilek. This, however, did not suit Theodore's object; so, after listening to the charges and counter-charges against the fidelity of his Mágdala "children," and taking into his royal consideration the fact that one of their great Chiefs had lately decamped with the connivance of others who still formed part of the garrison, his Majesty came to the conclusion that he could no longer trust them with the defence of the fortress, and accordingly ordered them to prepare to go down to Salámgê, from whence fresh troops were to be sent to replace them.

The charge alleged against the Commandant was utterly without foundation; his loyalty to Theodore was unimpeachable. Had he really wished to surrender Mágdala to Menilek, or to any other rebel Chief, during the royal absence, no one would have dared to oppose him. The fact is, his Majesty, for reasons best known to himself, wanted to send a fresh garrison to the fortress; but as it was not in his nature to act straightforwardly, he trumped up this case against the two Chiefs, who had been foremost in encouraging the troops to resistance, when Menilek appeared before Mágdala. The announced change of the garrison caused me no little concern, not only on account of the loss of many old and faithful friends which it would involve, but because I apprehended that it was the forerunner of still more serious consequences, especially as I had received private intimation that we were to be watched day and night by a large guard, some of whom were notorious for their antipathy to foreigners.

The Court closed at ten o'clock, and Theodore returned to Salámgé without fulfilling his promise of visiting me. On passing our inclosure he sent me the following message by Aito Samuel and my interpreters: "I hope you will excuse me for not having come to see you, as I intended. I have had some disputes among my Mágdala people to settle, and am now rather excited; I trust, however, to meet you shortly. Your brothers [British troops] are coming to liberate you. I am prepared to meet them, by the power of God." His Majesty fully expected a reply to this communication by Aito Samuel and my interpreter, for, on leaving the fortress on his return to Salámgé, he gave orders that the former should be allowed to pass, in the event of his being sent down with a message from me. The interpreter, as well as our Indian servants generally, had always been allowed that privilege from the time of our confinement in Mágdala; but Samuel was treated as a prisoner on *parole*. The answer which I sent was to the following effect: that I hoped to see his Majesty ere long; with regard to the British troops, I remarked that as I had come to Abyssinia on a friendly mission, my sincere hope was that I should leave the country in peace. To this Theodore replied in these words, through the messengers: "As far as I am concerned, I am desirous of nothing but peace; and I pray God that your brothers are coming with a good intention." I judged it prudent to take no notice of the delicate topic thus broached,

especially on finding, shortly after the delivery of the
message, that we were surrounded by a host of new jailors
who had been sent to guard us most strictly, and who eyed
us with evident animosity. As soon as the King reached
Salámgê, he dispatched a thousand men to the fortress under
the command of Bitwáddad Hásani, a native of Métcha,
and one of those lucky men who had never incurred the
royal displeasure. His orders were, to take charge of the
Treasury and all its appurtenances, and then to see that all
the native and European prisoners were made over to him,
after due identification. When the Abyssinian captives had
been thus consigned to their keeping, all the new officials came
to our quarters, accompanied by the old Chiefs, to go through
a similar form. We were all summoned to be counted, but just
as I was leaving my room I was told to remain where I was, as,
not being then in chains, the King had not given any instructions about my enumeration with the rest, and that when the
new Commandant had finished his task outside he would look
in upon me. That, however, he declined to do, on the plea
that his master had not ordered him to count me, and that
on no other ground could he venture to approach me without
the King's special permission. Although I received many
visits subsequently from this Chief, by Theodore's orders, he
uniformly refused to be seated in my room, and only once
ventured to enter it, alleging as a reason that evil-disposed
people might be led to say of him, as they had of others, that
he had sold himself to me. He swore that, for the same
reason, he would not even take a cup of coffee with me;
nevertheless, he pledged his word to befriend me and to assist
me in obtaining anything I stood in need of; "but," he
added, "if ordered by the King to do a certain duty, no
matter what it may be, I shall discharge it faithfully, as I

am bound to do, without the least regard to private friendship." The austere Chief was quite correct in his appreciation of the Mágdala people, for there were some even among the Europeans who doubted whether a native was capable of a generous action, except at the price of a gratuity or bribe. On the other hand, I can vouch for many a good turn done me by Abyssinians who absolutely refused any remuneration for their services. Moreover, there was not a courtier, royal messenger, or Chief, who would not have befriended me as far as lay in his power, and whose conjoined friendship, if only available on purchase—seeing that many of them were in possession of our secrets—would have necessitated an outlay of at least half a million of dollars, and even then I should still have been as much in their power as ever.

After Bitwáddad Hásani left me, I found to my great delight that three of the new guards placed in charge of us were old acquaintances of mine, who still remembered the night of the 3rd of July, 1866, when they were appointed to a similar duty during our confinement in the Treasury at Debra Tábor. On being introduced to me this evening, they reminded me how they had been turned out into the wet and cold by the King, who paid me a visit there, and how after his Majesty's departure I had called them in and directed Samuel to provide them with refreshments.

28*th*.—This morning Theodore countermanded the removal of the old Mágdala troops to Salámgê; the new garrison was to reinforce the place, but all the former Chiefs, with the exception of Bitwáddad Wâsi, were to be deprived of their commands. At about 10 P.M. Bitwáddad Hásani came within our inclosure, bringing orders from the King that all my fellow-captives were to sleep in one room, and to be strictly guarded, and that I also should be watched in my hut during the night. Luckily, Mrs. Rosenthal was not included in the arbitrary order. It was clear that our fortunes were entering a new phase, and that still greater trials awaited us. The King sent me no message to-day, so that altogether our prospects were very gloomy. As one hut was not large enough to contain the twelve captives, they were located in the hut of my companions, and in that of Messrs. Stern and Rosenthal. Two of my old acquaintances were appointed to watch me, and as Samuel had been ordered to keep me company, he also considered himself in the light of a prisoner. My watchmen gave me no trouble; they were exceptionally clean in their dress, and never used butter on their heads, which they kept close shaved; and as Samuel generally washed his hair with hot water and soap, I was spared the usual disagreeable odour arising from the persons of the natives. The men ensconced themselves near the door, as far from my bedstead as possible, and fell asleep as soon as I re-occupied it. There were at least one hundred soldiers on guard over us during the night, and not one of our servants was allowed to stir from his place. By way of consolation, Bitwáddad Hásani sent to tell me, before his return to the royal camp, that I was not to attribute the stringent measures which he had taken to the King; they had emanated entirely from himself, as the party responsible for our safe custody. The message was kindly meant, but I was fully aware at the time that he would as soon have cast himself over the Mágdala precipices as place a guard within my room without special orders from his master. The fact is, the friendly disposition of the Chiefs generally led them to do all in their power to prevent an open rupture between me and the King, while there was still a chance of matters being brought to a favourable termination.

29th.—By the advice of the old Chiefs and Aito Samuel, I sent a message to the King, informing him that I had slept well and hoped he had spent a comfortable night. To this I received a prompt reply, assuring me that, owing to my good wishes, his Majesty was in excellent spirits. At about 2 P.M. it was announced that Theodore was coming to the fortress, and as the people generally expected anything but a propitious visit from their Sovereign, especially after their experience of his proceedings on the last occasion, we were anxious to rid ourselves of all documents likely to compromise us in any way, to prevent their possible seizure by his Majesty's orders. Accordingly, each began secreting what papers he could in the thatch of the roof, burning those which could not well be disposed of in that manner. At this time I had some most dangerous letters in my possession, and that same afternoon a messenger had arrived with a missive from Menilek, King of Shoa, inclosing Lord Stanley's dispatch to him of the 19th of August, 1867, which he wished me to translate. I had also a letter from the Wakshum Gobazé, referring to different subjects connected with the march of the British troops; and another from Imâm Ahmed, the Chief of the Wello-Gallas, requesting me to surrender the fortress to him, and promising, in the event of my acceding to the proposal, to conduct me to the coast with honour and safety! I tried at first to conceal all these papers in the roof of my hut, but my Abyssinian friends advised me not to trust to such an expedient, assuring me that if Theodore intended to institute a search, the roof would not stand in his way. I accordingly committed the whole to the flames, together with the English document.

At 3 P.M. his Majesty entered the fortress, and on passing our house he sent Mr. Flad to say that he had come up on business, and if possible he would call upon me. I said in reply that I should be happy to meet him. Mr. Flad returned immediately after with the following answer:—

"I am going to visit the church of my country. I have been called 'Frank' by some of my priests. I am not ashamed of the name, because both you and I believe in one Trinity, which is the foundation of the Christian faith. Had I been accused of being a Mohammedan, or of any other sect of unbelievers, I should have acted differently towards those bad priests. I would rather lose my head than hold any other faith save that in Christ. Prepare yourself to meet me."

Soon after Mr. Flad, Mr. Mayer was sent with the subjoined message:—

"The reason I have ill-treated you was because I wanted the people of your country to come to me. I am glad they are coming. Whether they beat me or I beat them, I shall always be your friend. I wish to have an interview with you on the plain outside your house, and I want you to appear before me in the same dress in which you used formerly to come to me. I will send for you when I am ready."

I lost no time in putting on my uniform, and was barely dressed when Bitwáddad Hásani appeared with a summons for me to repair to the King's presence. Messrs. Flad and Mayer, and Aito Samuel, accompanied me to the royal pavilion. There were as many as five hundred officers in attendance, all anxiously waiting to witness my reception by their Sovereign—who it appears had been in a bad humour throughout the day, and just before my arrival had worked himself into a towering rage by recalling to mind the late Metropolitan and some of my fellow-captives, swearing in his fury that he would pierce the latter through and through with the lance which he held in his hand; and then, suiting the action to the word, aimed at a new carpet and drove the weapon into it. Under these circumstances, the bystanders augured anything but a favourable reception being accorded to me; but on my arrival his Majesty immediately changed his demeanour, and appeared quite gay. The same tent in which he had received the Mission on our first interview with him in Dámôt, at the end of January, 1866, was pitched in front of our prison-house for the occasion, and about 2,000 square yards of ground in the immediate vicinity were covered with carpets. When I left our inclosure, the King was inside the tent, together with all his European artisans, but on my approach he walked towards the tent door to welcome me. I was glad to notice a smile on his countenance, and as I deemed it prudent to put the best face upon our misfortunes, I endeavoured to look as pleased as if I had never been put into chains by the despot, and were not even then his prisoner. He received me most courteously, with his *shámma* thrown loosely over his shoulders, extending his right arm to shake me by the hand, remarking that, on that day, "we must all be English."

As soon as we had sat down, I on his Majesty's right hand and the European artisans on his left, in a circle round the tent, the King told me that the reason he had dispensed with his throne on that occasion was, that he wished to sit on the same level with me, his friend, and the representative of the Queen of England. He then looked pointedly at me, and said, "Why, Mr. Rassam, I heard that you had become quite gray; but I do not see one gray hair on your head. Look at me, and see how gray I have become since we parted." I was certainly surprised to see what a great change had taken place in the colour of his hair, and also in his countenance, since my last interview with him at Debra Tábor, at the end of June, 1866. There were only a few gray hairs visible then; now the gray largely predominated, and he looked altogether ten years older. To give the subject a jocular turn, I replied, "It is not to be wondered at that your Majesty has grown gray, considering that you have been enjoying the happiness of wedded life, whereas I am still unencumbered with the trouble and care of a wife." The banter contained in this reply drew a smile from the King, and placing his hands over his face he remarked, "There you hit me hard, my friend Rassam." *Tèj* was then brought, and served in the tumblers which I had presented to him. The first glass filled was handed to him; after tasting it, in accordance with Abyssinian usage, he rose a little and handed it to me, saying, "In our country drinking *tèj* together is a sign of friendship." His politeness on that occasion was extreme, and he was all smiles, except when alluding to the Bishop, Consul Cameron and the Rev. Mr. Stern. I endeavoured to soothe him when he broached these topics, and succeeded in cooling him down. He referred several times to the impending war, sometimes saying that he would fight even at the risk of being beaten; and, then, that it would be absurd in him to think of encountering a disciplined army. In either case, he said, I should remain his friend. "One day," he added, "you may see me dead; and while you stand by my corpse, it may be that you will curse me for my bad conduct towards you. You may say then, 'This wicked man ought not to be buried; let his remains rot above ground;' but I trust to your generosity." I again expressed a hope that, as I had come to his country as a friend, I should leave him in peace; and with reference to what he had said about his death, I begged that he would not mention such a calamity.

I may record here, as another proof of Theodore's excessive condescension on this occasion, that before the European artisans sat down he requested me to allow them to be seated. In spite of my remonstrance that it was his Majesty's prerogative and not mine to give such directions, he insisted on my doing so, and then joined me in according the necessary permission.

The King then alluded to a report which had reached him of the English having invented a variety of improved guns and other fire-arms, and that such muskets as his own soldiers carried were out of date, and regarded as "rubbish" by the British Army. "However," he added, "as your troops are coming to take you away, I must watch over you, for I cannot let you leave me. It is true that I have put you in fetters, after the barbarous usage of my country—which I admit to be a bad custom; but have you seen a hand-chain? That, I assure you, is still worse to bear." He then went on to say that his only reason for detaining me was that he wanted my countrymen to come and "open his eyes." After this, he suddenly asked me who were the sons of Abraham. I replied, Isaac and Jacob. "Who were their sons?" was the rejoinder. Guessing what the royal catechist was driving at, I skipped over all intermediate genealogy, and said, "David and Solomon." "And who was their son?" was the next question; to which I made answer, "From what I have heard, your Majesty is their offspring." Thereupon he laughed, and remarked that he wished for nothing more, and that if his enemies and those who abused him would only acknowledge him as such, he was ready to forgive them all. His Majesty then introduced me to my old acquaintance, Afa-Negûs Báhri, who was one of my guards the previous night, telling me that he had served under Râs 'Ali, and knew Plowden; "and, being a very old man," Theodore went on to say, " he will be able to tell you that the former Emperors of Abyssinia and the independent Chiefs very rarely saw a European—some of them, indeed, never saw one in the whole course of their lives, whereas I like them so much that I keep a number of them about me "— pointing to the six artisans, including M. Bardel, who were sitting in the tent. I replied that in former times Abyssinia was only read of in books, but that his Majesty's name had become so notorious that even children knew who Theodore was. He then gravely asked, " Why ? " " Because," said I, " your Majesty has put me in chains." No sooner had I uttered this speech than he burst out laughing, and, looking towards the European artisans, exclaimed, " Hear what Rassam says! Hear what Rassam says ! " One of them, named Zander, remarked, " Mr. Rassam has forgotten to mention America also." I rejoined, "If his Majesty will allow me, I will add the other two quarters of the globe as well." Thereat the King was so convulsed with laughter that all he could say was, " Oh, my friend, Rassam ! my friend ! " After a while, he proceeded to observe that two persons had accompanied me for whom he had neither love nor hatred ; but inasmuch as they had come to Abyssinia with me he would unfetter them for my sake, provided I stood security for them. I replied, that as they were my companions he would gratify me greatly by unchaining them, and that I would hold myself responsible for whatever Dr. Blanc and Lieutenant Prideaux might do. On his requesting me to send and have them unshackled, I begged Mr. Flad and Aito Samuel to go on the errand. They accordingly went, accompanied by Bitwäddad Hásani, and after removing their fetters returned with the two officers, agreeably with the King's orders. His Majesty received them well, and assured

u 2

them they had nothing to fear, whatever the upshot of the war might be. "You three be of good cheer," he continued, "because you are my children, and came to me when you knew of my having imprisoned Mr. Cameron, and had heard of his doings." Then, turning to me, he likened himself to a woman with child, who might either bring forth a son or a daughter, or might die of miscarriage, and said that he looked to me to assist him in giving birth to a son; to which he added, that a person might die either in youth, or old age, or in the prime of life, and expressed a hope that the last would not be his lot.

Referring next to his European employés, Theodore remarked that they were compelled to make the cannons and mortars which he had brought to Mágdala, adding, "They were as much obliged to cast them as you were to remain in Abyssinia; indeed, I forced them to perform the task." Then, turning to Mr. Waldmeier, he stated that that esteemed servant of his had lost no opportunity of speaking to him in my favour, and that the only time he had been angry with him was when he had ventured to recommend that he, the King, should assume a friendly attitude towards the invading British force. (We had heard of this fact when it occurred, and that Mr. Waldmeier had narrowly escaped a beating for having presumed to offer such advice.) In the course of the interview Theodore, regarding me with a disconsolate look, said in a subdued tone, "I hope, Mr. Rassam, that when your people [the British troops] arrive, they will not despise me because I am black; God has given us all the same faculties and heart." Then, remembering what he had said to me at Zagê, on the 25th of March, 1866, about the guardianship of his sons, he inquired whether Dajjáj 'Alamâyo had been introduced to me. On my replying in the negative, he said to the lad, "'Alamâyo, why do you not go to your father, Rassam?" Whereupon the boy approached and kissed the pillow on which I was leaning. After some further friendly conversation my companions and I were dismissed, his Majesty directing the young Prince and the European artisans to escort us back to our prison-house. Before his return to Salámgê he ordered that no guards were to sleep either in my room or in that of my companions; the remainder of the captives were to be watched as before. As Consul Cameron was unwell, the Chiefs, at the intercession of Samuel, allowed him to sleep in his own apartment, with Mr. Kerans to attend upon him; but Messrs. Stern, Rosenthal and Pietro were obliged to sleep in one room, under a guard, until we were released. We were told afterwards that the reason the King had caused us to be so strictly guarded the preceding night was owing to certain evil-disposed persons having reported that some of my party had been overheard boasting of the approach of the British troops, and that his Majesty had consequently come up that afternoon with no friendly feelings towards the captives. Luckily, something happened to please him after he entered the fortress, which led him to treat me with unusual affability.

On reaching Salámgê, however, he had another access of ill-humour. Seating himself on a rock in front of the royal tent, he summoned all the old Mágdala Chiefs before him, and began abusing them indiscriminately. The burden of his objurgation was that they were "asses," and did not understand me; that they had allowed me to do as I pleased on the mountain, without any check; that they had repeatedly sent to tell him that I was his friend, whereas I was in daily correspondence with my Government, urging them to dispatch an army to chastise him. "You asses and slaves," he went on to say, "Mr. Rassam has made fools of you and of me likewise by his professions of friendship for me. Did either you or your forefathers ever hear of a friend sending for troops to slaughter his friend's valiant men, ravish their wives, and reduce his people to bondage? Nevertheless, such a friend is Mr. Rassam, who, by playing upon your imagination, has managed to ingratiate himself into your favour. And yet the fault is mine, for I behaved unjustly towards him; he came to me as a friend, and I treated him as an enemy. Tell me, however, if you are prepared to fight Rassam's brothers, who are coming against you with guns that dazzle the sight, and muskets that shoot and stab simultaneously? We must keep Rassam with us at all risks, and watch him with every eye, until I see what is about to happen." The disconcerted Chiefs were at a loss what to say to this diatribe: they hesitated to abuse me, fearing that Theodore might then turn against them and take my part; they accordingly restricted themselves to assuring their liege lord that nothing would daunt them from carrying havoc into the ranks of the "white b——d asses, who had dared to leave their own country to invade the dominions of the mighty King of kings." Poor Damash, who was imprudent enough to open his mouth on the occasion, received a severe rebuff from Theodore for having ventured to brag against the "sons of the English," whereas, as his Majesty contemptuously reminded him, he was not a match even for the cowardly Gallas, who had despoiled him of his arms and horses. This sneer levelled against the unfortunate Chief was in allusion to a sally made by a detachment of the Magdala garrison upon the Worohaimano, a sub-tribe of the Wello-Gallas, on the morning of the 6th of September, 1867. As the affair occurred during our captivity, and was attended with a variety of circumstances illustrative of the mutual relations subsisting between the Amháras and their Galla neighbours, a succinct account of its origin and results may not be uninteresting to the reader.

Two days previous to the date above-mentioned Rás Bisáwwir, the good-natured Commandant, under the pretext that they wanted to weed their adjacent corn-fields, had permitted a young Afá-Negûs, named Mashí-ha, and Bajirwand Kánfu, an officer attached to the Treasury, to go beyond the gates of the fortress. It was soon discovered, however, that both had deserted to one of the Galla villages on the south-east of Mágdala, and that Bajirwand had robbed the Treasury of a pair of pistols and a rifle, which he made off with, the former secreted in a bag of chick-peas, which he told the guards at the gates he was going to sow, and the latter ostensibly as his own. The rifle belonged to the King, and was highly prized by him. It had been his companion from boyhood, and he alleged that he had borne it in all his battles. He looked upon it as a talisman, and for greater security had sent it to Mágdala at the end of 1866, believing —so it is said—that its possession would secure him greater renown than any of his predecessors. He entertained a similar notion with regard to Mágdala itself, and the superstition was shared by a number of his Chiefs, that even if despoiled of all his other territories, yet if he succeeded in retaining that Amba he would eventually go forth from thence, and reconquer his lost dominions, and subdue half the world besides. My firm belief is, that this persuasion induced Theodore to repair to Mágdala on hearing of the approach of the British force. As far as our interests were concerned, his credulity in this respect contributed in no small degree to the favourable termination of all our Abyssinian difficulties; for if, instead of spending three months in the neighbourhood of that fortress, he had carried us off to some distant stronghold—his native Kwâra, for instance—the war would have been indefinitely prolonged, and not one of the captives would have been rescued alive.

When the Mágdala Chiefs found that the charmed rifle had been taken away, and that there was a chance of its being conveyed to King Menilek, in case the deserters succeeded in reaching Shoa, they decided to pursue the runagates to their hiding-place, which had been revealed to them by some Galla spies. This step, however, was in direct violation of the King's orders, who had forbidden the garrison to leave the fortress on any warlike expedition, and restricted their duties to protecting his family and guarding his throne and crown, which were deposited in the Treasury; or, in plainer terms, they were to act on the defensive only. Of the two evils likely to incur the royal displeasure—the loss of the rifle and an interdicted raid—they chose the most hazardous; for had the Gallas been apprised of their approach, in the course of a couple of hours they might have mustered a body of five thousand horse, who would have effectually cut off their retreat, and slaughtered and mutilated them wholesale, ere they retraced their steps over the fifteen miles of Wello-Galla plateau which separated them from Mágdala.* Luckily for the assailants,

---

* The Gallas generally are notorious for mutilating all male prisoners, taken in war, in a most horrible manner. The same barbarous custom prevailed among the professedly Christian people of Shoa in the time of Sáhĕla Sĕlássĕ, but was abolished by Theodore when he conquered that country. In the present instance, the special grievance of the Amháras was enhanced by a desire to punish the Worohaimane, for having killed many helpless women and children who had gone beyond the gates of Mágdala to collect wood and grass. These outrages occurred during the period of our captivity.

their enemies, who had ceased keeping watch since the King left the neighbourhood at the end of 1865, were fast asleep; for who, thought they, among the Amhâras would dare to cross the deep chasm which lay between them and Mágdala but the dreaded Theodore?

The expeditionary force, which was headed by Bitwáddad Wûsi, consisted of 150 Musketeers and 250 Lancers, the former commanded by Bitwáddad Damâsh, and the latter by Dajjáj Gojjé. They left Mágdala at sunset, and before joining his detachment Damâsh called to take leave of me, and begged that in the event of his death I would look after his family. The wretched man evidently believed that he was going on a forlorn hope. They reached the village about midnight, and halted in a hollow till daybreak. It had been originally intended to surround the place at once, but just as they began to move some one reported that he heard a noise; of course, every one thought the same when the words of command "Listen!" "Silence!" were given. A council of war was then held by the three members of Council and the petty Chiefs who were to lead the assault, and it was unanimously decided that operations should commence forthwith. When within two hundred yards of the first hut, however, a squabble arose among the soldiers which of them should invest the village, and which should engage in the attack—all being equally anxious to take the latter duty, which afforded a better prospect of plunder. Meanwhile, Afâ-Negús Mashísha and his companion, who had passed the night with the local Galla Chief in a small hut at the other end of the village, situated in a wooded ravine, overhearing the wrangling among the soldiers, and suspecting that something was in the wind, hurried out into the cover, where they awaited their host, who had mounted a horse and started off at full gallop towards another large Galla village, about three miles distant, to give the alarm. The Mágdala Chiefs, on the other hand, finding all their efforts to maintain discipline unavailing, ordered the entire party to push on together. As the Galla Chief's house was thought to contain the most desirable prizes, including the Chief himself, the two deserters, and the most valuable booty, a combined rush was made in that direction. After seizing and securing two of the Chief's cousins, his brother, wife and sister, together with three children, who were all fast asleep at the time, a general search was made for plunder and the two runaway officials. One hut where the Chief's horses were kept was attacked by a Christianized Galla, and two men showing fight in defence of their master's property were speared down by the assailant. Three others were killed in the village while attempting to escape; the remainder, to the number of thirty-one souls, including women and children, who had not managed to get out of the way before daylight, were captured. It was then resolved by the Council to dispatch the prisoners in advance, together with all the cattle, horses and mules that had been seized, in charge of Dajjáj Gojjé's Lancers, while Bitwáddad Damásh and his Musketeers were to bring up the rear, to ward off pursuit. The Mágdala warriors were in the highest spirits, congratulating themselves upon having taught the Gallas a lesson which they were not likely soon to forget; but their exultation was premature. They continued their homeward journey for three hours without noticing any movement on the part of the enemy, when suddenly Galla horsemen were espied galloping towards them from every direction. At this juncture, Damásh, who was about two miles behind the Lancers, judging that the Gallas would first attempt to rescue the captives and the plunder—never dreaming that they would venture to attack a party armed with muskets—ordered his men to push on and overtake their comrades. In less than half an hour about twenty horsemen approached, headed by the Chief of the village, who was heard calling out to his followers to attack the Christian "Káfirs" and seize their muskets. In the mean time the assailants were receiving fresh additions to their numbers, the Gallas for twenty miles round having been apprised that something was amiss by the light of three burning houses which the Mágdala detachment had fired before they left the village. On recognizing the Galla Chief, the Musketeers bawled out, "Shoot him down!" whereupon a native of Kwâra aimed at him and shot him dead. A couple of horses, also, were killed by the fire of the party, and five horsemen were wounded, two of whom died shortly after. The lifeless body of the Chief was immediately picked up and borne away on horseback by his men, to the great relief of Damâsh, who was glad to see his deadly enemies retreat. This incident checked the Gallas for a time, and enabled the wary Gojjé and Bitwáddad Wâsi to descend into the valley with the prisoners and booty, where they were safe from pursuit. Meanwhile the Gallas had re-assembled in force, and poor Damâsh, who could not boast of being a good soldier, much less a leader, lost his wits. He was then about a mile from the difficult pass leading down to the valley which surrounds Mágdala, and instead of placing his men where they might easily have protected the rear of the Lancers and kept the Gallas at bay at the same time, he ordered them to "run." Thereupon, as might have been expected, a regular panic ensued among the soldiers; all tried to be the first to escape through the narrow pass, which admitted only a few abreast, and in that state of utter disorganization—many of them actually falling down from sheer fright—they were pounced upon by about two hundred of the Galla horsemen, who dismounted and rushed upon the terrified Amhâras with spears, swords and stones. Among the assailants on the occasion was one of Damâsh's own men, who used to thatch the roofs of our huts, and who had deserted to the Worohaimano a few days before. On recognizing his old commanding officer, who was rather infirm owing to long illness, and was consequently left in the lurch, the fellow bawled out to his new associates, "There is that villain, Damâsh; let us seize him alive!" At the mention of his name, which was hated at Mágdala and throughout the neighbourhood, a party of Gallas fell upon him and deprived him of his arms. They then endeavoured to secure him as a hostage, in order to exchange him against their captured countrymen, whose release was now hopeless, as they had already been conveyed into the valley. Damâsh would inevitably have been borne away had not Bâsha Kâsha, a countryman of his and one of his petty officers, bawled out to his men, "Shall we not be called cowards if we see our Chief carried off before our eyes, without attempting to rescue him? Shame upon us! Let us go and deliver him out of the hands of the Muslim slaves." He accordingly returned with twenty Musketeers, and a well-aimed discharge from the party killed one and wounded three of the Gallas who were engaged in binding their prisoner. Damâsh was now free to run, and taking to his heels tumbled down the valley, heedless of all impediments, and regardless of the risk to life and limb, intent only on getting beyond the reach of his deadly enemies. Fortunately, he did not try to escape by the pass; had he done so, he must have fallen once more into the hands of the Gallas, who regarded him as a great prize. The deserters, Afa-Negûs Mashisha and his companion, now appeared on the scene armed to the teeth, the latter carrying the King's rifle, which he discharged with deadly effect upon the fugitives. One of his victims was the brave Bâsha Kâsha, who received a shot through the leg, just above the knee. By seven o'clock about five hundred Gallas were assembled on the edge of the precipice, all engaged in throwing spears and sticks and hurling stones on the retreating Amhâras, who were scrambling down the rough valley as best they could. Had their assailants possessed the pluck to follow the runagates, not one of the latter would have escaped, for they were utterly panic-stricken, and most of them had thrown away their arms in the stampedo.

This disaster cast a gloom over Mágdala, and nearly drove the crest-fallen Commandant out of his senses. Damâsh, who had received a scratch on one of his legs in leaping over the precipice, feigned to be badly wounded, and got himself conveyed into the fortress on the back of a mule, supported by a couple of men on each side, and looking more dead than alive. He was obliged to keep up the deception, and was consequently confined to his couch for more than a month. A case of fractured skull, and another of a petty Chief, one of whose legs was nearly severed—both wounds inflicted by the stones thrown by the Gallas—were brought to Dr. Blanc, but they were beyond medical treatment, and the two men died a few days after.

30th.—Sent our compliments to the King early this morning, and shortly after I received a message from his Majesty, asking me to send down to Salámgé five of my fellow-captives —namely, Messrs. Staiger, Brandeis, Schiller, Essler and Macraire — to assist in making stone shot for the large mortar. My reply was, that I had no objection to the proposal, if the individuals themselves agreed to it. On their consent being obtained, hand-chains were substituted for their fetters, and they were conducted down to Salámgê. The couriers who brought me this message were charged with another, to the effect that his Majesty was desirous of befriending all the captives for my sake, and hoped shortly to release them from their chains. This intimation led me to apprehend that he intended asking the rest of my fellow-captives, except my fellow-officials, to work for him; but the subject was not mooted again.

I received letters this afternoon from Colonel Merewether and M. Munzinger, which apprised us, to our great delight, that the British force had reached Ashángi.

Mr. Flad called on me in the morning, and told me that the King had inquired of him how I felt after our interview the day before. On learning that I was happy, his Majesty went on to say, "I thought of him all last night, and I had sweet dreams in consequence. I wish I lived next to him, as you do, for I should then be able to see him; but for the present I am too busy."

31st.—In the afternoon Mr. Waldmeier came to me from the King with a request that I would become security for the five Europeans who joined him yesterday, otherwise he would be obliged to keep them in chains. I stated in reply that it was quite out of the question for me to assume such a responsibility on behalf of persons over whom I had no control; that the individuals referred to were living at Salámgê and working there for his Majesty, whereas I was shut up in Mágdala, and knew nothing of what took place in the royal camp. Theodore subsequently sent word to say that he was quite satisfied with my answer, and had foreseen that I knew better than to undertake the proposed suretyship. The artisans, however, were eventually released from their fetters, having found some of their fellow-employés at Salámgê to stand security for them.

1st April.—Sent compliments to Theodore this morning, and dispatched letters to the British camp during the day.

2nd.—The members of the Mission received an invitation from the King early this morning to witness the bringing up of the mortar to the plateau by the new road which his Majesty had made below the southern slope of Salámgê. We accordingly equipped ourselves in uniform, and went down, accompanied by the old and new Commandants and Aito Samuel—the latter by special licence, without which he could not have ventured to join us. We found Theodore superintending the operation. He welcomed us most graciously, and bade us be seated behind him, on the edge of a precipice overlooking the soldiers, who were busy dragging the different mortars and guns which were cast at Debra Tâbor last year up the incline. As soon as the large mortar, which the King had named "Sevastopol," reached the bend in the road below us, his Majesty asked me to look at it and tell him what I thought of it. I replied that it was a splendid piece of artillery, adding that I hoped it would not be long ere the British army would be viewing it with the same amicable feelings that then animated me. The King smiled, and said, "I hope so too." I thought this a good opportunity to ask him to "gladden my heart" by releasing the remaining five captives—namely, Messrs. Cameron, Stern, Rosenthal, Kerans and Pietro—of their chains. Samuel hesitated at first, through fear, to translate my request, but on his Majesty's asking what I had said, the request was repeated by me, and interpreted to him. He replied, "I'sh-shi" (very well); and forthwith ordered an officer to go and strike off their chains at once.

The monster mortar, borne on a strong waggon, had to be dragged by main force above a hundred feet up an acclivity at an angle of forty-five degrees. The weight of it, I was told, was at least seventy tons, and as many as five hundred men were engaged in moving it, encouraged and assisted by all the Chiefs of note, who ever and anon placed stones under the wheels to prevent them from turning backwards. Occasionally, one or more of the strips of cow-hide which bound mortar and carriage together snapped asunder, threatening the momentary precipitation of the huge mass into the valley below, at the imminent peril of those who might happen to be in its way. When the "Sevastopol" reached level ground, the King asked us to mount the waggon and inspect it. It was unquestionably a wonderful piece of ordnance for its size, and more wonderful still as the workmanship of his Majesty's European artisans, who had previously had no experience of casting cannon. As I knew that Theodore expected me to say something on the occasion, I sent to tell him—he was then superintending the transport of other mortars and guns up the ascent—that since the time of the great King Menilek no one in Abyssinia had ever accomplished such a feat. He then invited me to sit by his side again, on the edge of the precipice, and began questioning me about European warfare: how peace was concluded between two contending parties; how the words of command were given in our army; what was the range of our soldiers' rifles; what number of British troops had been sent against him, and how they manœuvred. After I had replied to all his queries, with the exception of such as were purely military, on which subjects, I told his Majesty, I was unable to enlighten him, he said, "I know you are a man of tongue;" and then subjoined, "Were I as

THE GREAT MORTAR "SEVASTOPOL."

powerful as I once was, I should certainly have gone down to the coast to meet your people on landing; or I would have sent and asked them what they wanted in my country. As it is, I have lost all Abyssinia but this rock"—he looked up and pointed to Mágdala—"and it would therefore be absurd in me to say anything. However, I am ready to meet them here, and I resign myself to the protection of my Creator." He remarked, further, that he had been in constant trouble since we left him in July, 1866, owing to the refusal of his people to pay the regular taxes. The whole country had risen against him, and the rebels had driven him to desperation. "But," he added, "whenever I caught any of them I caused them to be burnt; while they, on their side, did not spare any of my subjects who fell into their hands. During the last six months especially, while on the way from Debra Tabor to this place, I have been harassed day and night by the robbers, and have been driven to support my soldiers on plunder. You yourself have witnessed what trouble making these roads and moving these guns has given me; but," he concluded, "I hope you do not imagine that I had the guns cast out of any animosity towards your people. I had them made to use against my own countrymen." He next reverted to the subject of Consul Cameron having re-entered Abyssinia without bringing an answer to his letter addressed to our Queen, and then said in an angry tone, "After his return to my country I waited five days before I learnt that he had come back without an answer. At the expiration of that time, I sent and asked him what had brought him back to my country, seeing that he had come without an answer to my letter. Receiving no satisfactory reply, I said no more." He then dilated anew on the abuse heaped upon him by Messrs. Stern and

Rosenthal; but for all that, he went on to say, the former had felt constrained to call him "a wonderful man" in his book ('Wanderings among the Falashas'), and he, the King, had detained him because Mr. Cameron had brought no reply to his letter. He knew, he said, that my companions (Blanc and Prideaux) and I were great men, and admitted that he had ill-used us without any just cause, for which he felt very sorry; in future, however, he would always treat us as friends. He then ordered a tent to be pitched, and directed Messrs. Waldmeier and Salmüller to provide breakfast for us within it, evidently under the impression that the wives of those gentlemen, who were the daughters of the late Mr. Bell, would be able to serve us with some European dishes. When Mr. Flad announced that everything was ready, the King rose and led the way, we following him. Theodore looked very sad, and although he made several attempts to be cheerful, he could not hide the care which was weighing on his mind. I never saw him so calm as he was on that day, and I shall never forget the melancholy expression of his countenance when, glancing at the half-clad men who were hauling up the guns, he exclaimed, "How can I show those ragged soldiers of mine to your well-dressed troops!" On our way to the tent, he asked me what I thought would be a proper charge for the large mortar. I replied that I could not tell him, as I was not an artilleryman, nor in any way conversant with military matters.

On the King's return to his own tent, he sent me word that the day on which "Sevastopol" was successfully cast, and to-day, when he had met me again in health and prosperity, had been the happiest days he had experienced since our separation at Debra Tabor. He therefore asked me to allow him to have a salute fired in honour of the auspicious event; accordingly, shortly after, the roar of artillery was heard mingled with the *Ellel*, or exulting shouts of the women, both on Salámgê and Mágdala. Before we took leave of Theodore he sent Messrs. Flad and Waldmeier to me to say, that a live coal, not larger than a pea, if not extinguished, might create a great conflagration. Samuel understood by this remark that his Majesty meant to intimate that he looked to me to put the fire out at once.

At about 3 p.m. we returned to our prison-house, escorted by the old and new Commandants. On reaching the inclosure, I hardly believed that it was the same place; for all my fellow-captives had been unshackled, and the dismal rattling of their chains was no longer heard. In the course of the afternoon I received a few lines from M. Munzinger, apprising me that our deliverers were not far distant.

3rd.—Wrote a few lines to Colonel Merewether this morning, and dispatched them out of Mágdala and through the royal camp by no less than five different channels. I also sent our compliments to the King, and requested him to allow Messrs. Flad and Waldmeier to come to me, in order that I might transmit an important message to him, through them. He acquiesced at once; whereupon I solicited his permission to write and apprise the Commander-in-Chief of the British army of the civility which we had lately received at his Majesty's hands. (I intended this as a feeler, and hoped that it might induce him to open communications with Sir Robert Napier.) His immediate reply was, that I had mistaken the motives of his recent conduct towards me; that he had released my fellow-captives from their fetters, not because he was afraid of the expected force, or out of any regard for the prisoners, but simply to gratify me, and as a proof of his personal esteem; hence, he did not see the use of my reporting a matter which in no way concerned a third person. He, moreover, desired Messrs. Flad and Waldmeier to convey to me the assurance of his continued friendship, and remarked to the latter that if I asked him to breakfast and dine with me, he would accept the invitation, rather than disappoint me. On the strength of this speech, Mr. and Mrs. Flad, who were then residing in Mágdala, felt at perfect liberty to accept an invitation from me, without applying for the royal permission. When Mr. Flad returned to Salámgê, Theodore inquired whether I had received his reply graciously. To an affirmative answer he remarked, "Mr. Rassam and I know each other well."

The King started off in the afternoon with the bulk of his army. One report was that he was bound on a plundering expedition; another, that he had gone to reconnoitre the movements of our troops. Rain fell during the afternoon.

4th.—News arrived this morning that the King was plundering all the country between the Bâshilo river and the fortress, and had not even spared some huts, situated below the Kâfir-Bär Gate, on the north-eastern side of Mágdala, although they belonged to Christianized Gallas who were in the royal service. This intelligence excited no little apprehension among the residents on the Amba generally—even the royal troops were not without fears that their property might be seized; consequently, every one was intent on hiding all he could from the grasp of the dreaded Sovereign. It was reported that Theodore had been driven to these harsh measures in order to provide food for his starving army. The resistance of the peasantry led to frequent encounters with the royal troops, and many were killed on both sides. My agents on the Bâshilo were also despoiled, but by all accounts they fought bravely in defence of their belongings. The communication which I had sent through them to Colonel Merewether the day before they concealed in the ground, and forwarded it to the British camp during the night. Theodore returned from his infamous expedition this afternoon, and, yielding to the advice of the Mágdala Chiefs, I sent a message congratulating him on his safe arrival.

5th.—Theodore sent me his compliments this morning. After Divine Service in my hut, Bitwáddad Hásani and Rás Bisáwwir, the old and new Commandants, paid me a visit, having received special orders from the King to see me often and attend to my wants. There was a little rain in the evening.

6th.—Sent compliments to Theodore this morning, and at noon Bitwáddad Hásani, with three ex-members of the Mágdala Council, namely, Rás Bisáwwir, Bitwáddad Damásh and Dajjáj Gojjé, called on me, by his Majesty's command, to reciprocate my compliments, and to sit with and "comfort" me. As the new Commandant was present, none of my old friends dared to drink even a cup of coffee, though poor Gojjé winked at me, in a way giving me to understand that he wished the interloper at land's end, as he was longing for a glass of *téj*— a beverage which he had not tasted since his removal from office.

After these visitors left, Messrs. Flad and Waldmeier came and informed me that the King was anxious to hear from the Commander-in-Chief of the British army, and that he had requested the former to send one of his servants to our camp to collect news. Thereupon, Mr. Flad told his Majesty that I had expected a communication from Sir Robert Napier for the last two days, but owing, as he supposed, to the disturbed state of the neighbourhood, the messengers were probably afraid to approach. To this the King replied, that those who carried such messages were afraid of him too. For the last three days Theodore has done scarcely anything but ascend the height of Salássê, scanning with a telescope the country towards Dalanta, from which direction he had been told the British force was advancing. Whenever his spies brought him any intelligence of its movements, he invariably sent and communicated it to me.

7th.—Theodore has been busy with his telescope throughout the day, and it was reported that he had espied some of our troops descending into the Báshilo. He is now anxious to hear from the Commander-in-Chief and to ascertain his fate.

The old and new Commandants of Mágdala came to me this evening with the King's compliments, and told me that he wished to see me at Salámgê early to-morrow morning, with all my fellow-captives, from which we inferred that he intended to retain us with him. The native prisoners were also ordered down. This news, we feared, portended no good to any of us.

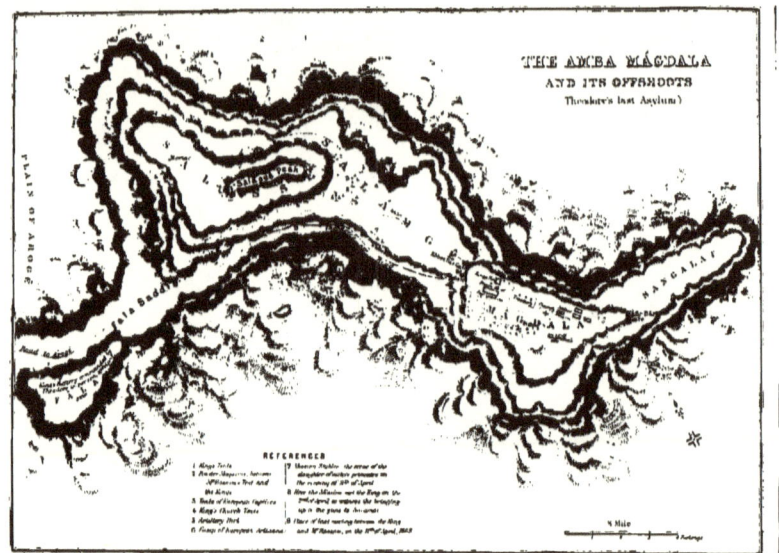

CHAPTER XXVI.

THE FALL OF THEODORE.

The European Captives summoned to Salámgê by the King — Theodore harangues his troops on the impending invasion by the British — Declines communicating with Sir Robert Napier — Release of some of the native prisoners — Cruel massacre of the remainder — The European Captives sent back to Mágdala — Letter arrives for Theodore from Sir Robert Napier, which he refuses to receive — The native troops are massed at Salámgê — Theodore attacks the British, is defeated, and wishes for peace — Lieutenant Prideaux dispatched to Sir Robert Napier and returns to Salámgê — Is dispatched again with an angry letter from Theodore — The Author and his fellow-captives directed to go to the British camp — The Author's interview with Theodore previous to his departure — The Captives reach the British camp in safety — Theodore's letter of apology and proffered gift of cattle to Sir Robert Napier on the morning of Easter Sunday — The Commander-in-Chief's message in reply — Theodore sets all the European artisans at liberty — Was Theodore deceived ? — The Author's justification.

AT dawn on the 8th of April, Wald-Gâbir, the royal valet, came to say that the King wished me to go down to Salámgê immediately, with all my fellow-captives, as he desired me to act as a judge between him and the people who were coming to fight him. It was surmised that the spy who had come to him the day before had communicated some disquieting news. The King had never before summoned the European captives and the native prisoners simultaneously, and it was apprehended that we were going to be put together and treated alike. However, when we reached the royal presence the King rose and welcomed us, and desired me to approach with my companions. He was examining some guns, and wore a new style of dress on the occasion, made of Lyons silk worked with gold—it is now in the South Kensington Museum— and instead of the common nether garments of the country he had on a pair made of white tinsel; in fact, he looked more like a harlequin than a sovereign in this novel motley suit. He walked on towards his tent, bidding my party to follow, and when he had taken his seat in front of his pavilion he asked Dr. Blanc, Lieutenant Prideaux, Consul Cameron and myself to sit near him, the rest of our fellow-captives remaining a little distance off. We talked on different matters for more than an hour in the open air, and in the course of the conversation the King told me that the reason he had brought us down was, that he might leave us in a safe place when our troops arrived. Being with him, he said he could protect us and look after our comfort; whereas if we were at Mágdala when our army reached, his soldiers might illtreat us. "Wherever the Empress and my son are," he added, "there you shall be. I have brought them both down to Salámgê for security." He told me to send for our tents, in order that we might pitch them near his. After this we left him, and repaired to a silk tent which he had erected for us, not more than fifty yards from his own, there to rest until our tents were forthcoming. Theodore was very absent during this interview; his countenance, despite the forced smiles which ever and anon played upon it, betraying that he really did feel like another Damocles—to whom he compared himself—and that his fate now hung upon a thread.

Immediately on entering the tent above-mentioned we heard that all the troops had been mustered, and about half-an-hour afterwards we were surprised to see the King himself standing on a rock not more than fifteen yards from us, haranguing his soldiers on the approaching invaders of his

country. He told them that in a day or two, perhaps, they would be obliged to encounter men who were far superior to them in strength and arms—whose very dress was bedecked with gold, to say nothing of their treasures, which could only be borne by elephants. "Are you ready to fight?" he continued, with increasing animation, "and enrich yourselves with the spoils of the white slaves, or will you disgrace me by leaving me in the lurch?" Afâ-Negûs Bâhri, whose name has already been mentioned, stepped forward and bawled out, "Only wait, your Majesty, until these asses make their appearance, when we will tear them to pieces, and those of them who are lucky enough to escape will have a sorry tale to tell on returning to their own country." The King, on hearing this vaunt, instead of commending the poor old man for his bombastic enthusiasm, as any rational being would have done under the circumstances, proceeded forthwith to damp the courage of his troops in this style:—
"What say you, old fool? Have you ever seen an English soldier to know what he is like, and what weapons he carries? Be assured that before you know where you are, your belly will be filled with bullets." Even the Abyssinian soldiery would have been provoked into merriment by such a speech coming from any other than the dreaded Theodore; as it was, they pretended to look grave, and were forthwith dismissed.

About an hour after we parted, the King went to superintend the fortification of a point against the attack of our troops. As he passed our tent he called me out, and indicated a clean spot, about one hundred feet from his own pavilion, where I might pitch my tent. (*Vide* Plan, page 277). He then entered into friendly conversation with me about communicating with the Commander-in-Chief, a step which

I had always urged him to take. He said, "What is the use of my doing so? The die is cast, and things must take their course. We shall see what will come to pass. However, as far as you are concerned, do not fear; no harm shall befall you."

When the King returned from his work I went out with my fellow-captives to welcome him. He told us that he had seen through a telescope some baggage and elephants coming down the Báshilo. In the afternoon he sent to ask me why our people advanced so slowly.

Early on the 9th of April he sent me compliments, and then went to see to the defence of another spot, and returned at about three in the afternoon. As soon as he entered his tent he again sent to tell me that he had seen more baggage coming down the valley, and had noticed small white animals with it, and asked if I could tell him what they were. I said they might be Somáli sheep.

When the native prisoners, 570 in number, came down after us from Mágdala, on the 8th, they were confined in my stables, in front of the royal household-establishment, and our mules and servants were turned out for their accommodation. That day, the whole of the children and women, amounting to 186, were released, together with thirty-seven Chiefs, including Kántiba Hailo and Balambarás Tasámma, the Master of the Horse. The day following he ordered the remainder to be released, excepting a few political prisoners. By 4 P.M. ninety-five more prisoners had been released, and as the process of opening the chains was rather slow, owing to the few hands told off to the work, those who were still unshackled became somewhat impatient. On hearing this Theodore fell into a rage, saying, "Do these people think they can oblige me to strike off their chains?" and rushed out in a frenzy, sword in hand, and called to his soldiers to follow him to the quarters of the native prisoners. A friendly courtier came running to me, and said, "The King has gone to make a general slaughter of the captives; tell your people to remain in their tents and keep quiet."

The King had not been away ten minutes before we heard the discharge of musketry, which lasted till 6.30 P.M. The place of execution was not more than 200 yards from our encampment. The unfortunate prisoners were dragged before him, one by one; and after the name and offence of the individual had been repeated, he ordered the victim to be thrown over the precipice. Those who did not die by the fall were to be shot by the Musketeers, who had been sent below for the purpose. After this indiscriminate slaughter had continued for two hours the King cooled down, and said "Enough;" not, however, until he had caused the destruction of no less than 197 hapless victims, only thirty-five of whom had committed any crime—the rest having been confined for trivial offences, or for having incurred the royal displeasure by laughing amongst themselves when the King was in a bad temper. I'ngădă Wark had been imprisoned for losing a rifle, and for being unable to pay the price at which Theodore had valued it. When brought before his master he said, "Have I not served you faithfully? Why do you kill me?" "Hurl the villain down! Have you not brought the Franks on me?" was the savage rejoinder. One of the most innocent of the victims was a youth, named Kidâna Máryam, who had been one of the King's pages, and had frequently been sent to me with his Majesty's compliments. He had dared to laugh while conversing with one Zaudi, of the royal body-guard, when Theodore was out of humour. Zaudi also was executed on this occasion, simply because a musket which he had loaded for the King missed fire when the latter attempted to discharge it at a rebel who was deriding him at a distance.

On that dreadful afternoon the King, in my opinion, must have been quite insane; and if any one instance goes to prove this more than another it is the following. Among the unfortunate prisoners was a man who had been confined on a charge of having attempted to take liberties with one of the royal concubines; and as Theodore generally made the relatives of the accused party suffer as well as the principal, he ordered two lads, between twelve and fifteen years of age, sons of the offender, to be imprisoned with their father. Soon after the King had commenced the slaughter, these unhappy boys were dragged before him, and on being apprised that they were the offspring of the man who had misbehaved himself, as aforesaid, his Majesty shouted out, "Away with them!" whereupon they were instantly hurled down the precipice and dashed to pieces. When the father of the two boys was produced, Theodore's rage had somewhat subsided, and after hearing the culprit's crime rehearsed by the proper officer, he said, "Open his chains and let him go."

That indiscriminate carnage disgusted the troops more than anything that had occurred before, as a great number of them had to assist either in the destruction of a relative or friend. Courage to resist they had none; they could only bewail their misery in the darkness of the night, out of the hearing of eavesdroppers.

Very early next morning (Good Friday, the 10th April) the King sent to bid me go up at once to Mágdala, with my eight fellow-captives, Mrs. Rosenthal being now added to our number. That Theodore was in an awful mood was evident from another message which I then received from him. I had repeatedly advised him to communicate with Sir Robert Napier, but he gave no heed to what I said. He now sent to say, "Do you want me to write to that man? No, I will do no such thing, inasmuch as he has been sent by a woman."

As we were starting, on our way back to Mágdala, a letter reached me from Sir Robert Napier, addressed to the King; whereupon I sent immediately to ask his Majesty's permission to forward it to him, with the messenger. He returned me an indignant answer, saying that he did not wish to see either the letter or the bearer, warning me at the same time against communicating with the camp. "If you write to them," (the British), he said, "my friendship with you will be at an end, and the blood of the messenger who carries your missive will be on your head. Beware!"

The following is a copy of Sir Robert Napier's letter above referred to, as published in the Abyssinian 'Blue-Book:'—

"From &c., &c., to King Theodorus.

"By command of the Queen of England I am approaching Mágdala with my army, in order to recover from your hands Envoy Rassam, Consul Cameron, Dr. Blanc, Lieutenant Prideaux, and the other Europeans now in your Majesty's power.

"I request your Majesty to send them to my camp, as soon as it is sufficiently near to admit of their coming in safety."

On that morning all the troops, both at Mágdala and Salámgê, were ordered to assemble, and only fifty men were left to guard the fortress—thirty over the native prisoners, and twenty at the gates. When the King was asked who was to guard the European captives, he replied, "Is not Mr. Rassam there? He is quite sufficient." For all that, our old warders watched us very strictly that day, and we could neither laugh nor talk without their saying, "Hush! you will vex his Majesty." A little after noon we heard that the British troops had reached A'rogê, and were taking up a position on different hillocks around Mágdala. About 3 p.m. it was rumoured that the King had taken the great body of his troops, and had gone to attack the advanced guard of our army. We heard continual firing for nearly two hours after, but could not determine whether the Abyssinians were only making a demonstration—as is their wont on similar occasions—or were regularly engaged with our troops. The gates of the fortress had been closed, and no communication was allowed between Salámgê and Mágdala until the morning. We retired to sleep, therefore, uncertain whether the King had actually attacked the British force, or had merely feigned to do so.

At 10·30 p.m., however, I was awoke from a sound sleep by Aito Samuel, who told me that Messrs. Flad and Waldmeier had come to me with a message from the King. I immediately called them in, when they delivered the following communication from the King:—"How have you passed the day? Thank God, I am well. I, being a King, could not allow people to come and fight me without attacking them first. I have done so, and my troops have been beaten. I thought your people were women, but I find they are men. They fought very bravely. Seeing that I am unable to cope with them, I must ask you to reconcile me to them." To this I replied that I was now powerless, as hostilities had already commenced; I could only send one of my companions, Lieutenant Prideaux, to the Commander-in-Chief, to see what could be done. I advised his Majesty, at the same time, to send an Abyssinian of high rank on his part, and to allow Mr. Flad to accompany them, he being a mutual friend. I owe it to Lieutenant Prideaux to state that he accepted the proposed duty most willingly.

At dawn the following morning, the 11th, Mr. Flad returned, and informed me that the King concurred in my proposal, and begged me to do as I had suggested; whereupon Lieutenant Prideaux accompanied Mr. Flad to the King. His Majesty appointed Dajjâj 'Âlami, a Chief who had married his favourite consort's daughter, to go with them, and then sent them off to the British camp.

I had dispatched Dasta, one of my interpreters, with Lieutenant Prideaux, thinking that he might prove useful to him on the road, or with the King. When his Majesty saw him he approved of his appointment, but ordered him to return to him as soon as the Commission had been received by the British authorities, and give an account of their reception. When they all left, the King went up to Salássê, and watched their movements through a telescope. Dasta returned about noon and informed the King, who was still sitting on Salássê, of the handsome reception accorded to his Chief. Whereupon his Majesty told him to come and communicate the happy tidings to me. After that, I heard nothing more, except that the King had worked himself into a fearful mood on the return of the Commissioners, and had sent Messrs. Prideaux and Flad back to Sir Robert Napier, with an angry letter,* and had refused to send his own

---

* The following are copies of the letters which passed on this occasion between the Commander-in-Chief and King Theodore, as published in the 'Blue-Books:'—

"*Copy of Letter from* Sir R. Napier *to* Theodore, *dated* '*British Camp, Affajo,* 11*th April,* 1868;' *sent in reply to the Verbal Message brought by* Lieutenant Prideaux, Mr. Flad, *and the* Dajazmaj Alamee, *the Son-in-Law of the King.*

"Your Majesty has fought like a brave man, and has been overcome by the superior power of the British Army.

deputy, Dajjâj 'Âlami, again to our camp, as he was against coming to any terms. The Dajjâj advised him to resort to

> "It is my desire that no more blood may be shed. If, therefore, your Majesty will submit to the Queen of England, and bring all the Europeans now in your Majesty's hands, and deliver them safely, this day, in the British Camp, I guarantee honourable treatment for yourself, and all the members of your Majesty's family."

KING THEODORE TO SIR ROBERT NAPIER.

"*Delivered by Lieut. Prideaux and the Dajaz Alamie on* 11*th April,* 1868.

"(Note, without superscription, seal, signature, or date. Along with it was returned the Commander-in-Chief's letter of that morning, in which the King was called upon to submit.)

"In the name of the Father, and the Son, and the Holy Ghost—one God in His Trinity and His Unity.

"Kassa, whose trust is in Christ, thus speaks:—

"O people of Abyssinia, will it always be thus that you flee before the enemy, when I myself, by the power of God, go not forth with you to encourage you?

"Believing that all power had been given to me, I had established my Christian people in this heathen spot. In my city are multitudes whom I have fed: maidens protected and maidens unprotected; women whom yesterday made widows; and aged parents who have no children. God has given you the power. See that you forsake not these people. It is a heathen land.

"My countrymen have turned their backs on me and have hated me, because I imposed tribute on them, and sought to bring them under military discipline. You have prevailed against me by means of people brought into a state of discipline.

"My followers who loved me were frightened by one bullet, and fled in spite of my commands. When you defeated them I was not with the fugitives.

"Believing myself to be a great Lord I gave you battle; but, by reason of the worthlessness of my artillery, all my pains were as nought.

"The people of my country, by taunting me with having embraced the religion of the Franks, and by saying that I had become a Musalman, and in ten different ways, had provoked me to anger against them. Out of what I have done of evil towards them may God bring good. His will be done. I had intended, if God had so decreed, to conquer the whole world; and it was my desire to die if my purpose could not be fulfilled. Since the day of my birth till now no man has dared to lay hand on me. When-

friendly measures, as there was nothing to be gained by fighting the English. The only answer he elicited was that he should hold his tongue.

About 4 P.M. the old and new Commandants of Mágdala came to me, with dejected countenances, to say that the King their master had sent them to tell me to go down to the British camp and take all my fellow-captives with me. Every Abyssinian who was apprised of the royal mandate came running with melancholy faces to see the upshot, as the general opinion was that the King meant to have us massacred on the road, or to keep us close prisoners until he had come to terms with the Commander-in-Chief. If he had really entertained any such design he was induced to change his mind when we met—probably in the hope that by sending me at once to our camp he would secure peace. Had the idea ever occurred to him that he would be required to surrender himself a prisoner, he would assuredly have had us cut to pieces rather than give us up.

As soon as Samuel heard the Chiefs' communication he said to me, "I advise you, Mr. Rassam, not to attempt to go to your camp before seeing the King." I replied that I must do so, as his Majesty had not expressed a desire to see me. "At all events," he said, "send and obtain permission from the King, and say that you could not think of leaving for your camp without wishing him farewell, and thanking him for his kindness and civility." I rejoined that

---

ever my soldiers began to waver in battle, it was mine to arise and rally them. Last night the darkness hindered me from doing so.

"Your people who have passed the night in joy; may God not do unto you as he has done to me. I had hoped, after subduing all my enemies in Abyssinia, to lead my army against Jerusalem, and expel from it the Turks. A warrior who has dandled strong men in his arms like infants will never suffer himself to be dandled in the arms of others."

he (Samuel) knew very well that ever since my arrival in Abyssinia I had never taken the initiative in such cases, and that at that critical juncture especially I could not do so, as his Majesty might easily have sent for me, had he wished to see me before I went away. Samuel then went and spoke to the Chiefs who had brought me the message and were waiting to escort me and my fellow-captives. They both urged me to take Samuel's advice. I told them that they knew their master's temper, and that if I sent to him myself and asked for an interview he might take it amiss and become furious; but, if they liked, Dr. Blanc and I would put on our uniforms and be ready to appear before the King, should he express a wish to see us.

The reason why Samuel and the Commandants of Mágdala were so anxious that I should see Theodore before going to the British camp was this:—All the Chiefs and courtiers who knew the footing on which I had been with the King were impressed with the idea that my meeting him would suffice to allay the royal anger; and as on this particular occasion every Abyssinian fully expected that we should be put to death, the above-named individuals judged that the only way to avert our doom was to bring about an interview between me and their Sovereign, which they eventually effected, at great personal risk.

As our three friendly advisers concurred in the suggested arrangement, Dr. Blanc and I dressed in uniform and went to Salámgê, with our fellow-captives, Consul Cameron, the Rev. Mr. Stern, Mr. and Mrs. Rosenthal, and Messrs. Kerans and Pietro. As soon as we descended from the fortress a follower of Râs Bisáwwir, the ex-Commandant of Mágdala, came running to that Chief with orders from the King to take me to him, if I wished to see him; his Majesty would see me only, and none of my fellow-captives were to accompany me. I then discovered that, although I had refused to send to the King, the Chiefs had agreed to do so themselves, and had sent to say that I had expressed a wish to see him, and to thank him for his kindness. I was accordingly separated from my fellow-captives and taken to the Sovereign. I had scarcely walked fifty yards when Mr. Waldmeier came to warn me against taking any of my fellow-captives with me into his Majesty's presence, as he would not see any one but me. We then walked on towards the spot where the King was said to be awaiting me. I found him standing at the junction of the upper and lower roads leading to the British camp, with about twenty picked Musketeers around him, and his European artisans in attendance. (See Plan, p. 227). On seeing me he asked how I had passed the day, and beckoned to me with his hand to approach. On my coming up to him he looked towards the sun, and said abruptly, " Do you not think it is late for you to go this afternoon to your camp? Would you rather go at once or spend the night with me, and in the morning I will send you straight to your people?" I answered that whatever pleased his Majesty pleased me. He then said, "Good; you had better go now; but," he added, "sit down for a short time, and let me have a few words with you before you depart." After I had seated myself on the ground near him, he said, "You know, Mr. Rassam, that you and I have always been on good terms. God knows your heart, but, as far as I am concerned, I have always had a sincere regard for you. It is true that I have behaved ill to you, but that was through the conduct of bad men. However, the past cannot be helped now, and, I can only say, God's will be done. I want you to bear this in mind—that unless you befriend me, I shall either kill myself or become a monk. Now, good-bye; it is getting late; try and come to see me to-morrow, if you can." I then thanked him for his kindness, and said, "I will come to see your Majesty, if possible." He asked again, "Will you come to-morrow?" I replied that it all depended upon the orders of the Commander-in-Chief. He then rose, shook hands with me, wept and said, "Farewell: be quick, it is getting late." I rejoined, "I thank your Majesty; but my companions are behind." His only answer was—and these words were the last I heard from his lips—"You had better go." I was now anxious about my fellow-captives, and after walking on a few paces I stopped. The King was still standing on a rock, surrounded by his Musketeers, and holding a double-barrelled rifle in his hands. When he saw me stop and look round, he motioned me with his hand to go on. My fears then began to increase; still I apprehended that if I said anything we should all be shot down, so I proceeded a few steps farther and stood still, when, to my intense joy, I saw my fellow-captives coming down the hill towards me. As soon as they joined me we went on towards our camp, but did not feel safe until we were within our pickets, knowing that the fickle Theodore might have recalled us at any moment. Before I parted with the King he ordered Dajjâj 'Âlami, Aito Samuel, and Messrs. Waldmeier, Salmüller, Mayer and Moritz to escort me to our camp. Soon after I left, I dispatched Mr. Mayer in advance, to notify our approach, and also to stop Messrs. Prideaux and Flad, in case they were on their way back. Luckily, he arrived just in time to detain them, or they might have started for Salámgé and missed us in the dark.

Some officers who were on guard conducted us to Sir Robert Napier's tent, on the outside of which we were cordially received by his Excellency and Colonel Merewether.

The latter welcomed us with his usual kindness, and, feeling as I did how deeply indebted all the liberated captives were to his assiduous sympathy and valuable assistance from first to last, I was rejoiced to have this early occasion of expressing my gratitude for his unwearied exertions on our behalf. Without Colonel Merewether's foresight and zealous cöoperation, our misfortunes might have come to a widely different termination.

The King having asked me to go up and see him again, I communicated his wish to the Commander-in-Chief, who, of course, objected to my placing myself once more in jeopardy, and thereby adding to the existing complications.

On the morning of Easter Sunday, the 12th of April, Theodore wrote a letter of apology, containing the offer of a present of cows and sheep, and sent it by Aläkâ I'ngădă, his chief Amharic scribe, with instructions to come to me, in order that I might accompany him to Sir Robert Napier. The following is a translation of this remarkable document, copied from the Abyssinian 'Blue-Book:'—

"In the name of the Father, of the Son, and of the Holy Ghost—one Lord:

"The King of Kings, Theodorus:

"May it reach the beloved servant of the Great Queen of England.

"I am writing to you, without being able to address you by name, because our intercourse has arisen so unexpectedly.

"I am grieved at having sent you my writing of yesterday, and at having quarrelled with you, my friend. When I saw your manner of fighting, and the discipline of your army, and when my people failed to execute my orders, then I was consumed with sorrow to think that although I killed and punished my soldiers, yet they would not return to the battle. Whilst the fire of jealousy burned within me, Satan came to me in the night, and tempted me to kill myself with my own pistol. But, reflecting that God would be angry with me if I were to go in this manner, and leave my army without a protector, I sent to you in a hurry, lest I might die, and all things be in confusion before my message should reach you. After my messenger had gone I cocked my pistol, and, putting it to my mouth, pulled the trigger. Though I pulled and pulled, yet it would not go off. But when my people rushed upon me, and laid hold of the pistol, it was discharged just as they had drawn it from my mouth. God having thus signified to me that I should not die, but live, I sent to you Mr. Rassam that same evening, that your heart might be made easy.

"To-day is Easter; be pleased to let me send a few cows to you.

"The reason of my returning to you your letter yesterday was, that I believed at that time that we should meet one another in heaven, but never on earth.

"I let the night pass without sending for the body of my friend Fitaurari Gabrie, because I thought that after my death we should both be buried together; but since I have lived, be pleased to allow him to be buried.

"You require from me all the Europeans, even to my best friend, Waldmeier. Well, be it so. They shall go. But now that we are friends you must not leave me without artisans, as I am a lover of the mechanical arts."

On receiving this communication I went to Colonel Merewether, and we repaired to the Commander-in-Chief's tent together, when I was requested by Sir Robert Napier to give him a literal translation of the letter. With the assistance of Samuel, who rendered the Amharic into Arabic, I translated the whole into English, sentence by sentence. That done, Samuel—who had been ordered by Theodore to return with the answer, and then to assist in bringing down the European artisans and their families—wished to know what reply he was to carry back to the King respecting the proffered present of sheep and cows. On my repeating this question to the Commander-in-Chief, his Excellency said, "I accept them;" and that was the message which I gave to Samuel.

A little before sunset that evening, all the European artisans, with their wives and families and the whole of their effects, arrived safely in the British Camp, the King having given them permission to leave Mágdala immediately after he received the Commander-in-Chief's message. A little after sunset, Samuel came to the British camp and informed me that the King had ordered him to go up to Mágdala and bring down our effects, and had also given him permission at the same time to remove his family and all his belongings from Mágdala to our camp. This last offer Samuel thought it advisable to decline, fearing that by accepting it he might create suspicion in the King's mind, who might be irritated on finding that every one wished to leave him. The King insisted, however, on his coming to our camp in charge of my moveables and those of my companions, and also to convey his compliments to me. His Majesty's words were, "How are you, my friend? I hope you are well. I know you have no longer any power; so do not think about me. God's will be done." This was the last message I received from Theodore. At a quarter past four in the afternoon of the following day I saw him dead. He had committed suicide in the presence of his valet, Wald-Gâbir, who told me that his master shot himself just as our troops reached the second gate.

It has been insinuated from more quarters than one, that Theodore was deceived with regard to the reply sent to his proffered gift of sheep and cattle, and that I was the author of the deception. It is not within my province to discuss the former question; the latter I utterly deny. Even when a prisoner with the King, I never gave him any reason to believe that I could shield him from the consequences of his obstinacy; on the contrary, I assured him again and again that, with our troops in the field, his fate rested in other hands than mine. In the matter of the present, I acted as I was bound to act, on superior authority, and was merely the channel through which the Commander-in-Chief's message was delivered to the King's officer. The innuendo referred to, however, was only one among several disparaging strictures on my conduct which obtained currency immediately after my release from captivity. Such ungenerous reflections were hard to bear, under the circumstances; but Time is the great repairer of injuries, and, moreover, I have the satisfaction of knowing that they had respect to matters far too trivial to be repeated here, and were either utterly unfounded, or based on words and actions which were grossly distorted.

CHAPTER XXVII.

ALL'S WELL THAT ENDS WELL.

Narrative of events between the 11th and 13th April, 1868 — Dispatch of the proffered cattle to the British camp — Theodore's impression that hostilities were at an end — Mr. Speedy — The King prepares to escape on hearing that his present had not been accepted — His troops decline to accompany him — Prepares for defence — Is abandoned by most of his followers — Some of the Chiefs surrender themselves to Sir Robert Napier — Theodore attacks a party of British Cavalry — Retreats with a handful of followers and secures the Gates of Mágdala — The fortress stormed by the British — Theodore shoots himself — A summary of his career — His surviving wives and children — Did Theodore, before his death, curse the Author? — Visit to Mágdala after its fall — The Author charged with the burial of Theodore and the care of his family — Disposal of the Chiefs and people of Mágdala — Contrast — Divine intervention — The Army of Rescue — Burial of Theodore — His son, 'Alamáyo, made over by his mother to the care of the British — Dismissal of the Mágdala Chiefs — The Author proceeds to Dalanta with the royal family — Mágdala in flames — Review of the Expeditionary force — Illness and death of the Queen Těrn-Wark — Dismissal of all Abyssinian followers at Senáfé — Arrival at Zoolla — Journey to Europe — Dispersion of the late European Captives — On British soil once more — Reception by old friends — Recognition by Government of the services and sufferings of the Mission to Abyssinia — Conclusion.

So many conflicting accounts have been given of what took place at the royal camp from the afternoon of the 11th of April, when I took leave of the King, until the morning of the 13th, that the reader may very naturally expect to hear my version of the subject. Without venturing either to impugn or reconcile the statements of other writers, I shall give a brief narrative of the principal events which occurred during that interval, on the authority of several trustworthy persons who were present at the time.

After the King had dispatched the 1,000 cows and 500 sheep—they were all he possessed—to Sir Robert Napier, on the mistaken idea that peace had been initiated between him and the British, he seemed quite cheerful, and continued so throughout the greater part of Sunday, the 12th of April, and allowed all his European artisans, together with their families and effects, to repair to our camp. He had appointed one Agafári Mashîsha, formerly the head executioner but whom he had recently raised to the rank of Dajazmátsh, to convey the live stock to the British lines. This man was stopped at the outlying pickets and kept waiting there. About sunset he sent a messenger to his master, stating that the cattle had not yet been taken over, and requesting orders as to what was to be done, as the animals were likely to die for want of water. He also reported that "Bàsha Fallákô" (Mr. Speedy) had been to examine the cattle, but had not told him whether he was to remain or return. As soon as the King heard the name of Fallákô, whom he always called an "enemy," he inferred that his visit boded him no good. He also concluded, from the fact of the cattle having been kept so long outside the camp without having been received by the Commander-in-Chief, that his confident anticipation of peace was doomed to be disappointed. He accordingly began to make preparations to decamp, and, summoning all the Chiefs of his troops on Salámgê, he ordered them to be in readiness to march with him during the night. In the course of an hour he was told that none could follow him that night, as they could procure neither animals nor carriers to transport their families and effects at so short a notice; nevertheless, about two hundred Chiefs volunteered to accompany him at once, leaving their families behind. As this did not satisfy Theodore, he went up to Mágdala and issued similar orders there, stating that he intended starting for his native province forthwith, and that they would be able to reach the Jejáho Valley next morning, from whence they might proceed onward to the Lake, without fear of molestation. Thereupon the Chiefs consulted with their men, and it was unanimously resolved to disregard the royal mandate, on the ground that for want of carriage they would be obliged to abandon their families— a step to which they had the strongest objection. They counselled his Majesty at the same time to come to terms with the invaders, and thereby save them and their families from the destructive devouring fire of the English, which all the people in Abyssinia, if combined against them, could not extinguish. The King then upbraided them for their disloyalty and cowardice; they, in return, blaming him for having surrendered me and my fellow-captives before exacting favourable conditions from the British. "Had the European captives still been with your Majesty," they argued, "you might have revenged upon them the refusal of their brothers to accept your offers of peace, and thereby have made their hearts smart; as it is, you have everything to lose. We are your Majesty's children unto death, if you will only listen to our advice and come to terms with the *Franchotsh*." After this incident, Theodore seated himself near the Salámgê Gate and was silent for about two hours. He then ordered Damâsh and other Chiefs to collect four hundred men to assist in placing some mortars on the road leading up from Salámgê, with the evident intention of making a show of defence, in the event of an attack by the British. Râs Bisáwwir, the old Commandant of Mágdala, returned to him in the course of half an hour, and reported that every petty Chief both of the old and new garrisons had sworn that they would not stir a finger in any attempt to fight the English; but that if he were willing to make peace, they were all ready to go before the great "English Râs," with stones on their necks, and sue for pardon. Before this message was delivered to Theodore, some of the highest Chiefs, including Râs I'ngădă, consulted what course they should pursue in case the King took it into his head to order the slaughter of some individuals of the garrison, with the object of intimidating the remainder into obedience. They all resolved, and sealed the determination with a solemn oath, that they would disobey any such order, even if issued against one of the common prisoners; and, moreover, that they would thereupon bind the King, if necessary, to prevent him from shedding any more innocent blood. Theodore did not visit his family at Mágdala on this occasion, and on receiving Râs Bisúwwir's answer he returned to Salámgê, saying to that Chief as he left, "Let those who still bear me any attachment follow me, and we shall see what assistance is to be got below." Between forty and fifty Chiefs accompanied him, and towards dawn he set about his absurd project of moving some mortars on the road leading up to Mágdala; but as it was no easy task to drag such heavy pieces of artillery, over rocks and stones, up a steep incline, especially as only a few hands could be got together to co-operate in the work, he eventually abandoned the attempt, and reverted to the former scheme of retiring from the place. He asked those who had come down with him from Mágdala, whether they would accompany him if he went to Gishen, and from thence make their way to Kwâra, by the safest route. On receiving an affirmative reply, he next summoned the Chiefs of the troops at Salámgê, who had promised the day before to go with him, if he wished them to attend him. He sent for them twice, but as they refused to come he left and returned to Mágdala, to try his luck there once more. In the mean time, some of the foremost Chiefs at Salámgê, thinking that Theodore was about to retreat with the Chiefs who had gone up with him to Mágdala, hurried off to the British camp and surrendered themselves to the Commander-in-Chief, proffering at the same time the submission of all the royal troops on Salámgê. The King, on the other hand, having tried in vain, for the space of an hour, to obtain more help from Mágdala to enable him to move the mortars and make a better defence, returned to Salámgê, at his wit's end what course to pursue. To his chagrin, he found the soldiers there, on whose loyalty he had implicitly relied, hurrying from their huts towards the British lines at A'rogê. Nothing daunted, however, by this sore mortification, he set to work, heart and soul, with his few remaining adherents, in placing the mortars in a good position for defence below the Salámgê Gate. While engaged on this bootless undertaking, he espied some cavalry belonging to Sir Charles Staveley's division on the height of Salássê. Thereupon the King immediately abandoned the work, mounted his horse, and set off towards that point, calling upon his party to follow him and die fighting. Most of his people, however, deeming that they would be safer in Mágdala, deserted him and returned to the fortress, only twelve persons accompanying him, including Rás I'ngŭdă, Bitwáddad Hásani, Rás Barráko, and Wald-Gábir, the royal valet. While Theodore was galloping about and challenging our troops to single combat, one of his party was shot in the arm, which induced the rest to entreat his Majesty to relinquish the rash demonstration and return to the defence of Mágdala. On reaching the fortress, he again appealed to the garrison to assist him in defending it; but all his solicitations were in vain. He succeeded, however, in securing the help of Râs Bisáwwir and Bitwáddad Damâsh, and their relatives, to pile huge stones behind the wooden gates; but before the task was accomplished the cannonading from our side began, which scared all the hands away, excepting the few persons who had gone up with him from Salámgê, and those Chiefs who had joined him in the fortress. Three of the former were killed by the explosion of a shell, and another by a rocket. As soon as Theodore saw one man fall, he went and seated himself in a passage cut between two rocks below the second gate, and bade those who remained with him depart, if they liked, and seek shelter elsewhere. None, however, would leave him, and all swore that they would remain where they were and die with him.

When the storming-party began the ascent, Theodore rejoined his few remaining adherents, and with five of them opened fire upon the advancing column. Four of his men, besides Râs I'ngǎdā and the Râs's brother, were shot dead by our troops. On seeing that the latter had attained the first gate, the King retired to the inner gate, bidding his diminished band follow him. Damâsh and another Chief were wounded while effecting this movement, and were immediately carried to their respective homes. Perceiving now that our troops had surmounted the wall of the outer gate, and that a few of them were approaching the spot where he stood, Theodore drew a pistol from his belt, and said, "Sooner than surrender into the hands of the Franks, I will shoot myself!" He forthwith put the muzzle of the pistol to his mouth and fired, the bullet coming out at the back of his head. Falling instantly on his back, he breathed his last.

Thus ended the career of Theodore, who had swayed the

Abyssinian sceptre for nearly fourteen years, during which time, as he himself told me, he had not enjoyed one day's rest. A warrior from boyhood, and elevated to the highest dignity by personal energy and dauntless courage, his early successes made him the idol of friends and the terror of foes. Had he possessed the requisite qualifications, Theodore might have consolidated his power over the feudal Chiefs, whose misrule had kept the country in a state of anarchy for centuries, fostered peaceful arts and sciences among his people, developed the resources of his kingdom, and made Christian Abyssinia a blessing to the surrounding heathen and barbarous races. The reforms which he initiated shortly after his accession to the throne show that he was capable of appreciating these and similar advantages. But he utterly lacked the talent for administration; or, if he possessed any, it was completely neutralized by inordinate military ambition and a thirst for martial fame. His efforts to carry out his schemes of conquest and aggrandizement excited first the passive, then the active resistance of his subjects, who banded together under their old leaders to withstand the oppressor. But his proud spirit could not brook opposition, and rivalry drove him to perpetrate those deeds of atrocity and cruelty which eventually stirred up Chief and peasant to compass his downfall. My own sincere conviction is, that this antagonism, perpetuated and intensified by the unwise measures which he took to repress it, so unsettled the mind of the haughty monarch that, at times, he was decidedly mad. On no other supposition can I account for his extraordinary conduct towards the Mission from first to last; although, when he ultimately decided to retain us as hostages, he most probably calculated on striking a bargain for our release, which he fondly hoped would have enabled him to regain his lost ascendancy. That there were a few loyal men who stood by him to the bitter end, evinces that Theodore must have had some noble qualities worthy of such devotion; that he was abandoned by all but that valiant little band, and died hemmed in on an isolated mountain, surrounded by thousands of his own people up in arms against him, proves that he had forfeited all claim to their allegiance, and deserved the fate which rid them and their country of an infatuated tyrant.

Theodore left three sons and three daughters, the Prince 'Alamâyo being the only one, however, who was born in wedlock, his mother Tĕru-Wark, the daughter of Dajjâj Oobê, having been married to the late King in the church, and the marriage confirmed by both parties receiving the holy Eucharist together. The other five were the issue of mothers who were married without any religious ceremony; consequently, according to Abyssinian Canon law, Dajjâj 'Alamâyo is the only legitimate child, although the present Civil law recognizes the secondary marriages as valid. Theodore's eldest son, Râs Mashîsha, now about twenty-three years of age, went away from Mágdala with a few followers, intending to make his way to Shoa, the day Mágdala was taken, but he eventually changed his mind and took refuge with his grandmother's family in Amhâra-Seint. Hailo Kâsa, the youngest son, was left in Tigrê with his mother, a Galla concubine, on the return of the British force to the coast. His eldest daughter, about twenty years old, who had been married to Menilek, King of Shoa, was made over by her father to a Tigrê Chief, named Bâria, when Menilek escaped from Mágdala and returned to his native province. His other two daughters, one about five and the other three years of age, were taken by their mothers to Bagámĕdĕr.

It was reported that before putting an end to his life, Theodore gnashed his teeth and invoked a malediction against Mr. Waldmeier and myself for having deceived him. I have never been able to discover how this story originated. Those who were in close attendance upon the King, from the evening of the 12th till the time of his death, assured me that they had not heard him utter a word either against me or any other person; the only time he mentioned my name was when he sent Samuel down with a message to me, in the evening of the 12th. Among those whom I questioned on this subject was Wald-Gâbir, the royal valet; his quaint answer was this:—"Master, why do you give heed to such reports? The day of lies, when through fear of the King no one would dare to moot such topics, has gone by; but Theodore is no more, and the English are here; therefore, if Mr. Waldmeier has told you this story, ask him to name the person who was with the King at the time, and related it to him (Mr. Waldmeier) and by that means you will arrive at the truth. I will pledge myself to become your slave for ever if, on investigation, you discover that any such person exists." Even if the story were true, Theodore's malediction, being wholly undeserved, would cause me no compunction. When I told him that I "hoped"—the word which I always used in my verbal as well as written communications to him—that matters would end peaceably, I really meant what I said. It was not my fault that he rejected wise counsels and persisted in his determination to resist, crowning his headstrong folly by attacking the vanguard of our army on Good Friday, the 10th of April, thereby causing the slaughter of so many of his hapless followers. My fellow-captives and I were shut up in Mágdala, and know nothing of what took place below the fortress from the morning of that day until the afternoon of the day following, when the King sent for us to Salámgé and dispatched us to the British camp. I had repeatedly warned the obstinate Sovereign against driving her Majesty's Government to extreme measures, and on the occasion of my previous visit to him at Salámgé I strongly urged him to make overtures to Sir Robert Napier. His reply to me, through Messrs. Flad and Waldmeier, was as already stated at p. 307.

If Mr. Waldmeier credits the story referred to, he is perfectly welcome to draw what inference he pleases from it; for my own part, I utterly disbelieve it. I was the last person to whom the King sent a civil message on the evening of the 12th, the pith of which was that he knew I was then powerless to assist him; and he also mentions my name in his last letter to the Commander-in-Chief, without the slightest indication that he entertained other than the most friendly feelings towards me. Further, the testimony of those who were present with the unhappy Sovereign, from that time until his suicide, wholly acquits him of the charge of having cursed any one on the occasion. Besides which, it should be borne in mind, that when Samuel was sent down to me on the evening of the 12th, the King had already heard that his present had been rejected.

In resuming my narrative I shall abstain from any attempt to describe the military operations of the campaign—a task which has already been so ably performed by Mr. C. R. Markham in his 'History of the Abyssinian Expedition'—and shall confine myself to matters connected with the capture of Mágdala and subsequent events in which I was personally engaged. Through the courtesy of Sir Robert Napier, I was allowed to accompany him in his attack upon the fortress; and was glad to find that, in conjunction with Samuel, I was able to render his Excellency some slight service as the medium of communication between him and the refugees whom we met running down from Salámgê towards A'rogê. At 4·30 P.M. Mágdala was captured, and the Commander-in-Chief entered the place in triumph, attended by his staff, myself among the number. On passing through the outer gate, I recognised Râs I'ngădă and Bitwáddad Bákal among those who had fallen on the spot, and on proceeding to the plateau above the inner gate I was called to identify the corpse of the King. It was unmistakable; there lay the "great Theodore," stretched on his back, with no other covering than a shirt and trowsers. On catching the first glimpse of the lifeless form I was strongly reminded of his strange speech, uttered on the 29th of March, just a fortnight before, when he said that ere long I might stand over his corpse, and begged that I would then forget his ill-treatment and see him decently interred.

When Sir Robert Napier had settled affairs at Mágdala and was returning to the camp at A'rogê, he appointed me to take charge of Theodore's remains, the Queens and their establishments, the Chiefs and the native political prisoners, and also to assist Brigadier-General Wilby, who had been made Commandant of the fortress for the time being, in all his requirements. Our first duty was to remove the corpse of the late King to the inclosure of our old prison-house, where we saw it deposited on Signor Pietro's couch, and placed under an European guard. On going thence to inquire after the Queens and the other members of the royal family, we found that they had left their residence, and had repaired for protection to mine, where they were received by Dr. Blanc, who happened to be in the house at the time. As it was the best in the inclosure, it was allotted to the two Queens and Dajjâj 'Alamâyo. Moreover, every available room within the fence, including Samuel's, was crowded with the male and female relatives—children and adults—of our old acquaintances, who had taken refuge there with what property they could bring with them, and the entire inclosure was thronged with the horses, mules and cattle which they had conveyed thither for greater safety. After General Wilby had placed a guard over the premises to keep out intruders, we collected all the Mágdala Chiefs and lodged them in Bitwáddad Damâsh's house for the night—also under a guard, to keep them together. We next notified to the rest of the inhabitants that they were to remain quietly in the open space until the morning, when all would be dismissed to their homes. Poor Damâsh, who was still suffering from the wounds which he had received that afternoon, got somewhat anxious after I left, apprehending that all those who had fought against the English were to be executed the following day. After seeing that every arrangement had been made for the comfort of the royal family, I repaired again to Damâsh's house, and in the course of my visit assured him and his companions that they need be under no dread of retaliation on the part of the British Commander-in-Chief. Bitwáddad Wási was the only one among them whose face wore a smile; the remainder were absent, and looked like men who thought that their doom was sealed. I took Rás Bisáwwir and Bitwáddad Hásani, the two ex-Commandants, to sleep in a room near the royal family, in order that their proximity might inspire the unfortunate Queens and their relatives with confidence;—the former was cousin to the late King, and had always been intrusted with the royal *Ilfing*. I also quartered with them the Etshêgê, or Superior of the monks, and two other priests who were held in great veneration at Mágdala. Mr. Waldmeier kindly volunteered to assist in the several duties which devolved upon me during our further stay in the fortress, and I feel bound to recognize his ready and valuable co-operation.

The extraordinary changes which, in the course of a few eventful hours had succeeded each other so rapidly, kept me awake nearly the whole night. I was unable to realize the idea that the dreaded monarch who, only two days before, held the lives of so many Europeans in his power, was now a lifeless mass, sheltered within one of the *Franchotsh's* huts; that the Chiefs who had been our jailors, and who from sheer timidity would not have hesitated, at the despot's fiat, to stain their hands with our blood, were at that moment guarded by British sentinels; and that my old prison-house, where I had lingered out an anxious existence for twenty-two months, had been converted into an asylum for the royal family. Ever and anon I fancied myself in a dream; then, again, I felt sure that we were free, and that the fear of an ignominious death had passed away. Truly, the deliverance was marvellous; no wonder, therefore, that for a time it should seem doubtful. God moves in a mysterious way; but the agency of His superintending Providence in the liberation of the captives was too manifest not to call forth from all a humble tribute of praise and thanksgiving for His merciful intervention.

Of the rescuing army—officers and men, soldiers and sailors, British and Indian—through which that intervention was wrought out, England may justly feel proud. Bloodless as was the campaign on our side, it was, nevertheless, signalized by a display of the noblest qualities which can adorn the true warrior—self-restraint, patient endurance, and indomitable perseverance. Incompetent as I am to make any remarks on the purely military conduct and manoeuvres of the Abyssinian Expedition, those are qualities alike appreciable by all, and, therefore, humble as the foregoing testimony may be, a deep sense of admiration and gratitude impels me to record it.

14th.—This afternoon Dr. Lumsdaine and Dr. Blanc having examined the bullet-wound in the head of Theodore's corpse reported officially that the King had died by his own hand. The ball had passed outwards from the mouth, which was blackened and scorched by the charge, and the palate had been blown away.

Sir Robert Napier could not have conferred a greater compliment upon me than that of intrusting the remains of Theodore and the supervision of his bereaved family to my care, thereby enabling me to prove to the Abyssinians that their late Sovereign had not vainly styled me his "friend." There was nothing, indeed, which the kind-hearted Commander-in-Chief would not have done to alleviate the sorrow and add to the comfort of the King's surviving relatives. I had only to submit a request on their behalf, either to him directly or through Colonel Merewether, and it was granted at once.

Orders having been received after the post-mortem examination that the King's remains were to be interred, I directed the Etshêgê, Aito Samuel, Theodore's confessor, and two other priests, to have the corpse prepared for burial, according to the Abyssinian custom, wrapped in a suitable shroud, which was generously provided by Samuel. It was an affecting sight to witness the reverence with which the dignitaries of the Church performed these last offices for their departed Sovereign. They approached the lifeless body with their *shámmas* girt; and their whole behaviour on the mournful occasion proved that, even in death, Theodore had not wholly lost the affection of, at least, some of his subjects. The grave had been previously dug in the church at Mágdala, and when all the preliminaries were completed, I made over the corpse to the old Chiefs, who accompanied the clergy to see it buried. Samuel and I were unable to be present at the funeral, as Colonel Merewether had just come up to the fortress to make arrangements for the future movements of the Queens and the Prince Dajjâj 'Alamâyo; also to dispose of the political prisoners and the inhabitants of Mágdala. In reply to Colonel Merewether's question, what her wishes were regarding her son 'Alamâyo, the Itêgê Teru-Wark said, that as his father, when alive, had made him over to the English, through me, she preferred abiding by his wishes, and was herself ready to follow him wherever he went. The Itêgê Itamanyo, Theodore's favourite ex-Queen, expressed a desire to return to her native Yadjow, and would leave us in Wâdala, the nearest place to that district. I then accompanied Colonel Merewether to witness the dismissal of the old Mágdala Chiefs and the political prisoners. The gallant Colonel had a kindly word for all, bade them not fear, and assured them, on the part of the Commander-in-Chief, of a safe-conduct through the Gallas and other deadly enemies, of whom they were in great dread. He also promised to provide all with animals for themselves and their wives, in order to enable them to reach their respective homes with greater ease. Some evil-disposed person having had the cruelty to tell the Chiefs that they would be retained as prisoners, and that several of them would probably be hanged, this authoritative announcement was hailed by them with intense satisfaction.

Early the following morning, I returned to Mágdala from the head-quarters at A'rogê, with instructions to provide the Chiefs and their families with the proper number of mules and horses from those which had been seized after the capture of the fortress. Almost the whole day was spent on this task, and when the hour came for starting towards A'rogê, which was the route which I had been directed to take, we found the road so blocked up by a relief which was going on at the time between two European regiments, that I had to postpone our departure till next day.

16th.—Early this morning I was informed that one of the gateways leading to Salámgê had fallen, and that we could not pass that way until the road was cleared. As the Commander-in-Chief had ordered that all the Abyssinians should leave the Amba as soon as possible, and as I was moreover anxious to see the royal family safely located at head-quarters, I determined to wait no longer. I accordingly took the Queens, who had been furnished with a guard of honour by General Wilby, and tried to escort them to A'rogê by the Kafir-Bär Gate; but on beginning the descent by the narrow path at its entrance, it was discovered that the loads carried by the mules were too bulky to pass that way, without being first discharged and then reloaded beyond the gate. As that process would have occupied an hour or two, we retraced our steps to our old quarters, and on arriving there found that the Salámgê Gate had been rendered passable. Thereupon I accompanied the cortège for some distance, and then leaving the Queens in Mr. Waldmeier's charge went to Salássê to distribute swords, shields and spears to the late inhabitants of Mágdala, Sir Robert Napier having most considerately ordered that they should be provided with these arms, in order to be able to defend themselves against attack on the way back to their respective homes. That done, I rejoined Mr. Waldmeier and his charge within half a mile of the pickets, and reached head-quarters towards evening. My tent, which I had brought from Aden, and which was the largest in the camp, had already been pitched for me; and having ushered the royal party into it, I gave them all the carpets with which the late King had presented me, and which now proved very useful. Meanwhile, the released native political prisoners, the Mágdala people, and all other Abyssinians, were located beyond the pickets, between the camp and the Amba.

17th.—I received orders early this morning to proceed to Dalanta with the royal family, under the escort of a detachment which was going thither, and there await the arrival of head-quarters. We reached the halting-place at Abbába in the afternoon, and pitched our tents next to those of my liberated fellow-captives, and of some of the European artisans who had preceded us to the spot. On the way, while ascending the valley of the Báshilo, we had heard the loud consecutive reports caused by the blowing up of the gates of Mágdala, and on turning round I saw the lurid flames ascending from that late abode of iniquity, tyranny and bloodshed, proclaiming to the surrounding country far and near that the sceptre of the oppressor of his people was broken, and his last refuge reduced to a heap of ruins. Thousands of widows and orphans probably gazed with wonder at the sight, and invoked a blessing upon their English deliverers, who, besides vindicating their own national honour, and adding a fresh trophy to British fame, had saved many a doomed victim from the fate which had been reserved for them by the ruthless Theodore. The two Queens and their attendants could not resist casting a glance behind them, and as the cherished Itamanyo looked upon the glowing mass, she sighed and said, "Now that our lord has gone, may all Abyssinia be consumed by fire!" Nevertheless, this lady was always cheerful, spoke kindly to every one, and while she remained with us was a general favourite with the late King's followers. On the other hand, the Itêgê Teru-Wark, the *de jure* Queen Consort, was always silent and dejected, and on inquiring into the cause I was told that she was naturally taciturn and reserved, and had ever manifested a dislike for gossip.

In reply to an attempt which on one occasion I made to encourage and cheer her, assuring her that she could not have better protectors than the British, she said that she entertained no doubt whatever on that point, but she felt that her days were numbered, for which she was not sorry; and then added, "Mine has been a miserable existence since childhood, and I am now looking forward to that happiness which is promised me by our Saviour."

18th.—All the troops which had remained behind at A'rogê, together with the Commander-in-Chief and his Staff, reached Dalanta to-day, and on the 20th there was a grand review of the whole force, at which all the released captives were present. On the 21st the latter, myself excepted, were dispatched with the Second Brigade to Antâlo, there to await the arrival of head-quarters. I remained behind in charge of the ex-Queens and the young Prince, and started with them on the 23rd, in the rear of the army. On the 24th we crossed the Chetta valley. Sir Robert Napier having kindly attached an European guard to the royal suite, I was able to have a separate camp for them, outside that of the force, where all other Abyssinians also who were under the Commander-in-Chief's protection located themselves. While at Wâdala, before crossing the Tăkkăzê river, the Itêgê Itamanyo left with her retinue for her native district, Yadjow, under the protection of a new Chief who had rebelled against the Wakshum Gobazê.

The day before we left Abbába the Itêgê Têru-Wark fell sick, but as her ailment was reported to be nothing but a cold, no anxiety was felt as to the result. It turned out, however, that she was suffering from pulmonary disease. As soon as the Commander-in-Chief was apprised of her indisposition, he appointed his Staff Surgeon, Dr. Lumsdaine, to attend her; and as she felt rather weak the day after, a palanquin was placed at her disposal, with bearers to carry her. In fact, nothing was wanting on the part of Sir Robert Napier to relieve and comfort her. Dr. Lumsdaine's assiduity and kindness towards his royal patient could not be surpassed, and the poor lady frequently expressed her gratitude to me for the sympathy and attention which she received both from her medical attendant and the Commander-in-Chief. Despite all our efforts, however, her health gradually declined. Now and then there was a slight rally, but she succumbed at last, and died almost suddenly on the evening of the 15th of May, at Haik-hallet, near Chelicut. I had noticed throughout the journey that the state of the atmosphere had a wonderful effect upon her: when it was fine, her health seemingly improved; but wet or damp weather increased her malady and made her breathing more difficult. There was a heavy fall of rain the evening she died, and at about nine o'clock I ordered a basin of arrow-root with a little port wine to be prepared for her, but her attendant through whom I intended sending it, and who had just left the Queen, informed me that she was too ill to take any food. I then bade him go and ask whether she would like a little gruel; he came running back immediately with the melancholy tidings that she had breathed her last during his short absence from her. I forthwith repaired to the tent, which was always pitched a few yards from mine, and found that the sad intelligence was true. There lay the lifeless body, but the features were unchanged, and seemed composed as in a quiet sleep. The Commander-in-Chief, on receiving my report of the melancholy event, directed me to see that she was buried with the honours due to her station. I accordingly dispatched a messenger during the night to the priests of a large church at Chelicut, requesting them to come early the following morning to arrange for the interment. On discovering that the deceased Queen's paternal grandfather had been buried some years before in a vault in the same church, I directed that her remains should be deposited next to his, and that a suitable monument should be raised over the spot, for which services the priests received prepayment.

After the death of the Queen, her mother and most of her attendants returned to their respective homes, well provided for; the remainder, together with Samuel and other Abyssinians who were still under British protection, accompanied us to Senâfé. I am happy to say that Sir Robert Napier rewarded all those Abyssinians whose faithful services I brought to his notice; and a great number of the late King's followers, who had assisted me to the best of their power during their master's lifetime, were kindly cared for by his Excellency's orders, so long as they travelled with the army on its return to the coast.

At Senâfé all Abyssinian followers were dismissed, excepting two old dependents of the deceased Queen, to whom the Prince was strongly attached. His foster-mother, who belonged to a Shánkĕlá tribe, we were obliged to part with, as her services were no longer needed, and she would have proved a great incumbrance. The late Itĕgê having expressed a wish that her son should continue his Amharic studies, Lord Napier was kind enough, at my recommendation through General Merewether, to allow Alăkû Zánnab, the late Keeper of the Royal Archives, and a pious Christian, to be attached as tutor to Dajjâj 'Alamâyo. For some reason or other, the Alăkû was subsequently discharged, which, if regard be had to the Prince's eventual usefulness to his own country, is much to be regretted.

We reached Zoolla on the 27th of May, where, in pursuance of instructions to that effect, I consigned the young Prince to the care of the local political officer. On the 30th, I and my late fellow-captives, with the exception of Consul Cameron who remained behind, started in the Peninsular and Oriental Company's steamer 'Ottowa,' and in due course arrived at Suez, where we left Signor Pietro and all Theodore's late European servants. On the 13th, Messrs. Stern, Rosenthal and Flad, with the wives and children of the two latter gentlemen, left Alexandria with me for Brindisi; my late companions, Dr. Blanc and Lieutenant Prideaux, having left the day before by the route *viâ* Marseilles, preceded by Mr. Kerans, who had embarked on board a Liverpool steamer, on his way to Ireland. Mr. Flad and his family separated from us at Brindisi to go up the Adriatic, while the rest of our party went on to Paris. Leaving Mr. and Mrs. Rosenthal there, Mr. Stern and I started together for Calais, and reached British soil once more, in health and safety, on the 22nd of June, 1868. The welcome which awaited me from many old and valued friends, whose former hospitality had made England a home to me, outweighed the memory of past sufferings, and in the midst of their cordial sympathy and generous kindness the anxieties and perils of my sojourn in Abyssinia are fast fading away into the unreality of a dream.

The official Report to Government of my proceedings in Abyssinia having been submitted to Parliament, I received in due course the following gratifying reply and handsome acknowledgment of the services and endurances of the different members of the Mission from her Majesty's Principal Secretary of State for Foreign Affairs:—

"Foreign Office, December 5th, 1868.

"SIR,—I have directed a letter to be addressed to you in regard to your financial arrangements during your mission in Abyssinia, and as I must now hold your accounts to be virtually closed, beyond such information as you may still be able to afford, it is my duty to signify to you that I shall no longer detain you from your duties under the India Government.

"I cannot, however, close my correspondence with you without expressing the high sense entertained by Her Majesty's Government of your conduct during the difficult and arduous period of your employment under this Office. You appear throughout to have acted for the best, and your prudence, discretion, and good management, seem to have tended greatly to preserve the lives and thus to insure the ultimate release of the captives.

"Your companions, Dr. Blanc and Lieutenant Prideaux, are also entitled to the thanks of Her Majesty's Government, which I request you to convey to them, for the uniform and zealous support which they gave to you during very trying times.

"The sufferings which you all underwent have been deeply deplored by Her Majesty's Government, and as some compensation, therefore, as well as a testimony of appreciation of good service, they have resolved to present a sum of 5000*l.* to yourself, and sums of 2000*l.* each to Dr. Blanc and Lieutenant Prideaux.

"I am, &c.,

(Signed) "STANLEY."

"*Hormuzd Rassam, Esq.,*
&c., &c., &c."

Proud of having been judged worthy of such a testimonial from her Majesty's Government, I shall feel prouder still of the approval of the British public, to whose verdict this Narrative of the Mission to King Theodore is now submitted. A Chaldean by birth, Great Britain is the country of my adoption; but although I cannot boast of being an Englishman, I can glory in this—that, to the best of my ability, I have endeavoured to emulate the loyalty of her most loyal sons.

INDEX.

ABAI, RIVER.

A.

Abai, river, i. 292; ii. 1, 125.
Abû-Fâlek, ii. 183.
Abbába, halt at, ii. 345, 347.
'Abdallah-abu-Khumeir, acting Governor of Câsala, i. 152.
'Abdallah Effendi, Lieut.-Governor of Massowah, i, 60.
'Abdallah Khalîl, i. 33.
'Abd-ul-Melek, Coptic messenger, i. 154.
'Abd-ul-Kerîm, brother to the Nâyib of Harkiko, i. 71, 85, 88, 118, 122, 132; leaves the Mission at Câsala, 142.
'Abd-ur-Rahmân Bey, Envoy from Egypt, i. 192; ii. 24.
Ab-hûn, i. 71.
Abîtu, Lij, ii. 2, 95.
Abûna Salâma, the Metropolitan, Author's letters to, i. 7, 78; his character and death at Mágdala, ii. 193-5; his opinion of Abyssinian marriages, 220.
Abu-Sin, Sheikh of Kedârif, i. 153.
Abyssinians, character of, ii. 249; their kindness to servants, 256.
Acháffar, district, i. 232, 235.
Adam, Yashâlaka, ii. 185.
Adârdi, valley, i. 128.
Aden, departure of Mission from, i. 2; visit to, 113; return to Massowah from, 114.
Adîna, on lake Tâna, i. 308.
Adjuration "by the death of Theodore," i. 104 ii. 50.
Adventurers, European, in Abyssinia, i. 32, 303.
Adwa, or Adowa, i. 103.
Afa-Negûs Bahti, ii. 290.
Agafári Gólam, a chamberlain, sent to Mágdala to release old captives, ii. 5; dies of cholera, 129.
Agówmedêr, district, i. 235, 245, 291.
Agows, the, i. 236.
Ahmed Arây, Chief of the Danûkil, i. 37.
Ahmed, Imâm of the Wello-Gallas, writes to the Author and the Abûna to surrender Mágdala to him, ii. 250.
Aidee, i. 90.

AUTHOR.

Aigai, i. 133.
Ailât, i. 53; hot-springs at, 57.
'Ain, i. 85, 90, 120.
Aito, title, import of, 156-7.
—— Samuel, see Samuel.
Alâkâ I'ngadá, chief scribe, ii. 55.
'Alamâyo, Dajjâj, only legitimate son of Theodore, ii. 336; introduced to Author, 292; brought by Author to Zoolla, 349.
'Alami, Dajjâj, sent by Theodore to Sir Robert Napier, ii. 319.
Alexandria, visit of Mission to, i. 111.
Ambâa, i. 84, 120.
Ambâra, country and people, ii. 271.
Annesley Bay, i. 81.
Ansaba, i. 125.
Antâlo, ii. 316.
Arafát, i. 162.
Arai, Sheikh of the El-Bakhît, i. 129.
Ariko, i. 220.
Armenian, an, his adventures with Theodore, i. 17.
Army, Theodore's, i. 274; on the march, 292; King's care for, 293; cholera in, ii. 125.
——, British, of rescue, tribute to, ii. 311.
A'rogê, Theodore at, ii. 224; British camp at, 318, 339.
Artisans, Theodore's European, reach Korâta, ii. 14; their wives and families, 27; accompany Mission to Zagê, 56; general friendliness to the Mission, 67; dinner party to, 70; their final deliverance from Mágdala, 327.
A'shfa, meeting with Theodore at, i. 248; departure from, 274.
Asída, a native dish, i. 164.
Asûs, i. 71.
Atbara, river, i. 148; excursion to, 172.
Atté-Máryam, tribe, their conversion to Islâm, i. 87.
Author, his appointment to the Mission, i. 2; his first four letters to Theodore from Massowah, 5, 41, 61, 107; to the Abûna, 7, 78; to Col. Merewether, 100; his first interview with Theodore, 218; tries to prevent a meeting between Theodore and the old captives, ii. 27, 76; holds a court to try

INDEX.

AWÂSA.

captives, 35; his letter to Theodore on the subject, 40; is arraigned at Zagé, 84; becomes security for the captives, 98, 143; letter to Government on Theodore's demand for artisans, 102; remonstrates with the King, 104, 106; receives visits from Theodore, 108, 136, 155; arraigned at Debra Tábor, 141; a prisoner at Mágdala, 160; his chains lightened, 197; lady visitors to, 207; is unfettered, 273; suggests that Theodore should make overtures to Sir Robert Napier, 307; his last interview with the King, 323; did not deceive Theodore, 327; not cursed by him, 337; takes charge of the remains of Theodore and of his ex-Queens, 339, 345; safe return to England, 350.
Awâsa, raid on by Tukroories, i. 177, 182.
Awhé, i. 130.

B.

Bâat, i. 128.
Bagámēdĕr, district, revenue of, ii. 16.
Bajirwand Kánfu, steals Theodore's charmed rifle, ii. 295.
Báhri, Bitwáddad, ii. 179.
Bákal, Bitwáddad, ii. 180.
Balâl-bin-'Abdallah, a Shoho Chief, i. 81.
Bálas, i. 224.
Báldárábá, what, i. 271.
Balwáka, i. 192.
Baren, Muslims of, attack Christians of Bogós, i. 44; incursions of, 126; climate of, 129; visit from Chiefs of, *ib.*; bad water in, 133; etymology of name, *ib.*
Bardel, M., Theodore's charges against, ii. 34; obtains copy of a dangerous document, 66; his friendship with l'ngáda Wark, 66, 77; in royal favour, 93, 97; nicknamed "Shrimps," 117, 141; betrays projected escape of European artisans, 261.
Barrako, Rás, ii. 277, 333.
Barriyah, tribe and district of, 132-4.
Basabír, i, 156.
Básha, captain of Musketeers, ii. 191.
Baskets, native, i. 55.
Beitahór, Theodore at, ii. 256.
Beke, Dr., report of his arrival at Massowah, ii. 25; his letter reaches Theodore, 41; impolicy of his mission, 46-50; excites the suspicion of the King,

CHETTA.

67; reports his imprisonment at Halai to Theodore, 110; his return to Europe after promising to visit the King, 144.
Beni-Amir, tribe, i. 129-30; visit from Chief of, 131.
Biancheri, Vicar-Apostolic, i. 9; his opinion of Theodore, 29; death of, 30.
Bifáta, in Métcha, ii. 277, 292.
Biráad, i. 125.
Birds, at Mágdala, ii. 209.
Bisáwwir, Básha, a doorkeeper, ii. 185.
——, Bitwáddad, ii. 169; his trial for treason, 280.
Blanc, Dr., his appointment to the Mission, i. 2.
——, Mrs. i. 45.
Bogós, province, i. 23, 72, 85; visit from Collector of Customs in, 126.
Bourgaud, M., ii. 4; Madame, 27.
Brandeis, Mr., imprisoned at Mágdala, ii. 261.
Branté, river, i. 236.
Brundo, raw meat, how eaten, i. 198.
Busson, Count du, i. 44.

C.

Cameron, Consul, letters to the Author from, i. 63, 73, 75, 78; Theodore's charges against, 262, 299; ii. 33, 305.
Canoes, bulrush, on Lake Tána, i. 309.
Captives, old, are liberated and reach Koráta, ii. 28; to be tried, 31; Theodore's charges against, 33, 34; result of trial, 40; start homeward, 82; are brought back to Zagé in chains, 91; are unfettered, 98; march with King and Mission to Koráta, 128; at Gaffat, 133-5; sent to Mágdala, 159; placed in fetters, 161; their quarters at Mágdala, 161, 202; their fare at Mágdala, 203-4; placed under strict watch, 284; released from chains, 303; summoned with Mission to Salámgé, 311; sent back to Mágdala, 315; recalled to Salámgé, 321; dismissed to British camp, 324.
Carpendale, Lieut., i. 48, 53, 57, 105, 108.
Cásula, arrival at, i. 136; ruined state of, 137; country between it and Kedárif, 149.
Chálga, plateau of, i. 207.
Chelicut, ii. 348.
Chetta, valley, ii. 265.

INDEX.

CHOLERA.

Cholera, in the Hijâz, i. 78; at Massowah, 116; in Theodore's camp, ii. 124-8.
Church, Abyssinian, description of, i. 217.
Clergy, Abyssinian, lay contempt for, i. 235.
Coffin, Mrs., i. 22.
Communicants, in Abyssinian Church, i. 312.
Converts, from Islâm to Christianity at Mágdala, ii. 213.
Coptic Patriarch, Theodoro's charges against, ii. 62.
Crocodiles, in the Atbara, i. 148, 172.

D.

Dábtrâ Dasta, messenger, i. 213; decorated with the Royal Shirt, ii. 25; un-shirts himself, 50; in the royal robes, 51.
Dágree, valley, i. 72.
Dágussa, grain, i. 189.
Dák, island in Lake Tâna, i. 315; how reduced by Theodore, *ib.*
Dakla-Guargîs, Dajjâj, i. 81, 103.
Dakn-ul-Fil, i. 186.
Dalanta, people of, submit to Theodore, ii. 256; he breaks faith with them, 270.
'Dalhousie,' steamer, i. 2, 29.
Damâsh, Bitwáddad, one of Mágdala Council, ii. 171-4; tried for treason, 280; charged with cowardice, 294; his raid against the Gallas, 297; wounded at the storming of Mágdala, 334.
Dúmbća, district of, i. 215.
Dambća, lake of, *see* Tâna.
Dûmót, district of, i. 244, 273.
Dangwé, i. 241.
Dánka, i. 294.
Dankôra, i. 232, 308.
Dasait, i. 92.
Dasta, Dajjâj, petty Chief of Mágdala, ii. 262.
Dâwunt, atrocity of an insurgent of, ii. 242; its submission to Theodore, 269; he breaks faith with its people, 270.
Debra Tâbor, Theodore at, ii. 131; holds an assize on the Captives at, 141; Mission confined at, 145; trial of rebels at, 148.
Delmonte, Padre, i. 9, 26, 60, 113; ii. 4.
Dháfar, Bitwáddad, ii. 181.

VOL. II.

GÂBÊ-LUKÛM.

Dharita, a shrewd Mussulman of, i. 51.
Dissee, island, i. 37.
Dust-storms, at Massowah, i. 9, 19, 91, 103; at Cásala, 141.
Dwârkin, rivulet, i. 204.

E.

Earthquake, at Massowah, i. 30, 43.
Eipperle, Mr., i. 163, 171, 178, 185.
El-Agamât, i. 71.
El-'A'zâzâ, i. 151.
El-Bakhît, tribe, i. 129.
Elephants, i. 82, 128.
El-Gaidât, i. 157.
El-Ju'afara, i. 159.
El-Madág, i. 156.
El-Maradib, i. 187.
Essler, Mr., imprisoned at Mágdala, ii. 261.
Etiquette, Abyssinian, in eating, i. 228; in riding, 245, ii. 126; in address, 220, 224; in presentation, 225; in drinking, 226.
Etshégé, Superior of Monks, ii. 340-1.

F.

Fallûké, *see* Speedy.
Fúnta, a Góndar merchant, i. 114.
Faróhé, i. 309.
Fáttam, river, i. 241.
Fekêr-Kásâ, a friendly indemnity, ii. 35.
Festival, of the Drum, at Matámma, i. 174.
Fetteh-Negûst, code of Abyssinian law, ii. 104, 148.
Fish, of Lake Tûna, i. 224; flying-fish at Massowah, 103.
Flad, Mr., i. 50, 52; letters to Author from, 62, 75; joins Author at Korâta, ii. 11; sent with letter to the Queen from Theodore, 103; testimony to his kind exertions, 206; forwards Queen's reply to Theodore from Massowah, 231; his account of Theodore's views on the approach of the British army, 266; is allowed to reside at Mágdala, 272; sent by Theodore to Sir Robert Napier, 319.

G.

Gábama-Wadgunfalo, i. 125.
Gâbê-Lukûm, i. 127, 134.

2 A

GÁBRA.

Gábra, guide from Matámma, i. 186.
Gábra-Mádbanê 'Álam, Balambarás, Governor of Wandígé, i. 308 ; ii. 74, 90 ; rebels against Theodore, 276.
Gabriê, Fit-awrâri, ii. 276.
Gabriê, Râs, imprisoned at Mágdala, ii. 261.
Gábza, i. 70.
Gadarêt, i. 86, 90, 121.
Gádiro, ii. 128.
Gáffat, i. 50; captives arrive at, ii. 131.
Gaïnti Bisáwwir, Bitwáddad, one of Mágdala Council, ii. 181.
Gallabât, inhabitants of, i. 157 ; government of, 158; etymology of name, 158.
Gallas, contemptible as assailants, ii. 251 ; raid on the, 295; their mutilation of captives, 296.
Game, see Sport.
Gastineau, M., i. 21.
Gésho, a plant used in fermentation, ii. 119.
Géta and Gétotsh, import of the titles, 156-7.
Gint, i. 205.
"Girding," ii. 221-224.
Gishen, i. 206 ; ii. 332.
Gójja, i. 221 ; ii. 76.
Gójjamy Kása, i. 196, 233-4.
Gojjé, Dajjáj, one of Mágdala Council, ii. 180 ; on a raid against the Gallas, 297.
Góndar, old capital, rumoured sack of, i. 35; glimpse of. 214 ; sacked by Theodore, ii. 17, 230-1.
Gondâwa, river, i. 187.
Greek priest, mission of, to Theodore, i. 77 ; ii. 144.
Guangûl, ii. 192.
Guinea-worm, i. 151.
Gûks, native tournament, ii. 121-2.
Gumâra, river, ii. 130.
Gûna, Mt., ii. 159.

H.

Hagiography, Abyssinian, ii. 128.
Haik-hallet, death of the ex-Queen Téru-Wark at, ii. 317.
Hail, on Mount Gûna, ii. 159 ; hailstorm at Mágdala, 265.
Hailo, messenger, decorated with Royal Shirt, ii. 8 ; death of, 256.
Hailo, Bitwáddad, one of Mágdala Council, ii. 174-177 ; escapes from Mágdala, 276.

ITAMANYO.

Hailo, Bitwáddad, of Chálga, ii. 181.
Hailo Kása, Theodore's youngest son, ii. 336.
Haji Ádam Korman, story of his lost wife, i. 31 ; his opinion of the Abyssinians, 83 ; prognosticates the illsuccess of the Mission, 102.
Hall, Mr. Moritz, kissed by Theodore, ii. 113; dragged in chains to Mágdala, 277.
Hállet-ul-Kanz, i. 154.
Hállet-Wadabein, i. 152.
Hállet-Wadabsin, i. 152-3.
Hamarai, i. 128.
Hûmid, Sheikh of the Beni-Ámir, i. 131.
Hamûs-Gábia, market, i. 220.
Harânrua, tribe, i. 134.
Harkiko, i. 10 ; water at, 14 ; visit to, 37.
Hásan Effendi, Kawwâs, i. 44; his effrontery, 159 ; leaves the Mission at Matánma, 174.
Hásani, Bitwáddad, new Commandant at Mágdala, ii. 283.
Hawashêt, valley, i. 132.
Hibâb, tribe, i. 86, 88, 90, 122.
Hibûb, wells, i. 126.
Hippopotami, i. 312 ; a lucky shot at, 313.
Honey, from a tree, i. 173.
Hozât, i. 80.
Huts, moveable, i. 56; of Abyssinian soldiers, 275.
Hyænas, i. 48, 205, 212.

I.

Ibánkab, ii. 159.
Ibrahîm, messenger, i. 95 ; his marriage, 103.
Ibrahîm, a Shoho, a relative of Samuel, i. 66.
Idris-Dâr, i. 134.
Idris Hásan, ex-Náyib of Harkiko, i. 37 ; visit to, 46.
Ifabâd, i. 87.
Ikwâr, i. 55.
Ilfing, royal female establishment : captives' quarters at Mágdala near to, ii. 162.
I'ngádá, Rás, Theodore's Prime Minister, his history, i. 255-258.
I'ngádá Wark, i. 269, ii. 66, 150 ; is put to death, 315.
Injabara, valley, battle-field, i. 238.
I'rkina, a Chief of Dalanta, his fidelity to the Mission, ii. 247, 268, 272.
Itamanyo, Queen, her sympathy with the Captives, ii. 106; her robe presented to Author, 117 ; her origin and mar-

INDEX. 355

ITÉGÊ.

riage with Theodore, 218; her conversion to Christianity and religious devotion, 219; returns to her home after the death of Theodore, 346.
Itégê, Empress. *See* Itamanyo and Téru-Wark.
Iz-ud-Dîn, Prime Minister at Matámma, i. 162, 173.

J.

Jä'afara, i. 157.
Jâgê, i. 128.
Jarâr, point, at Massowah, i. 11, 79.
Jebel Tâyif, i. 108.
Jiddah, arrival of Mission at, 108; town of, 109.
Jumä'ah, Sheikh of Gallabát, i. 157; visit from, 164; harangues his troops, 175; farewell to, 182.

K.

Kalamât, i. 123.
Kaldur-koy, style of serving dinner, i. 38, 64.
Kamánts, their character and religion, i. 208.
Kánfar, i. 85, 92, 120.
Kánfu Dajjâj, Theodore's father, i. 229.
Kânôha, i. 224.
Kántiba Hailo, ex-Mayor of Góndar, ii. 13; his history, 16-20; urges Theodore to release the captives, 106; his credulity, 138; imprisoned at Mágdala, 261.
Karkuê, Mt., i. 132.
Kar-Obél, i. 128.
Kása, Aito, merchant of Korâta, i. 32; arraigned by Theodore, ii. 105.
Kásha, Básha, a brave Amhára, ii. 301.
Kása, Lij, *see* Theodore.
Kása, Lij, a courtier, ii. 2.
Kedárif, district, i. 151. (*See* Hállet-Wadabsin.)
Kedús Mikáil, church, i. 216.
Kerans, Mr., ii. 112, 111, 154, 319.
Khásm-ul-Ghirbah, i. 118.
Khatmin, i. 112.
Khoja Bedrós, i. 21, 77, 102.
Khoja Panagiotes Kozika, i. 139.
Khôr-Ithrib, i. 159.
Khôr-ul-Gash, i. 113.
Khôr-ul-Lailah, i. 187.
Kidâna Máryam, Râs, Commandant of Mágdala, ii. 160; his history, 167; is put in irons, 239.

MARCOPOLI.

Kidâna Máryam, a page, brutally massacred, ii. 315.
Kilté, river, i. 235, 308.
Kítba, i. 124.
Kokai, rivulet, i. 187.
Komâr, i. 187.
Korâta, i. 316, 319; sojourn of Mission at, ii. 1-80.
Kwâkûra, i. 236.
Kwâra, i. 207; ii. 296.

L.

Lagústa, i. 236.
Lákaba, i. 130.
Lebka, i. 86, 121.
Lejean, M., i. 39; Theodore's complaints against, ii. 60, 61.
Lent, Abyssinian, i. 311; ii. 268.
Lih, Yashâlaka, ii. 228, 273.
Lij, title, 197.
Lisag, i. 214.
Lions, i. 86, 123, 188; Theodore's tame, ii. 148.
Locusts, i. 80 121.
Lumsdaine, Dr., ii. 312; his assiduous attentions to Queen Téru-Wark during her illness, 347.

M.

Macraire, M., ii. 117, 145, 154, 261.
Magamayatât, i. 86, 90, 121.
Mágdala, dispatch of stores and letters to, i. 64; Captives arrive at, ii. 160; kindness of its Chiefs, 165; our guardians at, 167-186; our domestics at, 187; prison-discipline of, 189; our guards at, 191; gates of, 192; escape of captives from impracticable, 193; Captives' quarters at, 202; fare at, 203; entertainment of public guests at, 205; society, 205-6; water, soil, and climate, 208-9; birds, 210; religious reform among soldiery, 211; Divine Service at, 214; communication between it and royal camp cut off, 241; re-opened, 256; Chiefs and European artisans imprisoned at, 261; dismantled by Theodore, 278; Theodore's entrance into, 279; Theodore's superstitious views respecting, 305; stormed by British, 334; dismissal of Chiefs at, 343-4; in flames, 345.
Mahabar, i. 121.
Mahlab, i. 127.
Marcopoli, Signor, i. 120, 130, 142, 178, 185.

2 A 2

MÁRGAF.

Márgaf, robe, ii. 117.
Marisa, dish, i. 164.
Markets, Abyssinian, i. 220.
Markham, Mr. C. R., his 'History of the Abyssinian Expedition,' ii. 338.
Marmadiyât, watercourse. i. 148.
Marriages, Abyssinian, ii. 215-220; sacramental, 216; second-rate, 219; third-rate, 219.
Máryam-wáha, i. 185.
Mashisha, Afá-Negûs, deserts to the Gallas from Mágdala. ii. 295.
Mashisha, Râs, eldest son of Theodore, ii. 45; introduced to the Author, 57; escapes from Mágdala, 336.
Máshlat, i. 89, 90.
Mâsir, i. 72.
Mastyât. Queen of Wollo-Gallas, ii. 250.
Mâswâha, stream, i. 237.
Matámma, district, government of, i. 157; called by Arabs 'Sûk-ul-Gallabât,' 158; climate of, 165; produce. 167; fairs at, 167; slave-trade, 168; horses and cattle, *ib.*; revenue and army, 169; review of troops, 171; Festival of the Drum at, 172; return of troops from a raid, 182.
Match, cord, distinguishing Abyssinians from non-Christians, Kamánts forced to wear, i. 209; borne by converts, ii. 213.
Mátrah-Maddai, i. 72.
Mayer, Mr., ii. 24, 324.
McKelvie, ii. 112, 145.
Meat, slaughtered by Christians and Mussulmans, i. 88; raw, *see* Brundo.
Menilek, King of Shoa, proposes to attack Mágdala, ii. 250; his display and retreat, 251; sends money and a letter to Author, 261.
Merewether, Colonel, i. 1, 60, 113; his arrival at Antâlo, ii. 275; at Ashángi, 302; his exertions on behalf of the captives, 325; his kindness to the Mágdala Chiefs, 313.
Messages, verbal, custom of sending with letters, ii. 3, 5, 23, 27, 41, 76, *et passim*.
Messengers, Abyssinian, their fidelity, ii. 245-247.
Métcha, district, i. 273, 289.
Metropolitan, Abyssinian, *see* Abúna.
Millet, large. i. 151; different ways of cooking, 166.
Milwia, ravine, i. 145.
Mirând, Dajjâj, i. 65, 73.
Mircha Warkee, i. 8.
Mission, to King Theodore, arrives at Massowah, i. 3; leaves for Egypt,

NAFÂSA.

108; returns to Massowah, 114; departure for Cásala, 120; reaches Cásala, 136; starts for Kedârif, 142; reaches Hâllet-Wadabsin, 152;—Matámma, 160;— Wahné, 188;—Theodore's camp, 248;—Korâta, 316;— Zagê, ii. 56; disgraced, 83; under surveillance at Zagê, 89; to be retained as hostages, 100; march with the King and his army to Korâta, 124-128; arrive at Gáffât, 131; location of, there, 133-4; under watch at Debra Tâbor, 145; arraigned again at, 152; confined at, 153; start with Theodore towards Mágdala, 159; fettered at, 161; quarters at, 202; invited by Theodore to see mortar brought up to Salámgê, 303; in tents at Salámgê, 312; sent back to Mágdala, 316; liberated and sent to British camp, 325; arrival at Zoolla, 319; recognition of its services by Government, 350.
Mohammed Âdam, cousin to Nâyib of Harkiko, i. 37.
Mohammed-bin-'Abd-ur-Rahîm, Nâyib of Harkiko, i. 37; his admiration of Theodore, 38; his adventure with the King, 39.
Mohammed Sa'îd, messenger, statement of his interview with Theodore, i. 98; sent with Agafâri Gôlam to release old captives from Mágdala, ii. 5.
Mohammed Sibâwy, the lying messenger, i. 92, 194; a candidate for the Royal Shirt, ii. 7; Theodore's apology for him, 9; is raised to the rank of Ôna, 50.
Moncúlu, water at, i. 14; Consul Plowden's house at, 19; residence of Mission at, 23; heat at, 24; French Consul's house, 47; dinner given to Massowah authorities at, 61.
Monkeys, i. 70, 160.
Morland, Lieut., i. 2, 21, 48.
Mortar, Theodore's large, arrests his progress to Mágdala, ii. 257; is brought up to Salámgê, 303.
Mudir, of the Danâkil, i. 53.
Munzinger, M., i. 22, 43, 48. 82, 114; is appointed British Agent at Massowah, 115; sent in advance of the British expedition to reconnoitre, ii. 273; at Dalanta, 276.
Mutchler, Mr., i. 171, 178, 185.

N.

Nafâsa, i. 231, 308.

INDEX. 357

NAGADRÂS.

Nagadrás Gabra-Mádhen, ii. 11.
Napier, Sir Robert, his proclamation, ii. 255; his ultimatum, 265; letters to Theodore, 317, 319; message in reply to proffered present from, 327; kindness to Theodore's surviving family, 342; rewards faithful Abyssinians, 348.
Naturalists, German, i. 32, 33.
Nâyibs of Harkiko, i. 37; visit to, 37.
Negûsê, Básha, a religious reformer at Mágdala, ii. 212.
Nûr-Habibai, i. 85.

O.

Obsequies, Abyssinian, ii. 258, 260.
Occupations, of males and females in Abyssinia, i. 191, ii. 72.
Odisso, Aito, massacred by rebels of Dáwunt, ii. 242; Theodore's grief for him, 243.
'Omar 'Ali, interpreter, i. 22.
Ôna Mohammed, see Mohammed Sihâwy.
Ondo, ii. 130.
Oobê, Râs, late Chief of Tigré, defeated by Theodore, i. 284; imprisoned by Theodore, ii. 217.
Order, of the Cross and Solomon's Seal, ii. 44, 48.
Order, of the Shirt, see Shirt.

P.

Palgrave, Mr. Gifford, i. 104, 111.
'Pantaloon,' H.M.S., i. 29, 61.
Pietro, Signor, ii. 154.
Plowden, Consul, his Report on the military and political career of Theodore, i. 282-287.
Prideaux, Lieut., associated with the Mission, i. 66, 70; sent with message from Theodore to Sir Robert Napier, ii. 319.
Priests, trial of two Abyssinian, ii. 280.
Purtoo Effendi, Lieut.-Governor of Massowah, i. 3; his opinion of Theodore, 4; of Massowah, 25; leaves for the Hijâz, 32; meeting with at Jiddah, 109.
Purvis, Captain, i. 29, 60.

Q.

Queen, her Britannic Majesty, letters to King Theodore from, ii. 38, 231.
Queens, Theodore's, ii. 336. See Itumanyo and Tera-Wark.

SEVASTOPOL.

R.

Raines, General, i. 113.
Râro, i. 87.
Râs Harb, i. 108.
Reade, Consul, i. 111.
Revenue, of Abyssinia, ii. 16.
Rosenthal, Rev. Mr., i. 78; Theodore's charges against, 300; ii. 306.
Russell, Earl, suggests that a British officer should be attached to Mission, i. 65; his letter to Theodore by Consul Cameron, ii. 37.

S.

Sabdarât, i. 135; view from, 145.
Sâbunja, i. 237.
Sahâtee, i. 53, 60.
Sakôla, i. 276.
Salamgê, plateau, Theodore reaches, ii. 27; his large mortar brought to, 303.
Salâssê, attained by Theodore, ii. 277; watches British camp from, 319.
Samhâr, the, i. 85, 90.
Samuel, Aito, i. 244; his character and history, 258; appointed Baldarabá to the Mission, 260; his character vindicated, 262; his fidelity, 264; arraigned by Theodore, ii. 86, 105; takes part with the Captives, 145; accompanies Mission to Mágdala, 159; his position at, 161; services at, 165; death of his wife, 260; in disgrace with Theodore, 278; restored to royal favour, 280; his visit to British camp and return to Mágdala with Sir Robert Napier's reply to Theodore's proffered present of cattle, 327.
Sarâba, i. 208.
Sâraf-ul-Bawâdra, wells, i. 151.
Sar-Amba, i. 197, 206; ii. 167.
Sarmoutsh, creek, in Island of Dâk, i. 315.
Sar-wâha, rivulet, i. 216.
Schiller, Mr., imprisoned at Mágdala, ii. 261.
Schimper, Dr., i. 52; letters from, 62, 75; his opinion of the Abyssinians, ii. 14; his sketch map of Bagêmêdêr and ichthyological researches, 24.
Schweinfurth, Dr., i. 163.
Senâfé, Abyssinian followers dismissed at, ii. 318.
Servants, Abyssinian, fidelity of, ii. 244-249.
Sevastopol, Theodore's large mortar, ii. 303-4.

INDEX.

SHA'AB.

Shä'ab, i. 85, 91, 121.
Shä'alab, i. 127.
Shajarât, i. 149.
Shállaka-Shatûsh, i. 240.
Shámma, etiquette in wearing, ii. 221-224; enveloping head in, an insult, 226.
Shánkěkí, slaves taken from the, i. 168.
Sharo, Lij, i. 196.
Sheikh Hasb-Allah, i. 150.
Shells, between Cásala and Kedârif, i. 150.
Shirt, Abyssinian Order of the, i. 198; Theodore proposes to invest the Mission followers with, ii. 5; Theodore and European shirts, 71.
Shísharo, valley, i. 72, 73.
Shohos, the, i. 66, 81.
Shûkry, tribe, i. 140; cameleers, 152.
Slave-trade, at Massowah, i. 61, 68; in Abyssinia, 287-8.
Snakes, near Lake Tâna, i. 226.
Solíb, i. 129.
Soodán, mutiny in the, i. 141; etymology of name, 150.
Speedy, Mr., Theodore's complaints against, ii. 63; regarded him as an enemy, 330.
Spies, alleged, sent to Massowah, i. 42.
Sport, i. 24, 51, 56, 73; near Lake Tâna, 224.
Staiger, Mr., imprisoned at Mágdala, ii. 261.
Stanton, Colonel, i. 110; his opinion of Dr. Beke's mission, ii. 47.
Steamer, Theodore's imitation, ii. 120.
Stern, Rev. Mr., letters from, i. 63, 73; Theodore's charges against, 299, ii. 305; his missionary labours at Mágdala, 211; fidelity of his Abyssinian servants, 249.
Suez, arrival of Mission at, i. 110; return from, 111; homeward journey from, ii. 349.
"Sugar," see Súkkar.
Súkkar, Chief of the Atté-Máryam, i. 87-89, 122.
Sûk-ul-Gallabát, see Matámma.
Sunkwáha, i. 204.
Surúr, Mt., i. 132.

T.

Tábot, or Ark, i. 225-228; ii. 260.
Tacrarait, i. 129.
Tadla, Bitwaddad, sent to re-arrest old captives, ii. 80, 116; in charge of Captives sent to Mágdala, 152; imprisoned at, 262.

THEODORE.

Tadla Gwâlu, deserts from the royal camp and is proclaimed Chief of Gojjam, i. 238; battle between his followers and Theodore, 239.
Tágga, Râs, Commander of the Musketeers, ii. 45, 277.
Táka, plain of, i. 145.
Tákkazé, river, i. 35, 63.
Takroories, i. 157; etymology of name, 158; disobliging, 170.
Tána, Lake, passage across, i. 314-317; shores of, ii. 7; shooting with Theodore at, 109, 114; artillery-practice at, 111.
Tánkwal, i. 216.
Tartar, i. 150.
Tasámma, Balambarás, Master of the Horse, imprisoned at Mágdala, ii. 262.
Tasámma, Lij, i. 196, 200, 201, 202; his mother, 213.
Tasho, Lij, i. 196.
Téj, beverage, i. 198.
Téru-Wark, daughter of Dajjaj Oobé, married to Theodore, ii. 217, 277, 336; makes over her son, 'Alamáyo, to the British, 343; her death, 347.
Tigrêan, dialect, used at Massowah, i. 14.
T'issoo Gobazé, rebel Chief of Walkait, i. 35, 74, 102, 188.
T'issoo Hailo, head of Abyssinian merchants trading to Massowah, i. 34, 35; is imprisoned at Mágdala, ii. 262.
Theodore, King, first letter from to Author, i. 93, 115; his reception of the Mission, 248; his complaints against the old Captives, 248-251; orders their release, 265; his letter to the Queen, ib.; knowledge of Arabic, 270; not a beneficent ruler, 278; his parentage and early youth, ib.; early exploits, 280; receives a check at Kedârif, 281; marries Tóbet, Râs 'Ali's daughter, 281; overthrows Râs 'Ali and Râs Oobé, 282-284; is crowned Emperor, 284; his early reforms, 285-6; causes of his waning power, 288-9; his fits of melancholy, 290; rapidity of his marches, 291; care for his troops, 293; alleged reason for delaying answering the Author's letter, 295; sends order for release of old Captives, 297; his complaints against them, 299; offers to make a treaty, 301; presents Author with 5000 dollars, 305; arrives at Zagé, ii. 1; his ethics, 9; agrees to departure of European artisans with Author, 12; used to believe in the black art, 19; writes that he wishes to "consult" Author, 21; proposes to

THEODORE.

decorate members of Mission with the Royal Shirt, 22; intimates that the Captives are to be tried, 26; arrangements thereto, 31; seeks an indemnity, 32, 35; demands artisans from England, 39; forgives the Captives, 42; sends Author another 5000 dollars, 45; his reception of the Mission at Zagê, 57; consults Chiefs and European artisans about detaining the Mission, 58, 59; his complaints against the Coptic Patriarch and the Egyptian Government, 62, 63; against his own people, 64; directs Author to prepare to leave Abyssinia, 64; in European shirts, 71; returns a seized packet open to Author, 73; changes plan of our return journey, 76; agrees to Author's proposed route, 78; orders re-arrest of Captives on their way homeward, 80; his charges against the Author, 84-86; apologizes, 87, 92; arraigns the Captives at Zagê, 93; asks their pardon, 99; causes the petition from the relatives of the Captives to be read, ib.; his letter to Queen Victoria asking for artisans, 100; his presents to the members of the Mission, 107; restores part of cash taken from old Captives, 107; visits the Author at Zagê, 108; commemorates Queen Victoria's birth-day, 110; fells a suppliant with a billet of wood, 111; recounts his wars against Turks and Gallas, 113; his cruelty at Zagê, 115; proposes that the Author should wear a *Márgaf*, 117; attempts imitation of a steamer, 120; his views on taxation, 131; courtesy to Author at Gáffat, 132-3; his descent from Alexander, 137; praises the English for providing his people with Amharic bibles, 139; his charges against the Author at Debra Tábor, 141-2; claims India and half the world besides, 153; visits Captives at Debra Tábor, 155; believes himself mad, 156; proceeds with Captives towards Mágdala, 158; sends Captives on to Mágdala, 159; his remarks on hearing that Author was fettered, 163; returns to Debra Tábor, 164; his different marriages, 217-219; his first letter to Author at Mágdala, 228; forwards stores to Author, 229-238; forwards Queen's letter to him for perusal, 233; notifies that he will keep us at Mágdala, 234; declines a proffered present, 240; cut off from Mágdala, 241; his cruelties at that

TOLERATION.

period, 241; receives copy of Sir Robert Napier's proclamation, 254; reaches Beitahôr, 256; death of his sister, 258; reaches Chetta valley, 260; his talk about the Author, 264; reaches the Dalanta plateau, 267; breaks faith with the Dalanta people, 268; reaches the Báshilo, 271; speaks of a " blood bath," 272; sends his valuables to Mágdala, 276; reaches Salámgê, 277; enters Mágdala, 279; tries two priests for defamation, 280; tries Chiefs for treason, 281; returns to Salámgê, 282; visits Mágdala again, 286; alleged reason for detaining the Mission, 287; summons the Author to an interview, ib.; his altered appearance, ib.; refers to the impending attack by the British, 289; requests the Author to bury him in the event of his death, ib.; another alleged motive for detaining the Captives, 290; unfetters Blanc and Prideaux, 291; hopes the British will not despise him for his colour, 292; upbraids his Chiefs at Salámgê, 293; his charmed rifle, 295; his queries on European warfare, 304; recounts his troubles, 305; deplores the raggedness of his troops, 306; refuses to make overtures to Sir Robert Napier, 307; goes off on a plundering expedition, 308; is anxious to hear of the British army, 309; watches for its movements, 310; harangues his troops, 313; is determined to let matters take their course, 314; orders massacre of native prisoners, 315; refuses to receive Sir R. Napier's letter, 317; attacks British advanced guard, 318; requests Author to open communications with Sir R. Napier, 319; his letter to Sir Robert, 320; his anger at the result of the deputation to British camp, 319; his letter of apology to Sir Robert, 325; sends present of cattle to British camp, 330; prepares to decamp, ib.; his Chiefs and people refuse to obey him, 331; prepares for defence, 332; attacks our cavalry, 333; retires to the gates with a few followers, 334; shoots himself, ib.; summary of his character, 335; his wives and issue, 336; his burial, 343.

Tôbet, daughter of Râs 'Ali, marries Theodore, ii. 217.

Toleration, Abyssinian religious, i. 319.

INDEX.

TOLLS.

Tolls, ii. 16.
Tournament, native, ii. 123.

V.

'Victoria,' transport steamer, i. 48, 53, 60, 64, 104.

W.

Wádala, ii. 148, 270.
Wahné, i. 188.
Waitos, near Lake Tâna, i. 314.
Waízero Barîtu, i. 218.
Waízero Denké, i. 213, 219, 222, 310.
Waízero Mínyen, mother of Râs 'Ali, i. 281.
Wâka, i. 187.
Wakshum Gobazé, of Lasta, i. 35, 74, 81; proposes to attack Mágdala, ii. 250; retires from before Mágdala, 251; his friendliness to the British army, 252; designs to attack Theodore, 255; forwards copy of Sir Robert Napier's ultimatum to Author, 265.
Wakshum Tafâré, cousin to Wakshum Gobazé, ii. 239, 263.
Wald-Gâbir, Theodore's valet, i. 276; saw Theodore commit suicide, ii. 327; denies that his master cursed on the occasion, 337.
Wald-Gabriêl, interpreter, i. 187; decorated with Royal Shirt, ii. 13.
Wald-Máryam, lesser Chief of escort, i. 196.
Wald-Máryam, messenger, i. 43, 48, 65, 77, 104.
Waldmeier, Mr., his testimony to first success of Mission, ii. 43, 44; his zealous co-operation, 206; Theodore's testimony thereto, 292; escorts liberated Captives to British camp, 324; styled by Theodore his " best friend," 326; assists Author at Mágdala, 340.

ZÚGDA.

Wald-ul-'Amnâs, i. 156.
Wald-Salássé Gobazé, i. 69, 70, 231.
Waldt-Máryam, a native Joan of Arc, i. 218, 317.
Walkaït, i. 35, ii. 74.
Wandé, Aito, is presented with one of Theodore's dismissed wives, i. 220, 317; is arraigned by Theodore, ii. 105.
Wandígé, district, i. 308.
Wanzígé, village, i. 216.
Warké, Yasháloka, a doorkeeper at Mágdala, ii. 185.
Wâsi, Bitwáddad, one of Mágdala Council, ii. 177; heads a raid upon the Gallas, 297.
Wello - Gallas, Theodore's campaign against, i. 74.
Wilby, Brigadier-General, ii. 339, 344.
Worohaimano, Gallas, raid upon, ii. 294-301.

Y.

Yadjow, Gallas, ii. 218; intended to submit to Theodore, 270.
Yashálaka, a Captain of Lancers, ii. 191.
Yusmâla, i. 234, 308.

Z.

Zâga, i. 130.
Zagé, capital of Métcha, ii. 1; reception of Mission at, 56; arrested at, 83; Theodore's cruelties at, 115; peninsula of, its inhabitants and produce, 118-120.
Zánnab, 'Alâkû, keeper of the royal archives, ii. 192, 349.
Zanzalima, ii. 80.
Zaudi, ii. 315.
Zoolla, visit to, i. 81; return to, ii. 349.
Zûgda, i. 236, 307.

THE END.

LONDON: PRINTED BY WILLIAM CLOWES AND SONS, STAMFORD STREET,
AND CHARING CROSS.

www.ingramcontent.com/pod-product-compliance
Lightning Source LLC
Chambersburg PA
CBHW030405230426
43664CB00007BB/750